Praise for *FutureConsumer.Com*

Frank Feather is an encyclopedic genius. This amazing journey into the future is a seriously wonderful book. Every page is filled with insightful nuggets. Try it. You'll love it!
— Stan Davis, bestselling author of
Future Wealth and *Blur*

A fantastic painting of mind-boggling pictures. Excellent bedtime reading — except it prevents you from sleeping!
—Yrjö Neuvo, Executive Vice-President and
Chief Technical Officer, Nokia Mobile Phones

A pleasure to read, providing new insights into the future impact of the Internet on our personal and professional lives.
—Janice M. Scites, Vice-President,
Internet Implementation Strategy,
AT&T Corp.

In this first-rate compendium of Net-driven changes to come, Frank Feather knows how to get under the skin of every consumer company with the message: change or suffer.
—Kevin Maney, Technology Columnist,
USA Today

Weaves extraordinary scenarios as ordinary events, bringing shocking trends to life so we can better exploit a future where everyone will be a dot-com consumer.
—Walid Mougayar, author of *Opening Digital Markets*
and Vision Columnist, *Business 2.0*

Frank Feather has an eye for telling anecdotes and a knack for fearless predictions. This is a "must read" for any executive who expects to be employed in 2010.
– John Brandt, Publisher and Editor-in-Chief,
Industry Week and IndustryWeek.com

The new "retail train" is leaving the station. And this highly accurate, aptly named "FutureConsumer.Com" snapshot is essential for those scurrying to scramble aboard.
– William H. Baxter, CAE, President & CEO,
Retail Merchants Association of Greater Richmond

future consumer .com

The Webolution of Shopping to 2010

Second Edition

Frank Feather

Warwick Publishing
Toronto

FutureConsumer.Com: The Webolution of Shopping to 2010
Second Edition

©2000, 2002 Frank Feather and Glocal Marketing Consultants, P.O. Box 38, Aurora, Ontario, Canada, L4G 3H1
www.future-consumer.com

Care has been taken to trace ownership of copyright material contained in this text, and full acknowledgement is provided by way of the "Further Reading" section. The author and publisher will gladly take any information that will enable them to rectify any reference or credit in subsequent editions.

The words "Webolution," "webographics," "WebMobile" and "WebPhone" are trademarks of the author and Glocal Marketing Consultants. Other product/brand names used in the text are trademarks of their various owners.

Warwick Publishing acknowledges the financial support of the Government of Canada through the Book Publishing Industry Development Program for its publishing activities.

ISBN 1-894622-18-9

Published by Warwick Publishing Inc.
161 Frederick Street
Toronto, Ontario M5A 4P3 Canada
www.warwickgp.com

Distributed in Canada by:
General Distribution Services Ltd.
325 Humber College Blvd.
Toronto, ON M9W 7C3

Distributed in the United States by:
LPC Group
2 Broad Street
Milford, CT 06460

Cover Design: Kimberley Young
Author photo by Bernard Prost, B. Prost Photography Inc.
www.portfolios.com/photog/prost.b

Printed and bound in Canada

For
my beautiful wife, best friend
and intellectual companion
Tammie Min Tan
and
our beloved daughters
Melissa Shuang-Ying Feather
and
Ashley Chun-Yao Feather

CONTENTS

FUTURE CONSUMER.COM:
The "Webolution" of Shopping to 2010

> There will be more confusion in the business world int he
> next decade than in any decade in history. I can't think of
> any that brought the kind of topsy-turvy change that's start-
> ing to happen now. And the pace will only accelerate.
> — Steve case, chairman
> AOL Time Warner

FORGET THE "DOT-COM SHAKEOUT" and the Nasdaq meltdown of
2000. Every seven seconds somebody new buys something
online for the first time. The Internet Revolution, or "Webolution,"
rolls inexorably onward and e-commerce will soon rebound
stronger than ever. Online shopping is gathering strength and the
dot-com shakeout will ultimately be seen as a small hiccup.

The Web takes shopping out of the shops. By 2010, the Internet
will gobble up 30 percent of retail spending, leaving most brick-
and-mortar retailers in rubble. All but the most savvy will get
killed. Most strip malls and many shopping malls, along with half
the department stores, supermarkets, retail chains, banks, and
local shops, will vanish without a trace as click-and-buy e-tailing
takes over. Who needs thousands of banks, bookstores, grocery
stores, hardware stores, drug stores — or any other kind of store
— if you can buy everything from a few Web sites?

The head-spinning Webolution is not easy to forecast. However,
before it's done — around 2018 — it will reverse and unwind virtually everything that the Industrial Revolution put into place. It will
smash the mass consumption economy to smithereens and re-
center it on the home.

The Webolution is so big that few yet grasp its significance.
Since the dot-com shakeout, there have been many silly Web obit-

uaries. Doubtless, the plodding plowman didn't "get it" when the first steam train puffed past his field. Likewise, the metal-bending blacksmith didn't "get it" when the first "horseless carriage" sputtered past his shop. So it is with many journalists and economists today when they dismiss the Web.

But this Webolution will rock the world, again utterly transforming life and commerce. And the rewards will accrue fastest to those who embrace it first. Click-happy shoppers are flocking online and will stun short-sighted brick-and-mortar retailers who stubbornly insist that people will always come to their stores. Online sales will kick in big time in the years 2002–2005, and grow rapidly throughout the decade to top $1 trillion by 2010. By then, the Web will be a hundred times bigger than today — a tidal wave HyperWeb that will drown those who can't or won't surf.

The stunning AOL Time Warner merger of January 2000 validated the Web and is a signpost for the future of mainstream society. Every month, some 140 million consumers use AOL Time Warner brands. And well more than half of those consumers are already shopping online.

Ask yourself which *you* would rather do:

(a) drag the kids to the store, shove a laden shopping cart with a wobbly wheel up and down crowded aisles, and then hump the stuff home; or

(b) drag the stuff into an online shopping cart with your mouse and then kick back with the kids until it arrives on your doorstep at the time you select.

A no-brainer, right? The Internet is fast becoming a shopper's paradise. It is changing not only how people buy, but how often, when, what, why, and from where. By 2010, a majority of Americans will live what Bill Gates calls a "Web Lifestyle" and will do at least some e-shopping. Most of them will do most of their shopping online.

Where will people buy? Whether or not pure e-tail Web sites such as Amazon.com will still be a favorite of online shoppers in 2010 is an intriguing question. In any event, such sites now serve as a living laboratory of the future of retailing. For sure, the "first-movers" have left their offline brick-and-mortar competitors in catch-up mode.

Some people argue that old-world retailers should leverage their offline assets and brand name to create a seamless online presence that out-competes the upstarts. But such a hybrid "brick-and-click" approach fails to recognize a simple reality of the online world: Most Internet users maintain a "favorites" list of book-marked Web sites that they visit most frequently. More important, the average favorites list contains no more than two or three dozen Web sites.

So the debate about who will win — pure bricks, pure clicks, or bricks-and-clicks — misses the point. All retailers are competing for consumer attention. If consumers won't have more than 15 retail sites bookmarked on their favorites lists, then there will be no more than one or two winners in each major product category. Hence, due to the rapid ramp-up of online shopping and the limited space available on the average e-shopper's favorites list, each retail category faces a massive shakeout.

Clearly, the retail battle will be decided on the favorites lists. Web sites that don't get bookmarked either will constantly struggle to survive or be swept swiftly to oblivion. Conversely, those sites that garner most surfers' attention will win — big time!

And that's the story of this book.

What's New in the Second Edition?

As will become obvious as you read this second edition of *FutureConsumer.Com,* I am still extremely bullish about the Webolution of online shopping. Despite the dot-com shakeout and economic slowdown (both of which were anticipated in the first edition), the basic thrust of the book has not changed one iota. The book's structure and layout also is unchanged.

However, the first edition was completed in early 2000 and so we have another 18 months of online shopping under our belt. As predicted, some things are selling better than others; I have re-run the forecasts to 2010 for all product categories and made some modest changes here and there.

In terms of total online shopping by 2010, the first edition forecast that 31 percent of all retail sales would be made online by then. The new forecast comes out at 29.5 percent, so not much has changed there. Still, please bear in mind that we are in the early days of the Webolution, and also that I am not saying *all* shopping will go online, but that for even 30 percent to do so will take at least a decade. However, e-shopping is picking up steam and will ramp up rapidly as the economy rebounds.

The original text basically stands unchanged. Despite the first, rocky phase of the Webolution, none of it needed rewriting to any significant degree. But it has been updated in important ways:

◆ **The Introduction is all brand new material.** It explains the Nasdaq "bubble" and the dot-com shakeout, and shows how and why the Webolution nevertheless continues unabated. In doing so, the Introduction critiques an article by Harvard strategy guru Michael Porter, who wrongheadedly tries to argue that the Internet changes nothing. He couldn't be more wrong! And the ongoing Webolution will prove it. Indeed, the next phase of the Internet will see it become a HyperWeb that will turn retailing on its head.

◆ **The beginning chapters contain new and vital information.** This includes fast-changing topics such as m-commerce, plus fresh online shopper demographic and webographic trend data.

◆ **All 12 product category chapters have been updated.** Many new paragraphs of essential information have been added to reflect and explain three important types of change:

- how some companies have changed their online offerings or e-tail strategies;

- how evolving Web technologies are changing the marketing of some products; and

- how some dot-coms became dot-bombs, and the lessons to be learned.

◆ **The final section on e-Marketing Strategy is unchanged.** As argued in my critique of Michael Porter's view of the Internet in the Introduction, I believe the strategies present-ed in the first edition are solid, future-proof, and right in line with where the HyperWeb is heading.

◆ **The lists of "Which Web Sites Will Win" in various cate-gories have been reconsidered and sometimes modified.** I also have slightly modified the "Top 50" list of biggest retail Web sites in 2010. The list in the first edition deliber-ately did not include many dot-coms because I believed few would ever achieve sufficient volume to make that list, even if they survived. Even then, two that did make the list have closed down (eToys and Petopia), and one of what I called "The Big 5" (Webvan) went bankrupt and has been replaced on that list.

With that, please enjoy Act II, the HyperWebolution.

Frank Feather
October 2001

THE WEBOLUTION, ACT II
Past the Point of No Return;
Here Comes the HyperWeb

This is the biggest business event since the Industrial Revolution.
— Jack Welch, former chairman, GE

THE WEBOLUTION of shopping is unstoppable. Nothing about the Nasdaq meltdown or *short*-term dot-com shakeout of 2000–2001 changes my forecasts. In fact, it re-enforces everything in this book and just goes to prove that the *long*-term impact of the Internet on business and society remains vastly underrated. Most people just don't get it — yet.

In fact, e-shopping has taken off and you can't put the genie back in the bottle. We are past the point of no return. The Web is gaining critical mass and going mainstream. What remains is to anticipate which customers will switch their shopping behavior permanently from the old method to the new, and which products they most likely will buy in a mobile, wireless, speeded-up Web world. In turn, this will require brand new business strategies suited for the coming HyperWeb environment.

Let's consider what happened, where we are now, what happens next, and what business needs to do about it. Then I'll briefly outline what little has changed since the first edition of the book.

Why the "Bubble" Burst
To understand why the Nasdaq stock market melted down, let's first be clear that it did not have a lot to do with the dot-com shakeout per se, but more with a technology and Internet mania

that became totally irrational. People over-estimated how quickly the Internet would change business in the short term and they drove stock prices to ridiculously overvalued levels. When the tech-laden Nasdaq index was at 3000, I warned audiences that it was way ahead of itself, too high, would inevitably correct, and that the higher it went the farther it would fall. This is precisely what happened. After zooming to 5000, it then went too far the other way, below the 2000 level.

But the stock mania had little to do with dot-com start-ups; some of it had nothing to do with the Internet at all. Indeed, many Dow-listed stocks such as Coca Cola were trading at ridiculous multiples and the price of almost any tech stock was driven sky high. I recall Microsoft CEO Steve Balmer saying publicly that his company's stock was overvalued in 1999. Amazon's Jeff Bezos actually warned people not to buy his company's obviously overvalued stock. In fact, the Nasdaq meltdown had three main elements:

1. Y2K Hangover: There was bound to be a technology slowdown after the Y2K problem was solved. In the rundown to December 31, 1999, companies strived frantically to ensure their computer systems would not crash when the clock ticked over to the year 2000. In the end, instead of trying to fix their software, lots of companies simply threw in the towel and bought brand new software and Y2K-compliant computers, servers, and databases. That drove the sales of everything, from software to computers, servers, routers, phone switches, you name it. In turn, that drove up profits and share prices. But then, after January 1, 2000, most corporations stopped buying all those things and vendor sales peaked out. And it will be 2002 before most companies again feel it necessary to upgrade their computer systems.

2. Dot-Com Craze: New start-ups, not all of them in e-tailing, were making initial public offerings (IPOs) of their stocks at inflated prices that investors drove to astronomical levels on the first day of trading. Start-up company "executives," who had never run any kind of business before, became instant multi-millionaires. Most of these companies became dot-bombs, but not until they too had bought all kinds of technology from manufacturers, in turn driving tech company values to even more unsustainable levels. Then, as the dot-coms floundered, those sales of technology not only stopped but loads of barely used second-hand equipment were thrown onto the market, again causing technology-manufacturing company orders to dry up.

3. Telecom Scramble: There also was a mad scramble to build telephone, cable, and fiber-optic broadband networks. At one time it seemed as if all major players, plus many heavily indebted start-up telecom firms, were building global broadband networks that inevitably must lead to an over-supply. That's exactly what happened. All told, about 42 million miles of fiber-optic cable — enough to circle the earth 1,600 times! — costing some $95 billion, was laid in the U.S.A. between 1997 and 2000. And yet it is estimated that less than three percent of the available capacity is actually in use. This has put the network builders in heavy debt, with few customers, and has left the telecom equipment manufacturers (such as Cisco, Nortel, Lucent, and Corning) with empty order books. So the entire telecom sector saw its stock values plunge, and many telecom companies will not survive. The only "plus" in all this is that we will one day get access to very cheap bandwidth.

Clearly, then, the e-tailer dot-com shakeout was but one part of the "bubble" and the stock sell-off was long overdue, inevitable, salutary, and healthy. It weeded out the excesses and the weaklings. After all, how many online pet stores do you need? Yet after reading the newspaper headlines of 2000, you'd think that the Internet had gasped its last breath. In truth, exactly the opposite is the case. The Webolution is far too big to go *poof* with the stock bubble.

e-Shopping at the e-Winners

The dot-com shakeout itself has not dissuaded people from shopping online. On the contrary, e-consumers are shopping as if nothing happened. Some 52 percent of North American adults have already bought something online. In 2000, e-tail sales were double those of 1999 and will double again in 2001. Like I said, e-shopping is catching on fast.

Yes, the consolidation of the e-tail sector is sorting the winners from the losers. Not all newly hatched turtles reach the sea. Of the 30,000 e-tail Web site start-ups, at least 80 percent will inevitably vanish due to over-competition and the reality that vendors in some categories need enough volume to offset slim profit margins.

Only one thousand sites sell more than $500,000 a year. Hence, beyond a few hybrid brick-n-click niche players, the winners will be those that achieve the scale needed to reduce their systems costs and build competitive advantages. The latter will be pure-play dot-coms such as Amazon and traditional retailers who integrate and exploit multi-channel customer relationship models.

A few other winners will be small companies, often one-person e-businesses. About 40 percent of companies with fewer than 10 employees already make a profit online and, in some ways, these will be the hidden engines of e-commerce. By 2010, a clutch of today's tiniest e-tailers could account for an oversized chunk of the North American e-tail economy.

Consumers not only are gravitating in growing numbers to these winners, they are spending much more online than they have spent before. There was some initial consumer uncertainty caused by the negative and way overdone media tirade about failing dot-coms, but this was no different than in 1995 when consumers were told the Internet would collapse under its own weight. Consumers didn't believe such silliness then and neither did they believe that e-commerce would come to a grinding halt in 2000. The Web has become an accepted purchase medium and people are not going to stop shopping online any more than they will stop using the Web, toss out their PCs and cellphones, or stop driving their cars. The Web is becoming part of everyday life, dismal newspaper reports notwithstanding.

The untold story is that consumers are switching on brand new PCs, PDAs, and cellphones at the rate of three per second worldwide. Minute in, minute out, about a hundred new people are going online for the first time in their lives. Minute in, minute out, new online shoppers are buying something online for the first time. Minute in, minute out, e-shoppers are buying more than they've ever bought before. The Webolution of shopping clearly continues unabated. Throughout the mayhem of 2000, for example, Dell sold at least $10 million worth of PCs online every single day of the year. Indeed, the Dells and Amazons of the coming HyperWeb have not even been founded yet. Hence, the Internet juggernaut rolls ever onward, remaking the socio-economic landscape and continuing its Webolution of retailing.

Shakeouts Happen

Shakeouts happen in every major technological revolution and this has all happened before. Any true revolution is marked by surprises, twists and turns, and volatile swings. The corporate cycle of birth, maturity, and death is perfectly natural. Of the Fortune 500 companies in the year 1900, only 10 percent still exist. That's life.

During the Industrial Revolution in Britain, thousands of start-ups failed because their business models were wrong or their managers did not know how to operate in the paradigm shift from the old agrarian model to a new factory model. Scores of new start-ups in the textile industry went broke across the Pennines. There were hundreds of new start-ups in the canal business, even though nobody had ever before operated a canal. Entrepreneurs, funded by private venture capital, stock issues and bonds, rushed into the industry with the expectation of making a fortune transporting textiles, raw materials, and other factory goods to market. By 1840, there were about fifteen hundred canal companies, yet almost all of them went bankrupt. A few survived and prospered but even they were gradually replaced by the railroads.

The railroads promised faster, cheaper, and more reliable transport at a huge profit and, again, investors found them irresistible. Shares were snapped up by people who had never before owned a single stock of any kind. The U.K. railroad bubble burst in 1845 just as some twelve hundred new railroad issues were ready to come to market and when the collective debt of the railroads alone exceeded Britain's entire national debt. Companies collapsed, families were wiped out, and the few surviving railroad companies were consolidated.

In the United States, there were more than three thousand railroads at one time. Many people are under the impression that Vanderbilt made his fortune building railroads. In fact, he made most of his wealth by buying up failed railroads and integrating them into a standardized network. By 1930, there were only 163 "Class I" railroads, with Penn Central alone having been formed out of six hundred previous systems.

It was the same in the telephone business. It took Alexander Graham Bell years to get venture capital because nobody thought there was a market for a device that Bell initially thought was going to be used to broadcast stage plays. Soon, however, once the telephony prospect was realized, entrepreneurs rushed in and there were more than three thousand phone companies in North America by 1914. By 1929 that was down to about a hundred phone companies. How many are left today, and how many of that handful — if any — will survive the coming HyperWeb?

The automobile revolution repeated the pattern. Yes, there were more than three thousand automobile start-ups too. Today, the few survivors comprise the various model brand names of GM, Ford and Chrysler. Even Chrysler is no longer independent.

So it is with the Webolution. And any notion that this is not a "new" economy is ludicrous. There are three million digital switches for every person on Earth, a PC for every twelve people, a cellphone for every six. None of these is going away, other than to be replaced by even more fantastic devices that will create a Hyper-Web and change the world of business yet again. What will emerge is a handful of truly different business models that have no current or traditional equivalent.

Why Do Companies Fail?

Most corporate failures, regardless of the age of the company but especially for new businesses, are due to inadequate funding, poor management and marketing, or to simply having the wrong product. Even Procter & Gamble (P&G), the world's largest packaged goods company, bombs out on about 70 percent of its new product launches. As we shall see, it also is struggling to succeed online.

Most dot-coms simply came to market without enough capital to establish a beachhead or, due to the larger Nasdaq correction, were unable to return to the markets for more financing as planned. Those with enough money spent it frivolously on exorbitant Web site design or, even worse, on reckless advertising binges. Some had zero management capability and/or did not get any managerial guidance from the venture capital firms or incubators that spawned them.

Others did not know how to market their wares in the new Internet space — something with which even the very best brick-and-mortar companies such as Wal-Mart still struggle. Most online ventures had seriously flawed business models or execution strategies. They simply did not know how to extract value from the new product-distribution and service-delivery network infrastructure.

Many dot-coms have been heavily and fairly criticized for trying to carve out a market niche regardless of profitability. In some cases, however, this is an unfair and totally flawed criticism. Some of the most outstanding business success stories, in both the offline and online worlds, have been built on precisely such a strategy. The automobile industry, for example, spends billions of dollars in product R&D without knowing for sure whether a particular vehicle will sell in sufficient quantity to recoup those investments, never mind make a profit. In consumer electronics, Sony for years has introduced a string of winning products — from VCRs to Walkmans — that were edged into the market at great cost before a broader market success was achieved. In the Webolution, AOL built its brand and accumulated a subscriber base by mailing out millions of floppy discs and CD-ROMs and offering free trials of its service. In the process, it amassed 30 million paying subscribers and put itself in position to acquire Time Warner, the largest media company in the world.

Some people have pooh-poohed AOL's brilliant success, either downplaying it or saying it is the exception rather than the rule. For example, a stock analyst appeared on CNBC in late March of 2001 and basically dismissed all dot-coms as having been a waste of time. He also said that "in the end, all that AOL had managed to achieve was to take over an old-time media company." Hello? Some old-time media company! It makes you wonder how most of these analysts are able to keep a straight face and hold onto their vastly overpaid jobs. Indeed, after the Nasdaq fiasco, most investors are left wondering what 99 percent of stock analysts have ever done of constructive value.

The Web Changes Everything

There is a great danger that misguided conclusions about the early stages of the Internet might lead corporations into backward thinking and guaranteed failure. Strategy guru Michael Porter, for example, wrote what amounted to an "I-told-you-so" article in the March 2001 issue of *Harvard Business Review* under the title "Strategy and the Internet" about how dot-coms didn't understand basic business strategy. The main problem is that Porter doesn't understand the Internet.

His densely worded, rambling, six-page article basically tried to justify the strategy model he developed back in the 1980s — that is, pre-Microsoft, pre-PC revolution, pre-cellphone, pre-Internet, and pre-Webolution! Consequently, his article was full of contradictions and his arguments were so circular and full of holes that it doesn't stand reasoned scrutiny. I have neither the patience nor the space to untangle all his incredulous incongruities. But I will spend some time explaining some of his major errors in thinking to show how a proper vision of the HyperWeb will lead to entirely different strategy recommendations.

To begin, Porter brusquely brushes aside online success stories such as AOL as being "the exception rather than the rule." But that is precisely the point! The success stories of *all* technological revolutions are few and far between because they do *not* conform to the old ways of doing things; they rewrite the rules of business strategy, something Porter is unwilling to do. Contrary to what Porter pretends, major technology breakthroughs are *not* merely new tools to layer onto the old economy. Rather, they disrupt previous economic models and call for brand new strategies — not rebaked old ones out of Harvard.

Risk-averse Porter says it's dangerous to assume the Internet "changes everything." He says the Internet is really nothing new, dismissing it as "an enabling technology." (Yes, it enables you to thoroughly whack your competition!) He even has the audacity to assert that "the experiences companies have had with the Internet thus far must be largely discounted" and "many of the lessons learned must be forgotten." Rather, he says companies should stick to time-tested processes. Now, nobody can defend the reckless incompetence of many dot-coms, but neither can you dismiss the winners as "exceptions to the rule" from which no strategic lessons can be learned.

Porter says that "confronted with a new business phenomenon," we should "look to marketplace outcomes for guidance." However, he says, "it is hard to come to any firm understanding of the impact of the Internet on business by looking at the results to date." So how can market outcomes be "discounted" or "forgotten," especially if this is a "new business phenomenon"? And how can he sweep the Internet aside based on one year's experience if that is not a reliable guide? In fact, the Webolution has already shown that it *does* change everything and that old models and strategies will not survive its onslaught without serious re-jigging.

The old production-centric, product-push, factory-based, mass production, mass consumption, mass marketing, mass advertising business model is utterly obsolete. The Web blows it to bits. The Web brings a new customer-centric, product-pull, network-based, mass-customized, one-to-one (1:1), customer relations–based business model. Obviously, those consultants with their heads buried in dusty 1980s strategy tomes will not be able to see this. Neither, unfortunately, will their seriously misguided corporate clients.

Porter claims the Internet "weakens profitability" without providing any "proprietary operational advantages." This weakened profitability argument simply does not hold water. He bemoans the fact that some companies have used the Web "to shift the basis of competition" (yes, that's the general intention!) "away from quality, features, and service" (on the contrary, they boosted those features!) "toward price" (yes, the Internet does force down prices because it creates a more efficient market, which is what competition is supposed to be all about, is it not?). According to Porter, this makes it "harder for anyone" (anyone?) in their industries to turn a profit (oh, poor laggards!).

In the end, Porter says, market forces are playing out, that the old rules will "regain their currency" and "true economic value" will become the "final arbiter" of business success. True, but not in the way Porter contends.

Value Added and Intellectual Capital

For example, Porter argues that the Internet tends to "reduce variable costs and tilts cost structures toward fixed costs." In fact, the Internet reduces fixed *and* variable costs and may even eliminate some fixed costs by making traditional fixed assets obsolete. The Internet transforms fixed assets such as buildings, machines, and telephone wires into "dead" capital with diminishing returns. And it turns mobile human resources into "live" intellectual capital with increasing returns as that asset gets traded non-stop across hyper-speed networks.

This HyperWeb leads to faster growth with less traditional capital and at lower cost to yield higher value. The Web places by far the most value on the value-added aspects of human creativity and innovation — intellectual capital — that can be digitized and applied to yield constantly higher levels of value. A portfolio of innovations will yield more than traditional assets and the HyperWeb will speed up those returns enormously. Time no longer evaporates with the workplace 9–5 clock; time now truly becomes non-stop as global companies operate across time zones in real time. Real time is real money and time not used to the fullest is wasted intellectual capital. Consequently, the new management challenge is to productively spend intellectual capital non-stop so as to model, simulate, and prototype more non-stop value creation. The HyperWeb demands that companies hyper-innovate human capital in real time to help customers hyper-customize their real-time needs at ever increasing speeds and levels of value.

Rather than encouraging "destructive price competition" as Porter contends, the Web thus squeezes out costs and boosts value, to the benefit of both producer and consumer. Indeed, the online consumer becomes the producer — or what *Third Wave* author Alvin Toffler long ago called the "prosumer" of value. The old second-wave, pre-Web, product-driven company increased shareholder value by extracting it *from* customers. The new third-wave, post-Web, customer-driven company sees shareholders and customers as complementary, with value to be extracted from intellectual capital in the service *of* customers. Companies that focus on lifetime customer value — which Web-enabled 1:1 marketing now permits — see customers as assets from which they generate ongoing revenue streams. In this way, customers drive growth in corporate assets and stockholder equity, and the 1:1 Web provides an unprecedented way of achieving that.

Porter does admit that advantages in operational effectiveness can take myriad forms, including better technology, superior inputs, better-trained people, or a more effective management structure. Indeed, these myriad forms of operational effectiveness are precisely what the Internet brings to bear! Yet he tries to differentiate between "uses" of the Internet (such as online transactions) and Internet technologies themselves (such as site customization features). But you cannot separate the Internet from its technology platform. They both serve the same purpose: to generate sales, gain efficiencies in distribution, and increase customer satisfaction. Yet Porter says only the "uses" can generate value.

Porter fully agrees that companies have "no choice" but to deploy Internet technology to stay competitive and that the Internet provides "better opportunities to establish distinctive strategic positionings." Yet, in the same paragraph, he says "the Internet per se will rarely be a competitive advantage." Which is it? The key question, he says, is "how to deploy it," to which he answers "as a complement to traditional ways of competing." What circuitous nonsense! Porter hopelessly twists himself into an ever-tightening Gordian knot and still fails to justify his old strategy model.

In an increasingly high-tech world, high-touch human assets will be paramount. Companies that combine the utility of the lonely Web with the sensibility and sociability of human touch will be clear winners. Yet Porter criticizes Merrill Lynch's move into low-cost online trading as potentially undermining "its most precious advantage — its skilled brokers." Porter clearly doesn't understand how the Internet stratifies knowledge and commoditizes routine transactions. By offering online trading, Merrill Lynch in fact frees up its skilled people from routine order processing so they can offer high-tech/high-touch value-added financial planning advice to clients.

"B-Web" Partnerships

Porter decries partnering and outsourcing, which were happening successfully long before the Web came along. Yet look at the changes already wrought on industries and businesses as they reconfigure themselves with what Don Tapscott in his brilliant bestselling book *Digital Capital* calls "B-Webs." IBM, for example, no longer makes computers; its webified partners do. Boeing doesn't make airplanes; it is a webified systems integrator. GM says an automobile is a webified information appliance. If these are not transformational business models and strategies, then I don't know what are. This is not incremental but HyperWebolutionary change.

Yet Porter says it's a "myth" that partnering is a "win-win" way to boost industry economics. He says partnering makes companies more alike, which heats up rivalry, forces companies to balance conflicting objectives, and reduces barriers to entry. On the contrary, strategic "B-Web" partnerships overcome supplier coordination problems and allow companies to team together synergistically to thereby raise barriers to entry.

Yet Porter says outsourcing to partners has a "dark side" because competitors can turn to the same vendors, eroding differentiation and shifting power to the suppliers. He offers no evidence for this because, frankly, there isn't any. Try telling the original equipment manufacturers (OEMs) in the auto industry that they hold the power over the automakers. They will guffaw.

In various industries, there are many commodity products and component parts and numerous private label products made for different companies by one supplier. The true point of differentiation, of course, comes from "black box" innovation and intellectual capital, webified supply chain management, webified marketing and distribution, and in repeatedly satisfying customer needs. Why should a company own costly, commodity-like production assets when it already owns the proprietary intellectual property and the loyal customer relationships that actually drive the business? Indeed, Porter soon contradicts himself to quite properly acknowledge that broadband and other technologies will in fact make it easier for companies to differentiate themselves.

The always-on broadband Web will clearly and dramatically further lower the cost of inter-business, business-to-business and business-to-consumer communication, reducing the cost of transaction and interaction between them. As webified companies integrate the HyperWeb into every nook and cranny of their businesses, this inevitably will reorganize markets and their dynamics, placing a premium on innovation and customer information.

Customer demands already exceed the physical possibilities of traditional supply chain models, which thus become obsolete. In fact, the HyperWeb decouples Porter's own, linear, industrial "value chain" and reconfigures it into a holistic "value web" and, in turn, restructures businesses and industries into value networks, or B-Webs.

Contradicting his initial dismissal of the Internet's impact, Porter later admits that "the Internet has created some new industries, such as online auctions and digital marketplaces." He even grants that the Internet has had "its greatest impact, enabling the reconfiguring of existing industries that had been constrained by high costs for communicating, gathering information, or accomplishing transactions." Now, wait a minute! He first asserted that the Internet had no impact on industry structure and that, anyway, lower costs of production and distribution were "weakening profitability" without providing any "operational advantages." Again, which is it?

He also admits that the Internet "provides an efficient means to order products" but dismisses that vis-à-vis catalog retailers who "have been around for decades" using "toll-free numbers and automated fulfillment" and that the Internet "only changes the front-end of the process." Give us a break! The Internet changes the entire business model and value chain, from initial production and back-end integration of processes, all the way through to after-sales service. This is not merely another iteration of the catalog business. Again, Porter is stuck in the past.

Then, thinking that he has made his case that the Internet is nothing new and changes nothing, Porter trots out his well-worn five-force strategy model, saying that the attractiveness of an industry is determined by the intensity of rivalry, barriers to entry, threats of substitute products, bargaining power of suppliers, and bargaining power of buyers. Hasn't there been intense rivalry in almost every sector of online business? Isn't that why we've had a shakeout? Haven't there been barriers to entry? Yes, the Web lowers barriers to entry but those who don't pass muster get shaken out. Aren't digital downloads of music and e-books substitute products? And wasn't the bargaining power of suppliers shifting to buyers anyway long before the Internet came along? The Web reinforces these trends and puts the e-consumer in control. And these very impacts, without question, again change the competitive environment and again demand a new strategy model.

e-Marketing and e-Channels

While asserting that the Internet is nothing new, Porter also admits that the Internet does provide companies with "new, more direct avenues to customers" and helps them "expand the overall size of the market." But he says these impacts (which he prefers to call "trends" — presumably to avoid discussing the Web's true impacts) are negative because they bolster buyer bargaining power. Since the Web gives buyers easier access to information, he says, this "mitigates the need for such things as an established sales force or access to existing channels, reducing barriers to entry."

Now, I ask you, since when was it negative to reduce or eliminate a sales force or a costly distribution channel? Surely that boosts profits by allowing customers to sell products to themselves. For example, if it were not for the network of automated teller machines, North American banks would today require at least twice as many tellers and much larger branch buildings.

Porter also complains that by expanding the geographic market, the Internet brings "many more companies into competition with one another." Now, come on, no matter how you elect to enter a new market you are bound to face new competitors.

Then he gives us another string of contradictions, even while reeling off what he calls the Internet's "very benefits": "making information widely available" (having just said that was negative); "reducing the difficulty of purchasing, marketing, and distribution" (having just said that also was negative); "allowing buyers and sellers to find and transact business with one another more easily" (having just said that market expansion was a negative development). Ah, I see; he says these "very benefits" paradoxically "make it more difficult to capture those benefits as profits." How does he explain this oxymoron? He offers an example about buying a car online — an example that clearly illustrates Porter's ignorance of the Web and online purchasing. He says the Internet reduces the importance of location and widens the market "from local to regional or national." (Actually, it makes the market "glocal" — both global and local — with varying impacts on different business sectors.) This expanded market competition, he bemoans, drives down the price of cars.

Let's examine that. The Web does change the economics and logistics of distribution in dramatic ways, sometimes even making previous channels obsolete. To buy a book, for example, you can visit your local bookstore or you can go to Amazon and have it shipped across the miles. But if you want to buy a new or used automobile, you are not going to get one shipped more than, say, a hundred miles because the cost would be prohibitive. In fact, most automobiles are bought locally, within fifty miles of home, whether offline or online. So that example utterly fails to prove Porter's spurious assertion because, clearly, a wider auto market neither leads to over-competition nor product commoditization. Yes, new car prices are reduced by the Internet. But that is more than offset by reduced inventory and selling costs, as any Web-savvy auto dealership will attest. Hence, the auto industry example actually disproves the point he tries to argue.

Porter then selects eBay as a good, contrasting example of how the Internet can help companies build economies of scale, both in infrastructure and in the aggregation of many buyers and sellers, that deter new competitors or place them at a disadvantage. I give him no argument on eBay though, as noted in this book, it began as a fad. But note how Porter now says it is okay to aggregate many buyers and sellers because it deters competitors. Yet he had just finished saying that widening the (automobile) market was not a wise move because you inevitably would face *more* competitors. Even though he's actually wrong on the autos, he can't have it both ways.

First-Mover Advantage and Network Effect

What Porter does not mention is that eBay enjoyed a "first-mover advantage" and became a "winner-take-all" company in its sector — a concept that he dismisses as a myth.

"First-mover advantage" flows from the Web's ability to woo customers with personalized and customized Web sites, from which they are loath to switch. The entire concept of "favorites lists" explained in this book totally disproves Porter's contention that switching is easier online and that category leaders don't become "winner-take-all" successes. In fact, "favorites lists" lock in customers and lead to category dominance by those Web sites that make it onto the e-shoppers' "favorites lists."

Porter also says "network effects" have to be proprietary to one company to be valid. Yet the entire shopping Webolution is based on the "word-of-modem" network effect that leads users to send friends to their favorite Web sites and thereby create "first mover" brand names, such as eBay, Amazon, and AOL.

Laughably, Porter constantly tries to explain away any online success story, saying that those companies that avoided "strategic mistakes" (as he defines them) are "exceptions to the rule" (his rule), thus dismissing any company that does not follow his outmoded strategy handbook. Moreover, Porter says that even if a company is "lucky enough" to control a network effect — which he also wrongly claims requires a large investment to create — then the effect often "reaches a point of diminishing returns, once there is a critical mass of customers."

Really? In fact, the very aspect of a network effect is that you build it with diminishing incremental costs. Try to tell AOL or Amazon or eBay (among many) that they are just "lucky" and that they face "diminishing returns." AOL has 30 million subscribers, is growing at the rate of one million new subscribers a month, and has just increased its subscription fee. Amazon's 20-million-customer base is growing by 500,000 a month and it enjoys the highest repeat customer rate of any Web site. EBay has 30 million registered users and is growing business at the rate of 50 percent a year, and at an 82 percent gross profit margin. These companies are just "lucky"? They face "diminishing returns"? They are "exceptions to the rule"? No, they are "first movers" who are enjoying the "winner-take-all" advantages of exploiting network effects to achieve increasing returns. They have carved out a competitive advantage by doing something that simply does not fit Porter's framework, and he clearly is unable to handle that.

Personalization and Customization

Competitive advantage, Porter rightly says, stems from "strategic positioning — doing things differently from competitors in a way that delivers a unique type of value to customers" — by offering different features, services, or logistical arrangements.

This is exactly what the personalization, customization, and one-to-one positioning elements of e-marketing strategies are all about — as perfectly demonstrated and executed by the likes of Amazon. Indeed, Porter says the Web is "arguably the most powerful tool available today for enhancing operational effectiveness." Ah, maybe he gets it after all? Oh no! He says that simply improving operational effectiveness does *not* provide competitive advantage because rivals will tend to copy your approach. Copying, he says, will become easier as system development costs fall, making "best-of-breed" applications less durable, making distinctive positioning all the more important. Who has copied Amazon? Haven't they achieved durable, distinctive positioning?

In any event, how does he advise companies to achieve this positioning? Configure "a tailored value chain" that is "highly integrated" as a "self-reinforcing system" that "any competitor wishing to imitate must replicate" in its entirety. In other words, Porter, without realizing it, is now advocating that companies webify themselves because this is exactly the non-replicable advantage that constant innovation via the HyperWeb will deliver! In fact, he says later that the Internet makes it possible to build "truly integrated and customized systems" that reinforce competitive advantage — which is exactly what Amazon has done.

Porter is so out of touch that he says the Internet "will be used" (future tense) "to optimize the value system in real time" and that "early applications will involve . . . customized product design . . .

based on customer input." In fact, of course, Dell has sold mass-customized PCs online since the day it started. Where has Porter been?

Need for e-Strategies

As for traditional companies, Porter tells them to "stop deploying the Internet on a stand-alone basis." In general, that is sound advice. However, why did Procter & Gamble (P&G) — the world's number one packaged goods company and the inventor of 20th-century corporate marketing and advertising — feel it necessary to set up Reflect.com as an entirely separate entity in the cosmetics market in conjunction with a Silicon Valley strategic partner? The answer must be that the Web represents such a profound break from the past that P&G felt compelled to venture online separately from the company — and, please note, with a strategic partner — so as not to risk its established business model and strategy. No doubt P&G is gaining much "experience" with this stand-alone venture and is learning many "lessons" from it — experience and lessons, remember, that Porter says are worthless.

Not to worry. He says established companies have "inherent strengths in deploying Internet technology." They do? On the contrary, "old" economy leaders such as P&G, Wal-Mart, K-Mart, Barnes & Noble, and Home Depot, among others, have shown that they have no such inherent strengths and that, indeed, their once-valid brick-and-mortar strategies cannot simply be transposed onto the Internet. Either you are an e-business or you aren't.

But Porter concludes that we should shift our thinking from e-business to business, from e-strategy to strategy. Now, it is true that we shall certainly stop using "e-" prefixes and ".com" suffixes in the future because every business will be a webified business. However, for that to occur, Internet strategy should in fact drive overall strategy, not be included within it, as Porter insists. Implicitly, a webified business will be driven by its HyperWeb strategy.

The Enormity of the HyperWebolution

Porter's thinking is fundamentally flawed because it stems from an utterly inadequate understanding of what the Webolution is all about. After all, his book *Competitive Strategy* was published in 1980 — the year the first IBM desktop PC came to market, four years before the first cellphone, thirteen years before the first Web browser. Clearly, the very means of commerce have changed dramatically and will continue to change even more dramatically over the next decade as the coming HyperWeb evolves.

To grasp just the initial magnitude of the Webolution, let's think back a moment. The first transistorized IBM computer was built in 1954 and had 2,000 transistors. Intel's Pentium 4, by comparison, has about 42 million. In 1983 the "PC bubble" burst at a time when Microsoft wasn't even a public company yet. In 1986, a state-of-the-art PC (basically a word processor) ran at what then seemed like a super-fast speed of 16 megahertz. In 1991, there were fewer than one thousand pages of information on a very crude Internet. There was no Web browser until 1993. Today, a top-of-the-line 1.7 gigahertz, Pentium 4–powered PC pulls down millions of pages of information from 1.4 billion Web sites on the Google search engine in a split second.

And we ain't seen nothing yet. In mid-2001, Intel announced the world's fastest silicon transistors that run a thousand times faster than a Pentium 4 and are so tiny that 25 as many of them — one billion all together — can be packed onto a single Pentium 4 chip. Within five years, these and still better chips will drive speech recognition, language translation, and other powerful programs that today can only be run on a supercomputer. The HyperWeb is at hand.

The HyperWeb also is going mobile. Commerce and communications have always been two sides of the same coin. Venetian merchants used carrier pigeons to gather market information, moving business at the speed of birds and galley ships. The HyperWeb makes communications instantaneous at virtually zero cost and will dramatically alter the parameters of any business.

The HyperWeb will have more wireless users than fixed wire users by 2003 and, by 2005, companies will generate at least 20 percent of their business through m-commerce. By 2010, it will be 50 percent or more — much of it earned by pure dot-com operators, many from abroad that will invade every North American industry at hyper-speed via the HyperWeb. By then, at least a billion people will be using an always-on Web on a person-to-person or peer-to-peer (P2P) basis, modifying their behavior and defining the new hyper-economic value proposition of a HyperWeb Lifestyle. This HyperWeb will utterly dwarf the amount of change already wrought by the 1990s Internet. And this, contrary to Professor Porter, demands brand new competitive e-strategies.

Porter clearly does not grasp the profundity of the Webolution thus far — never mind where it is inescapably leading — nor of its impact on the firm and competitive strategy, which is supposed to be his forte. He sees the Internet as merely another level of information technology and shows no foresight as to the inevitable network effects of a wireless, broadband, always-on, multimedia HyperWeb platform on society and commerce. He is akin to the plodding ploughman who could not envision how the first steam engine chugging past his field was about to change the world. Porter's eyes are transfixed on the linear furrows of an old way of life that will soon be washed away by a HyperWeb dramatically different than even today's wonderment.

Webified businesses and industries will slash production and distribution costs to a fraction of what they are today. To the extent that Porter acknowledges this, he decries it, saying that by driving down costs the Web is destroying the old bases of competition. Exactly!

HyperWeb m-Commerce Strategies

Under HyperWeb m-commerce, traditional approaches to creating a sustainable competitive advantage will wither against this blistering pace of change. Strategy must be an e-Strategy that constantly and in real time seeks out temporary advantages through continuous hyper-innovation that will quickly spotlight the leaders and starkly expose the laggards. The marketing mix will change yet again to focus on a new proposition: the time, convenience, personalization, and proximity values of each individual m-commerce consumer.

The smarter old-line companies will not listen to Porter but will change the way they operate. They will learn to make decisions in a heartbeat, innovating very quickly, and looking for new ways to reach fast-moving customers. Those who hunker down and try to re-Porterize their companies will fail.

Companies must invest in intellectual capital, hyper-innovate, and revamp their ways of doing business like never before. Those with capital and talent should push forward, webify their business as rapidly as possible, and grasp the opportunity to widen their lead.

For example, Dell is turning up the heat on its competition by slashing prices ruthlessly, something that Porter decries as self-defeating. But it is not self-defeating for a webified business to do so. On the contrary, Dell can do this and still make a profit. Any Dell competitor that sticks to Porter's advice will find itself squeezed out. Amazon, which scared the heck out of traditional retailers — at least those who were not listening to Porter — is still the trailblazer of e-tailing and is widening its lead.

Those who prosper from the shakeout will be those that create or adopt new HyperWeb technology, experiment boldly with new business models, and expand aggressively online. They will use the HyperWeb to supercharge every aspect of their business.

Webify or Die

To understand where this leads we need to ponder what the world will look like in 10 or 20 years. From that standpoint, it is abundantly clear that this is a major turning point in human and economic affairs.

Today's new combination of hyper-technologies creates markets for products that never existed before by offering something familiar yet so dramatically improved that people are embracing it, en masse, and it will totally disrupt the old order.

Hence, Porter's 20-year-old strategy model is itself no longer strategically competitive. To use Porter's own words, its "experiences" have been "discounted" by time and its "lessons," though not entirely "forgotten," have largely become irrelevant due to the disruptive changes of the HyperWeb.

Disruptive changes foster new perceptions with which to exploit paradoxes and incongruities between what is and what will be. They clear obstacles and bottlenecks in the old system, which often gets turned upside down. In fact, as explained in this book, the Webolution reverses everything about the old industrial system.

After the shakeout, entry to the new Web-based economy will be largely foreclosed as the surviving Web pioneers will tend to dominate their sectors. The survivors of 2000–2001 have gained invaluable online experience and learned tough lessons of what works. Old corporations, created when conditions were far different, need to be re-created if they are to survive at all. They must webify or they will die.

Ready for Act II

Clearly, the year-2000 shakeout was only about 10 seconds after the HyperWeb's "big bang." It wrung the initial silliness out of the first phase of the new era. The HyperWeb isn't even a toddler yet, never mind running. This is a one-year-old that's going to live one hundred years. We see only the first one percent of it.

Whatever analogy you use, the HyperWeb is still young. That was just Act I — the end of the beginning, not the beginning of the end. The HyperWeb is re-making the world into something very difficult to imagine because it is a fast-changing hundred-act play. Let Act II begin.

PART I

— • —

The Webolution

You'd have to be an idiot not to believe that something big is happening.

— Tom Peters, management guru

W<small>E ALL NEED TO SHOP</small>. But while the world needs shopping services, it doesn't need traditional brick-and-mortar shops. To grasp the enormity of the coming retailing upheaval, we need to understand how the Internet Revolution, or Webolution, is changing life, society, and the economy.

Within a decade, half of us in North America will live a "Web Lifestyle" and will spend less and less time doing physical shopping. This section of the book describes how we will live our lives over the next 10 years and how, in turn, that will change the way society and the economy function.

These changes will occur due to the Webolution's "reversal effect," where the "WWW" of the World Wide Web becomes a "MMM" or Mobile Media Mode of everyday living. In turn, this will flip economics on its head and place power in the hands of a "Web Billion" of Webpreneurs — one billion independent Internet business owners who will drive online production and consumption.

These broad topics are explored in this section under three main headings:

- ◆ Web Lifestyles: Home-Based, Cyber-Spaced
- ◆ The Webolution: "WWW" Flips to "MMM"
- ◆ Web Economics: The Web Billions

1 WEB LIFESTYLES
Home-Based, Cyber-Spaced

We are crossing a technology threshold that will forever change the way we learn, work, socialize, and shop. It will affect all of us in ways far more pervasive than most people recognize.

— Bill Gates, chairman, Microsoft

BILL GATES, THE CHAIRMAN OF MICROSOFT, predicted in mid-1997 that the majority of North Americans would be living a "Web Lifestyle" within 10 years (that is, by 2007 at the latest).

There is no reason to doubt Gates' prediction. After all, Microsoft is investing billions of dollars to make this way of life possible. But can it all happen so quickly? Gates himself often says there is a real tendency to overestimate how much things will change in the short term. (That's why we had the Nasdaq "bubble.") However, he also adds that there is an equal tendency to underestimate how much things will change over 10 years.

So, what is a Web Lifestyle and how will we live it? Let's leap to the year 2010 to find out.

— • —

Life in 2010

It's morning in cyber-America 2010, and a Wichita family is preparing for the day.

Mom asks her always-on voice-activated WebPC wall display to graph the family's global investment portfolio based on overnight price changes in overseas markets. Then she asks it to print out her and her husband's customized e-news — published around the world since their last review — stories the computer "knows" they will be most interested in. Then, preparing for a drive to a working lunch with a new cross-town client, she uses her hand-held WebPhone to call up a mapping program. Linked to a satellite hovering above the earth, it will guide her to the exact location of the company she is to visit.

Once in her electric WebMobile, she'll download up-to-the-second traffic data so the self-driving car can take the easiest route. Before leaving, she downloads a cyber-cash weekly allowance onto each kid's WebPhone. She also asks her computer to search for potential Brazilian suppliers her client might need and to download that info to her in the car before she reaches the meeting.

Dad instructs his WebPC tablet: "Dial Mr. Fuji at Ford Asia. He'll be in the Air China lounge at Tokyo airport." Mr. Fuji's mobile WebPhone number pops onto the screen along with Ford Asia's home page in a window. Within seconds, Mr. Fuji's face appears on the tele-talk screen. He answers "*Moshi,*" which Dad's computer instantly translates to "Hello." Dad says, "Hello Mr. Fuji, how are you?" which the computer translates to "*Konnichi wa, Fuji-san, ogenki desu ka?*" And so it goes, each speaking their own language as the computers simultaneously translate.

They discuss their planned joint bid to take over Lucky Auto, a Chinese firm. As they talk, Dad asks his computer to bring up Lucky's home page and a list of news items on the firm since their last chat. They debate their final bid as Mr. Fuji calls up a credit report on Lucky. After further discussion, they agree on the offer Mr. Fuji will present in Beijing. They e-mail a co-signed memo to each other's president about the final bid and Mr. Fuji dashes for his flight.

Next, Dad asks the WebPhone to read out a list of urgent video-mail messages and, noticing the need to visit a client in Paris, instructs the WebPhone's smart agent to find next Monday's cheapest and most convenient flight options.

The couple's "screen-age" son also keeps his computer on constantly, alert for beeps that signal incoming M3 (multimedia mail) on final-exam results or confirmation of acceptance into the next global distance learning courses. In fact, most students use M3 and tele-chat to study collaboratively with fellow students around the world for courses monitored by an international roster of superstar professors.

Meanwhile, nine-year-old Missy is about to resume presiding over an online discussion group of 60 grown-ups who want to learn everything about the Web. Yesterday she told them how she first learned to use the Internet in kindergarten, later setting up her own personal Web page in second grade, and then began making "WebPals" all over the world. Today she'll show them how to assemble their own home page and how to surf the Web for any topic under the sun. Tomorrow she'll show them how to shop online.

Grandma, a member of Missy's Web class, is downloading her vital signs, blood readings, and last night's EKG scan to her physician's mobile office as part of her daily tele-medicine routine. If medical attention is required, the doctor will e-mail her to advise what time he will make a house call or to confirm that he has e-mailed a revised prescription to the pharmacy for home delivery within the hour.

— • —

Sounds far-fetched? Not so! This is not Oz. Many families, in Kansas and elsewhere, already live their lives at least partially this way.

We are at a historic turning point, a true watershed in human affairs. The Internet is not high-tech news hype; it is an earth-shaking event dramatically reshaping our lives. We are living through the collapse of an outworn way of life and a new one struggling to be born.

> The Internet is not hype; it is an earth-shaking event dramatically reshaping our lives.

Soon, all of us will be living our lives in even more fantastic ways, homesteading on the electronic frontier. Yes, rich and poor alike will have access to the Net. Today, even low-income people have phones, TVs, CD players, microwaves, and cars. Surely they also will soon acquire a PC that now is as cheap as a TV and getting cheaper.

By 2005 the Internet will be the ubiquitous "dial tone" of everyday modern life, the rule rather than the exception. Homes will have home-page WWW addresses as well as street addresses, zip codes, and phone numbers. By 2010, we'll wonder how we ever got along without the Net; by then, the Internet may *be* society!

Home-Based, Cyber-Spaced

When the Internet first comes into a home, it has a similar impact to that of the first color TV, which clearly changed family life, society, and commerce. At stake is not just the future of the living room, but global lifestyles in the 21st century. The Web extends personal space beyond the living room to the entire planet. Your computer is your world. And so the world is yours. Everybody connected to the Web will have their own home page that will serve as a mobile, ubiquitous personal portal. They will interact through that portal with everyone else, for every need, wherever they happen to be.

Life will be very different in cyber-society. Each and every one of us will have a powerful global tele-presence through our own personal home page on the Web. Personal home pages will be as common as — and will replace — today's phone listings in the white pages and display ads in the Yellow Pages. Of course, as with unlisted phone numbers, those who want to drop out of cyber-society simply won't put a home page on the Web. But if you really want to live life to the fullest in the exhilarating digital era, a personal home page will be essential to your 21st-century freedom and happiness.

Your confidential and secure home page will put your entire life online, in chronological order, searchable from your digital birth certificate onward. You will be able to interact with any computer anywhere (even more easily than you do with a telephone today) and immediately focus in on your lifestream — all of your interactions and transactions with everybody in the world, including those with your immediate family, will go through it. Families will exchange multimedia seasonal and New Year greetings, turning paper cards into museum curiosities. All your correspondence, billing records, product ownership manuals, catalogs, family snapshots and videos — everything, will be digitized.

Indeed, your home page will outlive you, making you immortal. Someone long ago set up a Virtual Memorial Garden on the Web where friends and family can display epitaphs and pictures of their deceased loved ones. Just as you see photos of ancestors pasted up at Asian family shrines or in Buddhist temples, even the dead will have a home page bearing testimony to their achievements.

Always-On, Everyday Web Habit

The promises are mesmerizing, the prospects dazzling. The Web creates a global pathway for work, education, shopping, and recreation. Each family will have a global database at its finger-tips for children's homework, for cross-border online shopping, for tele-working across the globe, and for staying in constant touch with friends, relatives, and colleagues. With an "always-on" Web, the Internet becomes the "Evernet" and the world will be con-stantly within reach.

Just as most people today turn automatically to the radio, TV or newspaper, millions of Internet-savvy people already use the Web daily — often several times a day — to check on weather, traffic, news, and sports. Yet more millions use the Web to manage their finances, watch their stocks, and file their tax returns. Even more millions use the Web to buy flowers, books, music, toys, clothing, airline tickets — even cars. In other words, millions of North Americans already use the Internet in much the same way that others still use the postal service, the Yellow Pages, the telephone, or go to the bank and go shopping in stores.

Now, if someone asked you why you make phone calls, watch TV programs, drive a car, or go shopping, you'd think they were crazy. Using a phone, TV or car, or going shopping are second nature; they are an integral part of life. By 2005, most of us will take the Web for granted; we won't even notice it. It will be second nature to turn to the Web for shopping, education, healthcare, entertain-ment, communication, and to earn a living. Web sites will be so sophisticated that interacting with them will be the most natural daily thing to do.

Within a decade, computers will "disappear" in the sense that we now take automobiles, microwave ovens, toasters, and tele-phones for granted. Truly useful technologies always take over the home to become "part of the furniture." Thirty years ago, the idea of a phone in the bedroom was considered ridiculous; today, they hang by the toilet. Whenever we bring a new technology home — whether cellphone, answering machine, fax machine, modem, or computer — it changes our ideas about convenience, about how we interact with the outside world, and about life itself.

Peek into any teenager's room and you'll glimpse the paradigms of the future. Like today's teenagers, we all will soon spend more time with our PCs than our TVs. In every way, the digital pathway into our homes will always be "live" — the always-connected way we communicate with the world to live every aspect of our lives — and will dramatically change how we learn, work, play, shop, and pay.

The Digital Family

The so-called nuclear family provided clear-cut, often rigid boundaries between private and public lives, between home and the outside world. The network family will be much different.

In North America today there is no such thing as a "typical" nuclear family. Now, it is more a state of mind than a household structure. In the networked world, family must be seen as a network of people. As relatives disperse, the Web becomes the gathering place where extended families come together to celebrate births, catch up on relatives, organize weddings and re-unions, or mourn deaths. Already, home pages and e-mails are used to share year-end letters and to show off baby photos and wedding albums.

The Web is sweeping aside the boring television as the family hearth. Indeed, this is the age of the digital hearth. In turn, family behavior is changing. Earlier, not all family members were equal before the TV set, either as to program choice or even seating arrangements. Generally speaking, the male preference for news and sports pushed aside the viewing preferences of other family members. When father was not home, the children had most choice over which program to watch. Women were least likely to choose what to watch on TV unless nobody else was home.

A similar pattern emerged when the family PC first entered the home, with Internet use initially dominated by men. But then children came into their own and finally, in 1999, women managed to draw alongside men on a 50-50 basis as online users.

At the same time, more and more families are becoming home-centered economic units. As a result, a different set of household rules and family practices will likely emerge. For example, the social function of keeping up family contacts will gravitate to the Web itself. Already, many members of today's households send e-mail messages to each other because they often are not home at the same time. In the future, families will be at home more often, but their communications with extended family members will all go over the Web.

The Family that Surfs Together, Stays Together

A handful of principles explains the future of Web-based society and what it all means. The main principle is "reversal." In the Internet age, for example, you don't "go" to work; work comes to you the moment you step into your home office and sit down with your always-on WebPC tablet or WebPhone. Similarly, you don't "go" to school, the bank, the video rental store, or anywhere that you do not physically need to go. Thanks to the Web, all these services come to you electronically, no matter where you or your family happen to be.

The Webolution is returning us to a family structure more like that of the Agricultural Age when life was home-based. There was no such thing as "work." The farmer did not say he was "going to work" but "to milk the cows," or "rake the hay." Life's daily tasks were done in and around the home. Children were educated there, those who became ill were treated and cared for there, as were the elderly. The Industrial Revolution swiftly shifted work to the factory, and later to the factory-like office. Kids went to factory-like schools, the sick were put in factory-like hospitals, and the elderly were confined to nursing homes.

> The main principle is "reversal" — you don't *go* to work; work comes to you.

The industrial-era family of bread-winner husband and home-maker/child-rearing wife will soon be a vestige of history. The edict of "job first, family second" only worked when the family depended on the bread winner's single pay packet. The work–family divide is being replaced by a new work–family pact where the Webolution makes the home again central to society. Home-based work not only blurs the distinction between work and family but replaces workplace conformity with new family roles and a desire for personal freedom.

For sure, the last 30 years of the Industrial Age (1950–1980) brought new gender roles. As women moved into the workplace after World War II, this meant a greater sharing of family tasks, especially parenting. The emergence of two-income families created a desire to have work and family as mutually reinforcing parts of a balanced life. However, a mid-1999 opinion poll showed that only 60 percent of North Americans thought they had achieved a satisfactory work–life balance. Indeed, 63 percent said they would work fewer hours if they could find a way to do so.

As a result, there is a growing urge by people to work at home, often for themselves. In any event, the loyalty tie that once bound people to their employers has been broken. People simply expect and demand both greater autonomy and greater concern for their individual interests.

The newly emerging patterns of life and work allow people to develop interests and activities that are similar to those of family members rather than work colleagues. While television and other mass media still show lifestyle images to which some people still strive to conform, the Web lets people pursue individual interests with like-minded people worldwide.

Families that are heavy Internet users describe themselves as far more family-oriented and believe that their families are more intact because they can stay together, work together, play together, and learn together. In these families, work and home have really become intertwined and inextricably linked in a new lifestyle where they grow together rather than grow apart.

Additional specific benefits of a home-centered work–family life balance are several. For example, work and household chores such as shopping can be done on a much more flexible time schedule. Childcare becomes automatic within the home as opposed to sending the child out to a caregiver. The flexible planning of household schedules allows family members to spend much more time together. And the care of aging parents or relatives becomes much easier and less stressful.

The Internet-based family also is much more communicative than the average family. Studies show that the average North American household sends and receives about one hundred messages per week, usually phone messages, written notes, and letter mail. In addition to simply having "more time to talk," Internet-based households also find that they use multiple voice-mail boxes, cellphones, sticky notes on the fridge, and e-mail at least one hundred and fifty times per week. By 2005, this is expected to double to three hundred messages a week, with fifty percent of households communicating to this extent. By 2010, the number of intra- and extra-household messages will average one hundred per day for the average Web Lifestyle family.

The "network" thus becomes the new social structure as people increasingly will hold the Web in their hand, everywhere they are. People who integrate this new and wonderfully empowering new multimedium into their lives will live a Web Lifestyle. They cannot imagine life without the Web any more than they could imagine life without a telephone or an automobile.

Digital Domiciles

And that's only the beginning. As people become simultaneously more virtually connected yet physically mobile, distance shrinks while explorable space expands, leaving us with only one fixed point of reference — home. In turn, as noted, homes increasingly will be places with WWW addresses. Indeed, if the phone companies and post office were smart, they would have given each household its own free home page on the Web long ago.

Digital homes will be equipped with what computer people call a "server" — basically a PC that will sit in a closet, utility room or basement, just like the electricity panel or telephone junction box. This server will be connected via a secure in-home network to individual room outlets. It will monitor and control all multimedia traffic flowing in and out of the home to every appliance in the home. Houses will have "smart," chip-based appliances such as furnaces, air conditioners, lighting and security systems. Microcircuits will be embedded everywhere: in walls, ceilings, floors, carpets, draperies — all silently monitoring your home.

Stand-alone wired desktop PCs and wireless portable devices such as PC tablets and WebPhones will communicate via the server. Typical applications will include Web access, telecommuting, distance learning, tele-medicine, video-telephony, home appliance management, security systems, power control, automated utility meter reading, multimedia on-demand gaming and entertainment, online shopping, financial services and bill payment — the list goes on.

You will be able to communicate with your digital domicile from your WebPhone wherever you are. On the way home you could call your home and tell it to change its control sequence to adjust the heat or air-con, put on your favorite music, fill up the Jacuzzi, or de-activate the security system to let in a specific neighbor or unexpected house guest whose arrival is imminent. If, while you're out, someone rings your doorbell, your WebPhone could automatically alert you and show you a live picture of who it is.

The home network will provide wireless high-speed, high-capacity Web access from all rooms and all devices, including WebPhones, WebTVs, stereos, kitchen appliances, and automobiles. The network will automatically control lighting, security systems, air conditioning, heating, lawn sprinkler systems, and so on. Empty rooms will adjust perfectly to preset temperatures when someone enters a room for the first time and again when they leave. Lights and window coverings will adjust automatically at dusk or dawn, at any time of year and according to your geographic location, without needing to be preset.

The system will learn the way that lights and appliances are connected and how you like to operate them. Then it can replay the same patterns later to make your home more comfortable while you're at home or make it look lived in while you're out. Your house also will have multi-scheme lighting where various light combinations achieve different effects. A simple voice command will darken or dim the seating area for watching WebTV or entertaining guests while brightening the kitchen counters or spotlighting artwork. Houses will come with pre-programmed, commonly used lighting schemes that you can customize to suit your own taste.

Digital Re-Modeling

To make all this possible, most North American homes will need to be re-modeled for the digital era. At the end of 2000, only 940,000 homes had some form of digital network installed. But the demand for high-speed broadband Web access will drive the expansion of home networking.

Broadband technology such as fiber optic or coaxial cable allows much faster transmission of voice/data/video content. By 2010, some 50 million homes will be digitally networked, mostly using wireless systems.

Broadband will also come to the home, both through souped-up phone wires and coaxial cable as well as small rooftop dish antennas that receive and send information wirelessly without being in line-of-sight of a transmission tower. These dishes — first developed in 1999 by Cisco — will capture and clearly transmit signals, even as they bounce off buildings, trees and hills.

In the digital home, the TV will no longer be the focus of the family room. Moreover, many tasks now performed on PCs will move to mobile devices such as Web tablets or WebPhones connected wirelessly to the always-on Internet. Home theaters or viewing rooms with giant screens and surround sound will be commonplace and relatively cheap. They will organize your downloaded music, video, and family photo collections into digital albums, distributing them for playing across the in-home network or in family automobiles.

Flat-panel screen displays of various sizes scattered throughout the home will be your family's link to the outside world. You can shop online, watch movies, or say "Hi!" to Grandma, all by voice command. Family members will play games of various kinds with each other or against opponents around the world. Virtual reality installations will allow golfers to improve their swings, and then let them pit their skills against PGA professionals — all without leaving the family room.

The family room and adjoining kitchen will continue to be the family communications hub. Walk into your kitchen and with a simple voice command scan your video messages from family and friends on a flat-panel display embedded in the countertop or a cupboard or fridge door panel. You will know immediately where everyone is and when they will be home for dinner. At the same time, the system will read out loud all your fax, e-mail, phone, and video doorbell messages. You will simply tell the system which ones to save, print, or delete as you go along.

Door handles with built-in fingerprint identifiers will be linked to your home's security system to allow or deny access to the house, garage, or any inside room. If you're going out, you simply tell your home and it immediately turns off all electrical outlets so that you do not accidentally leave on potentially dangerous items such as coffee pots or irons.

The smart house will also help you look after your health. The Japanese have invented a health-monitoring toilet that examines stool and urine for unhealthy levels of sugar, blood, fiber, and fat. The toilet also measures your weight, body temperature, and blood pressure. If something is seriously amiss, the toilet sends data over a secure home network to your doctor's office for electronic consultation. In less serious situations, the toilet may simply send a message to your smart fridge to tell it to order more spinach for you to eat.

Digital Appliances: The Online Fridge

The smart refrigerator will monitor its own contents and compile an electronic grocery list which, at the push of a button or with a voice command, you can zap to your food delivery company.

Alternatively, the fridge can let you know when it is running low on something like milk, sending a voice-mail to your WebPhone reminding you to buy more on your way home. The fridge can even remind you when perishable products are nearing their expiration date. Or, if you still go to the supermarket to shop, while there you can use your WebPhone to get a list from the fridge of all the groceries you need to buy as you browse the aisles. Your fridge has a tiny camera inside it so that you can actually see what it contains on your WebPhone display.

Such refrigerators already have been made in North America by Frigidaire and Whirlpool, in Europe by Electrolux, and in Japan by Panasonic. Each has a computer touch-screen built into its door panel and a small camera so that family members can leave video-mails for each other or send e-mail or video-mail to others. Family members have their own mailbox where both e-mail and video messages are stored. The fridge also lets you surf the Web while waiting for your eggs to boil. If you're not sure what to cook for dinner, the fridge can suggest a menu from its built-in cooking database. When you're ready to cook, the fridge can communicate to the oven and tell it how to cook the dish that you have selected or prepared.

The smart fridge will monitor its contents and make a grocery list you can zap to your food delivery company.

The smart fridge also plays video clips or lets you listen to music or the radio. All family members use the fridge to compile lists of things to do. Each family member has a personal Web page on the Internet and the system contains a family calendar. Thus everyone can remember every possible life event such as birthdays, scheduled children's sporting events, out-of-town trips, car care, home repair, lawn and garden maintenance, bill payment and investing, pet care, doctor and dentist appointments, even laundry needs.

The household laundry room also will be digital. Certain dishwashers, of course, already have complex program cycles that deal with various kinds of cutlery and glassware. Connected to the Web, they will download the program required for different wash cycles.

Similarly, the washing machine can be directly connected to the database of a cleaning product maker such as Procter & Gamble so that you can quickly find out how to remove a certain stain from a garment. Once this information is downloaded to the combination "wash-n-dry-clean" appliance, it will know exactly what to do and how much soap or dry cleaner is required and will automatically adjust its settings to do the best job. Countertop microwave clothes dryers will let you dry clean small loads using chemical drying agents that dry clothes without heat. Unfortunately, you'll still have to fold and stow away the clean clothes.

Hot WWWheel WebMobiles

By 2010, as noted, the Web will be as much a way of life as driving the family car. Indeed, the Web Lifestyle will be lived out in the car as much as in the home.

There are more than 220 million cars in North America today and their owners collectively spend 100 million hours a day in them. While much of this includes an average daily round-trip commute of 90 minutes that will be reduced, if not eliminated by a big shift to telecommuting, the car will be a big part of the mobile Web Lifestyle — and of online shopping.

Tomorrow's cars will run as much on information as gasoline. Today's modern car has at least one on-board computer to operate the engine, regulate fuel consumption and control exhaust emissions. Luxury cars have more than a dozen on-board processors. They operate the radio, tell the transmission when to shift gears, remember drivers' seat positions, adjust the interior temperature, adjust the suspension on rough roads, alert the driver to loss of tire pressure, and call for help automatically if the car becomes involved in a serious accident.

In addition, of course, people use their cars in many information-intensive ways. The radio and tape deck or CD player tend to be in constant use. The cellphone — which 99 percent of people once said they would never want in a car — is commonplace, and new cars come with built-in, voice-activated cellphones. Mobile workers even set up makeshift offices in their cars, either on the passenger seat in sedans or at a table and swivel chair in mini-vans. In short, as I told a conference of automobile engineers in 1994, the car is an "information appliance."

All technologies are extensions of human capabilities and senses; they are mediums of our expression. As such, the car in the Internet Age is a medium; it is a computerized content carriage. By 2003, Internet connectivity in cars will be available to anyone who wants it, either through built-in appliances or through a portable WebPhone. More and more, cars will be networked and permanently connected to the always-on Web; tomorrow's car will be the "Web-on-WWWheels" or a WebMobile.

In this context, cars will truly "click on all cylinders" and it won't be long before traffic cops hear the lame excuse, "Sorry officer, I was just surfing." By the way, there will be no stolen license plates in the future because cars will have electronic IDs embedded in the car's computer. Car licenses will be renewed online automatically — eliminating line-ups for sticker renewals.

With more than 70 percent of wireless phone minutes logged in vehicles, the automakers ought to be the largest resellers of wireless services — and that's what they aim to become. WebMobile drivers and passengers will be able to send and receive multimedia mail, track the latest sports scores or stock market quotes, surf the Web, play video games, and even gamble. Of course, to avoid fumbling with the WebPhone, e-mail systems will be operated by voice command so that the driver can listen and reply to messages without glancing away from the road. Indeed, chart data, graphs, diagrams, and video clips will be projected onto the windshield using the same kind of head-up displays now used by fighter pilots.

GM's OnStar system had 500,000 users by the end of 2000 and a million by mid-2001, with 5,000 more signing up daily. If something sounds peculiar in your engine, OnStar agents can remotely check everything from fluid levels to engine temperature, and even whether the ball joints are worn. Premium versions of OnStar include automated e-mail, news, stock quotes, traffic, weather, and even an audio edition of the *Wall Street Journal.* Users can download music and books or shop online for anything that catches their fancy — with GM earning a commission for mediating such m-commerce through its vehicles, all of which it aims to get hooked up to OnStar within the decade.

In mid-2000, Ford launched a joint venture with Qualcomm called Wingcast to deliver wireless services to automobiles, including phone, Internet, entertainment, navigation, and safety. Wingcast could be rolled out in one million Ford cars in 2002 and another three million in 2003. After 2004, Ford says that every vehicle it produces will have built-in Web access.

Cars will be so information intensive that their software will be upgradable, just like PC software. Downloading new functions to a car from the manufacturer will be routine and will vastly extend the life of the car, which will be driven much less anyway as more people work from home.

Telecommuting and Tripping Out

Surveys show that 37 percent of U.S. households include someone who has founded, tried to start, or help fund a small business, many of them home-based.

In addition, nearly 40 million people now work at home and about 34 percent of full-time workers have flexible schedules. As well, the number of remote and mobile workers is soaring. By 2002, more than half the 100-million-strong workforce will be categorized as remote and mobile workers: telecommuting, road-warrior, or bring-work-home types.

Commuting to work, of course, separates neighbors and families. Until the automobile came along, people knew their neighbors through school, work, and worship. But commuting to central workplaces, usually by automobile, created "bedroom" communities and erased neighborhood links. Often, people who live next door to each other don't even know each other's names. The reversal of work back into homes will have exactly the opposite effect. Digital homes are not that different from weavers' cottages: spinning wheels and weaving machines are replaced by hard drives and networked PCs.

In any event, when you think about it, the main purpose of a car is to "take a trip." WebMobile passengers will be able to "trip out" on a variety of entertainment and will undertake greatly enhanced educational excursions. Cars will come with flat satellite antennas embedded in their roofs so that they can receive super-fast Web access as they speed along. Satellite-distributed infotainment will be sent to multiple touch-screen displays where the driver and each passenger can customize their own content. Each passenger will use voice or touch-screen commands to check their multimedia mail, stock prices, sports scores, or watch individual movies or WebTV.

Already, children can play video games or watch movies on backseat displays. And more than one-third of consumers say they are interested in purchasing a passenger entertainment system in their next car. Initially, the main applications will be WebTV and video games played alone or with other passengers. Through Internet links, passengers will be able to interact with family or friends back home or with people traveling in other vehicles, sending messages back and forth and playing games together. As well as keeping the kids entertained, of course, software titles and

Web-based reference sources can help them with their distance education courses and online degree programs.

In terms of pure audio, WebMobile drivers or passengers will be able to listen to a reading of daily news stories, e-zine articles, or any one of thousands of e-books. This content will be downloaded, either overnight to the car in the garage or while driving along. Passengers also will be able to listen to their local radio station back home no matter where they happen to be.

For planning long-distance travel, mapping systems are already quite commonplace. However the real advantage of hooking the car to the Internet is that tourists can enjoy a guided tour through almost any facility, on the spur of the moment. For example, if you spot an exit sign to Gettysburg, you could download a detailed guided tour that can play on cue based on your car's precise satellite-determined position as you drive along. As you go past Little Round Top you'd get a history lesson and as you drive by Pickett's Charge you'd hear cannon shots, and so on, for a truly real-time, Disneyesque experience. Of course, you would no doubt pay a service charge for such tours. Indeed, this example provides a clear indication of the future of the car. As an information appliance permanently connected to the always-on Internet, the WebMobile will have its own Web address. The car thus becomes an e-commerce portal of huge potential. At the basic level, consumers will be able to buy mobility by the mile, paying an automobile maintenance charge as they go, and being billed for units of infotainment as they are consumed. This would create a new model of car ownership, replacing outright purchase or leasing plans. In fact, one company already sells auto insurance by the mile. In short, the WebMobile could be sold or rented on a subscription basis.

The Web Lifestyle will be lived out in the car as much as in the home.

Mobile Commerce

The e-commerce applications for the WebMobile are even more profound. New car buyers will become an instant, captive audience for mobile commerce — a sitting-in-the-car market that could be growing by 20 million vehicles a year by 2010. WebMobile commerce gives the auto companies an opportunity to communicate one-on-one with online consumers and to mediate a big chunk of their shopping transactions. For example, as the car drives along, the driver or individual passengers could be alerted to special deals at nearby stores. Therefore, the car companies and their e-tail partners have a unique opportunity to bring products and services to the attention of mobile e-consumers at exactly the right time.

This will be particularly important during the consumer transition from brick-and-mortar retailing to online e-tailing. Most products are bought close to home. And the WebMobile, knowing your neighborhood better than you do, will guide you to desirable brick-and-mortar or online product specials as you drive along.

America, the land of the automobile and inventor of the drive-thru, is the ultimate mobile society. Yet it has been slow to adopt mobile technologies such as smartcards and smart cellphones. The average U.S. consumer currently spends a mere $12 a month on wireless purchases. However, this is expected to top $75 a month by 2004 and wireless seems to be finally taking off.

Even airline passengers will get Web access very soon. For example, Boeing's Connexion service — offering high-speed in-flight Web surfing, e-mail, live TV, games, travel and tourism information, and shopping — will come available on Delta, United, and American Airlines domestic flights in late 2002. Duty free, anyone?

WebPhone-wielding shoppers on the go are driving the shift to m-commerce, especially in categories such as event tickets, books and CDs, flowers and gifts, health and beauty items, gasoline and tolls, and fast food. McDonald's has begun using ExxonMobil's "SpeedPass" automatic payment system in its restaurants. SpeedPass is a 1.5-inch-long plastic wand that dangles from a key-chain and lets users charge gasoline to a credit card by simply waving the wand in front of the pump. About five million people already use the system. SpeedPass intends to expand into other retail outlets, including grocers, video rental stores, and vending machines.

M-commerce and value-added services will evolve hand-in-hand. Just as the Web moved shopping from the shops to the laptop, m-commerce returns shopping back to the purse where it started. The WebPhone will function as an electronic purse — a sort of remote control through which we will live our Web Lifestyles.

Every new car on the road in 2010 will have these capabilities. As people everywhere live a home-centered, cyber-spaced but Web-mobile lifestyle, the implications for both transportation and e-commerce are profound.

2 THE WEBOLUTION
"WWW" Flips to "MMM"

The medium is the message.
— Marshall McLuhan

THE MESSAGE of the globally electrifying, digital multimedia Web is its all-embracing ubiquity — a Webolution that will utterly transform every aspect of life, society and commerce.

How We Got Here

To put the prospect of the next decade in context, let's first briefly review the history of computing and the Internet. Computer cost-effectiveness rose 100 million–fold from 1958 to 1997 — computers were 100,000-fold more powerful but their cost dropped 1,000-fold. Today, a brand-new PC is switched on for the first time in human history every second, 24 hours a day non-stop around the world. In 1993, there were only 5,000 computers connected to the Internet; by 2000, more than 240 million PCs were connected. By mid-2001, 407 million people worldwide were online.

There are now more cellphones sold every year than PCs and the newest phones are permanently connected to the Internet. It is estimated that by 2003 there will be one billion cellphones, half of them permanently online WebPhones.

As a result, the Internet is spreading across society and into our lives faster than any previous medium. To reach 50 million North American users, radio took 38 years and television took 13 years. The Internet reached 50 million people in only five years.

Moreover, Internet use is growing five times faster than television and ten times faster than radio.

We are fast approaching what scientists call a "singularity" or "inflection point" where networked information will become instantaneously available to perhaps a billion people. As this occurs, around 2005, the Web will have become an everyday fact of life for the majority of North Americans. More than 65 percent of North American households already have a PC and more than half of those households are online. Most of them are still learning the benefits of the Web and few people could yet claim to truly live a Web Lifestyle. But that will happen as people gain in online experience. Meanwhile, the Web is quietly changing household behavior and laying the groundwork for the Web Lifestyle.

The "Reversal Effect"

The Web Lifestyle will reflect some aspects of pre-Industrial times. In 1973, media guru Marshall McLuhan espoused a new medium's four inter-related effects as follows:

- enhance, amplify, inflate, or play up some aspect of life;
- obsolesce, impede, erode, replace, push aside, or play down some aspect of life;
- revive, retrieve, replay, or bring back what was previously obsolesced; and
- transform, reverse or flip, when pushed to extremes.

Thus, for example, the automobile enhanced privacy, obsolesced the horse and buggy, and revived the countryside as people took Sunday drives there. However, the car also transformed the countryside into sprawling bedroom communities and revived the city as a workplace.

McLuhan predicted that "global electric media" — such as today's Internet, which of course didn't exist at the time he wrote — would have the following effects:

- enhance speed, creating a simultaneous information environment;
- erode visual and logically connected order through information explosion;
- revive audile-tactile dialogue, tribal involvement, and the occult; and

- transform the sender: you're there and they're here, instantly, as discarnate minds.

The Internet thus speeds up everything to real-time simultaneity, erodes time and distance, revives human communication on a planet-wide basis, and puts everybody and everything immediately in touch. In sum, the Webolution reverses all previous processes and flips the old order on its head.

The broadband Web will be "always on"— you'll never have to boot up or log on.

We're all part of the Web — because the Web is us. And because the human sensorium is a broadband device, the coming broadband Web will be even cooler than today's Web; so cool that you won't believe it's the Web.

Today's Web — and all of life and commerce — will get flipped on its head. The broadband Web will be "always on": you'll never have to boot up your PC or log on through a service provider. It will just be there, invisible — part of the furniture, so to speak. Not to be on the Web will be as absurd as not having a phone or a TV.

WebWorld Explosion

The Web, of course, is still young. In 1993, a 23-year-old University of Illinois programmer named Marc Andreessen released the first Web browser software called Mosaic. At that time, there were only 50 computers in the world that hosted and served up Web documents. By mid-1994 there were 1,500 Web servers, and by mid-1995 tens of thousands of such computers were hosting an even larger number of individual Web sites created by companies, newspapers, magazines, universities, and government agencies. In the blink of an eye, hundreds of thousands of Web sites appeared.

That same year, the World Wide Web suddenly pierced mass consciousness when Andreessen's company Netscape — subsequently taken over by AOL — went public in one of Wall Street's most stratospheric stock offerings. In the fall of 1995, Bill Gates wrote a now-famous internal e-mail that, overnight, totally redirected Microsoft's focus to the Web.

Since then, a public bombarded with inescapable WWW messages has been flocking online. By mid-2001, there were some 407 million users globally, about half of them in North America. The next big wave of Web users will be families. Sooner rather than later, 98 percent of us will have two or three WebPhones, including one for the car, plus a WebTablet, a WebPC and a WebTV — all permanently online.

Internet Mania

It seems that all great technological breakthroughs start with a mania. Breakthrough technologies go through a "hype-to-maturity" cycle and then, if they turn out to have real socio-economic value, they enjoy widespread societal diffusion. This cycle is illustrated in the following diagram.

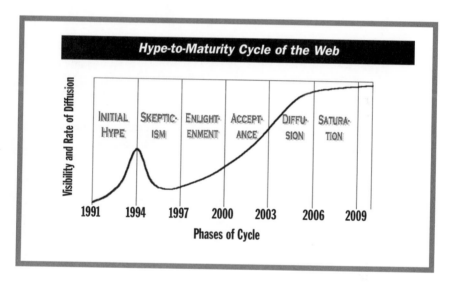

Upon the first appearance of a new technology that dramatically upsets the status quo, most potential buyers take a wait-and-see attitude. Upon wider acceptance, there comes a flash point when much of the marketplace shifts allegiance from the old to the new, and the product diffuses rapidly across society.

During the early stages, every new technology brings out the techno-skeptics, some of whom change their mind later. An interesting modern-day example is Ted Turner, the founder of CNN and now the vice chairman of AOL Time Warner. He himself launched CNN with much hype and in the face of many skeptics whom he subsequently proved wrong. When the Internet came along, he in turn was skeptical of it, at least vis-à-vis television. In 1994 he said, "Most people want to sit back and watch — interacting is hard work." Turner later sold CNN to Time Warner and became its vice chairman. Thus, when AOL took over Time Warner in January 2000, Turner found himself vice chairman of the world's largest Internet service provider.

As already noted, news of the AOL Time Warner blockbuster deal was a monumental validation of the Internet and marked the beginning of the enlightenment phase. Next will come widespread acceptance and diffusion, leading to market saturation. At that point, the Web will be as central to people's lives as the telephone, the television, and the automobile. Indeed, it will subsume all three of them. The majority of the population will live a mobile Web Lifestyle, carrying the Web with them in their pocket as they go.

Technology Denial and Skepticism

Every new technology has met with denial. Even the inventors of technology tend to perceive its future very narrowly. The steam engine, for example, was devised just to pump water out of flooded coal mines, yet it jump-started the Industrial Revolution. Alexander Graham Bell envisaged his telephone as a one-way radio device to broadcast news, symphonies, and stage plays (as it turns out, he will be proven correct as the always-on broadband Web evolves). Thomas Edison's phonogram was to be an office dictation machine, not a musical disc player. And cars were originally envisaged as "horseless" carriages that, hence, were free of polluting horse manure.

A slew of skeptics often will raise one or more objections: "It will never work," or "There's nothing new about this," or, failing those, "Nobody needs it." Indeed, nobody watched television when it first came out. And people wondered why anybody would want a cellphone in their car. The following examples of skepticism may be well known but are still amusing:

> *This "telephone" has too many shortcomings to be seriously considered as a means of communication. The device is inherently of no value to us.*
>
> — Western Union internal memo, 1876

> *Well, this is an absolutely fascinating device but what could I possibly do with it? (You could talk to people in other cities*

across the United States.) Why would I want to do that? I don't know any people in other cities.
— Mayor of New York, quizzing
Alexander Graham Bell, 1877

Everything that can be invented has been invented.
— Charles H. Duell, Commissioner,
U.S. Office of Patents, 1899

The wireless music box has no imaginable commercial value. Who would pay for a message sent to nobody in particular?
— David Sarnoff's associates,
rejecting pleas to invest in radio, 1920s

Who the hell wants to hear actors talk?
— Harry M. Warner,
Warner Bros., 1927

Television will never be a serious competitor for radio because people must sit and keep their eyes glued on a screen; the average American family hasn't the time for it.
— *New York Times* article, 1939

I think there is a world market for maybe five computers.
— Thomas Watson, chairman,
IBM, 1943

There is no reason for any individuals to have a computer in the home.
— Ken Olsen, chairman,
Digital Equipment Corp., 1977

There will be fewer than 900,000 cellphone subscribers in America in 2000.
— AT&T internal memo
upon cellphone invention, 1984

The Internet will collapse in 1996.
— Bob Metcalf,
Ethernet inventor and 3Com founder, 1995

New innovations follow a fairly consistent pattern: early imitators followed by a "gold rush" and, ultimately, many failures and a few resounding successes. For example, in 1855 there were more than 50 telegraph companies, and between 1894 and 1903 some 20,000 telephone companies were started in the United States. There used to be hundreds of North American automobile manufacturers; now there are just two.

In the first edition of this book, I warned that we would see a major consolidation of the Internet industry, with a few very successful companies dominating the market. For example, there still are about 1,500 shoe sites and more than 500 auction sites on the Net right now; few will survive the ongoing shakeout.

Web as Second Skin

But we won't be able to gauge the real impact of the Webolution for at least 20 years. What has happened already is bound to be very small in comparison to what lies ahead. By 2003, the majority of PC users will be regular Internet users and Internet shopping will have far outstripped catalog and 800-number shopping. By 2006, with broadband widely diffused, Internet video traffic will exceed voice and data traffic combined. From that point on, we will see rapid diffusion of the Internet which will begin to disappear into the woodwork of Web Lifestyle homes.

As mentioned, in comparison with previous media the uptake of the Internet is much more rapid. Here are some more comparisons: By 1970, 40 percent of American homes had color television, 25 years after its introduction. By 1997, 40 percent of homes had a PC, 17 years after its introduction. At the end of 2000, about 42 percent of homes were online and the 50 percent mark should be reached in 2002, only nine years after the introduction of the Mosaic browser. By 2005, about 70 percent of homes will be using the Internet regularly, many of them for several hours a day. By then, Internet usage will have surpassed TV watching.

Therefore, it is fairly easy to predict that 90 percent of households could be online by 2010. Once consumers go online, they never look back. During the latter part of this decade, a majority of many kinds of consumer household transactions — banking, stock trading, and much shopping — will occur over the Internet. As this decade draws to a close, one-to-one online shopping will have made mass marketing obsolete and driven many retailers to the wall. Thousands of retail establishments and malls will have vanished, numerous downtown office buildings will have lost their office workers and been converted into apartments and hotels, and many school and college campuses will have been abandoned.

And in this WebWorld, you won't have to know, type or speak a Web site's URL address. You won't even use a browser because all applications and access appliances will be Web-aware. You'll simply say, "Find me the latest Tom Clancy novel," or "Where's the latest Chinese movie playing?" You'll use the Web without thinking about it — just like driving a car — and won't even consider that you are using a fantastic computer network. You'll simply take it for granted. The Internet will be vastly important but just *there* — so embedded throughout our lives that we will wear it like a second skin.

> By 2010, online shopping will have made mass marketing obsolete and driven many retailers to the wall.

Embedded Chips

Computer chips no bigger than a fingernail are embedded everywhere. A simple musical greeting card contains the same amount of computing power that existed in the whole world in 1950.

First invented in 1971, by 1980 a single chip had 6,000 tiny transistor circuits etched into its surface. Today's chips have 25 million transistors squeezed onto them — transistors that once cost a dollar apiece. Now, one dollar buys 10 million transistors and, by 2005, a computer chip will cost less than a potato chip. Maybe we'll eat them as snacks. Don't laugh!

There are now scores of computer chips for every woman, man and child on the planet. By 2010, there will be at least 30,000 embedded chips for each of us. That's a staggering 200 trillion chips, each 10 million times more powerful than those of the year 2000. By 2010, 10-GHz chips — versus today's 1-GHz — will have one billion transistors and do 100 billion instructions per second (bips), perhaps matching the capability of the human brain. The earthly computing power at our disposal, and the enormous web of wealth that will flow from it, is unimaginable.

Today's Web is a mere 407 million people, mostly typing at each other and drilling for info buried in a billion unique documents. By 2010, the Web will be a constant flow of the collective multimedia interaction of two billion people and their 200 trillion chip-embedded objects, all talking with each other in their own language. When anything we look at, listen to, or touch is Web-connected, surfing will be as natural as speaking or reading or flipping a light switch.

These tiny crash-proof computer chips are embedded inside a growing number of everyday products. Here's a list of typical applications either already in place or coming over the horizon.

- Cars will be smart "chips-on-wheels" infotainment appliances.

- Cars approaching airports will talk with airplanes to get arrival/departure time and terminal gate info.

- Airplanes will talk with each other to coordinate flight paths, takeoff and landing slots, and airport gates.

- Luggage handles will recognize whether the true owner is picking them up, sounding an alarm on baggage thieves.

- Luggage will call home if it ever gets lost — which will be extremely unlikely in chip-embedded baggage-handling systems.

- Doorknobs will recognize who is trying to enter a room.

- Video cameras smaller than a little finger will be built in to all kinds of appliances.

- Toasters will recognize family members and brown their bread to their desired crispness.

- Harvest-ready fruit and vegetables will chat with robotic irrigators, pesticide sprayers, and harvesters.

- Food will communicate with food-delivery companies, restaurant chefs and smart fridges.

- Milk cartons will automatically re-order a replacement as soon as they are opened.

- Human body parts will be monitored constantly by wearable or implanted chips linked to doctors' offices.

- People will appear to have a photographic memory — which, indeed, they truly will as every signal sent to or by them gets recorded by wearable sensors.

The Web is becoming our eyes, ears, nose, mouth, and hands. As everything gets connected, the always-on Web will envelop us in a multimedia bubble that will accompany us everywhere. As media guru Marshall McLuhan observed, "the electric age . . . establishes a global network that has much of the character of our central nervous system; it constitutes a single unified field of experience." Clearly, the possibilities teeming from this "Webucopia" are endless.

World Wireless Web: WebPhones Replace PCs

The future of the Web is wireless. With data the fastest-growing segment in the telecom sphere, and broadband imminent, the wireless Web will generate a computing revolution dwarfing that of the PC.

In 1990, a Motorola MicroTac cellphone weighed more than 12 ounces and cost $2,995. By 1999, it weighed 3.8 ounces and cost $209. Today, many cellphone service providers give them away to subscribers. Thanks to their rapidly declining cost, 165 million cellphones were sold globally in 1998 — more units than PCs, PDAs, and automobiles combined. During 1999, the world population of cellphone subscribers jumped from 300 million to 450 million. This is expected to surge to 630 million by the end of 2001, 840 million by the end of 2002, and 1.1 billion by the end of 2003.

There is a brand new cellphone activated for the first time in history every half second and every day 150,000 people buy a Web-ready cellphone. Cellphones are now used by so many people that the phone companies are ripping out payphones. Some 15 percent of payphones have vanished in the U.S. in the last three years and the number of calls made on payphones is down 23 percent since 1998. This is only the start of a trend: BellSouth is removing all its 143,000 payphones from service by the end of 2002.

Even desk phones in offices are falling into disuse as people prefer to use their cellphone, pager, of PDA. Desk phones too will soon start to vanish from office cubicles. And some consumers are doing away with local phone service at home, relying instead on their much more convenient cellphones.

By 2003, the next-generation "Internet Protocol version 6" (IPv6) will allow trillions of devices to be connected to the Web. Also by then, there will be more cellphones on the planet than fixed-line phones. Today, of course, 50 percent of the world's people live more than two hours' travel time from the nearest telephone and thus have yet to make their very first phone call. Nevertheless, before this decade is out, it may be possible to give every man, woman and child on the planet a WebPhone that literally puts the Internet in everyone's pocket.

Upcoming third generation (3G) mobile networks will easily outstrip current Web connections and will enable travelers to use one phone — and one phone number — just about everywhere. As a result, Internet access — which now is 94 percent via the PC — will rapidly migrate to wireless devices which will account for about 35 percent of Internet access as early as 2002. The global standard of 3G mobile phone technology will deliver the bandwidth and speed required for wireless video and audio transmission. By 2003, there will be more mobile phones than PCs hooked to the Web.

In the interim, the Wireless Application Protocol (WAP) is sending data wirelessly at speeds of 100 Kbps. This is not fast enough to deliver multimedia but is more than enough for e-mail and for accessing information such as weather reports, stock quotes, and sports scores. By 2003, wireless Web speeds should hit two megabits — fast enough for high-quality music, Webcasts of TV shows, virtual reality games, and real-time videoconferencing across the globe. As this occurs, there no longer will be any such thing as a long distance phone call. Nor will there be any local calls. With an always-on wireless WebPhone, any global or local connection will be made instantly at zero cost — something the phone companies just don't grasp.

"WWW" Flips to "MMM"

Mobile access obviously will turn the telephone industry, the computer industry, and the Internet itself upside-down. WWW (World Wide Web) will become MMM (Mobile Media Mode) as business users and consumers increasingly use mobile phones, not PCs, to interact online.

By 2003, the Finnish cellphone maker Nokia claims that at least 50 percent of cellphones will have Web browsing capabilities — almost the same numbers of PCs with Web access in 1999. Of course, skeptics will say that AT&T tried Web browsing with its PocketNet service in 1996 and failed to generate a meaningful user base. In reality, PocketNet failed because the phones were too clunky and their battery life was woefully inadequate.

That was then. In 1999 in Japan, NTT's cellphone DoCoMo subsidiary (the name means "anywhere") gained one million customers within six months of launching an always-on wireless Web browsing service. By far the world's number one provider of mobile Web services, DoCoMo signed up 27 million subscribers for its iMode service in its first 27 months of operation to mid-2001 and currently signs up 500,000 new subscribers every week. Revenue topped $3.5 billion in 2000 and this will at least double in 2001.

DoCoMo's iMode is an always-on, 2G (second generation) mobile Web access service with more than 42,000 content sites. The Web is accessed by pushing a special "i" button on a feather-weight phone that boasts a 400-hour battery life. Its new Eggy phone has a built-in 350,000-pixel digital camera that can store 150 color pictures, as well as send and receive videos, and display either on a color screen. All this in a country where Web access over the PC lags the U.S. adoption rate by at least two years. Now, however, many Japanese are bypassing hard-wired PCs altogether as they go online wirelessly.

The Japanese clearly are the early adopters of the wireless Web. Compared with North American phones, the DoCoMo units are digital rather than analog, weigh half as much, and have four times the bandwidth. Such *keitai* (mobile) phones are giving Japan a headstart in developing high-speed Internet services such as moving pictures and interactive games. Surfers currently can use e-mail, maintain calendars, chat, swap pictures and play games. They also can download weather, horoscopes, phone directory listings, restaurant guides, and customized news from more than 15,000 Web sites that have been modified so that their contents fit the phone's small screen.

In October 2001, DoCoMo rolled out Foma, the world's first 3G (third-generation) super-fast Web access service. This delivers multimedia, location-based content that is personalized to the user, based on exactly where the user happens to be. Product and service providers thus can "meet" the customer online, at the precise moment of need, giving e-tailers a rare opportunity to differentiate themselves at that point of need. DoCoMo has allied separately with AT&T Wireless and AOL to develop mobile Web services in North America in 2002.

In early 2000, DoCoMo acquired a wireless network with data transmission capacity of 1.1 gigabit per second (gbps) — the same data amount that can be stored on 550 floppy disks — bringing its total wireless transmission output to more than nine gbps. As that bandwidth comes on stream, the limitations of screen size will no longer apply and, thanks to the invention of digital paper that can be rolled up like a scroll (discussed later in this book), WebPhones will come with page-size retractable screens that recoil inside the phone. By 2005, for example, Sharp expects "sheet computers" or e-paper to be commonplace.

Mobile Commerce (m-Commerce) is Next Web Killer App

As users start to dabble in a mobile Web Lifestyle, the demand for sophisticated applications of all kinds will further drive the growth of the mobile Web. In the business world, such capabilities as sales tracking and e-commerce will shift to a mobile environment. Indeed, major banks and retailers are already installing mobile data applications that will revolutionize business as much as fixed data networks did in the 1980s.

Consumers also want a mobile Web. A recent survey found that 42 percent of North American Internet users want to go online with a cellphone or personal organizer. Wider adoption of the wireless Web will fuel demand for universal messaging services where all e-mail, voice, traffic and paging services are combined. But shopping will be the killer application of the mobile Web, bringing m-commerce (mobile commerce) to the masses.

For example, you could be in a taxi with a friend who tells you about the latest electronic book she's reading and immediately download it for yourself. Alternatively, while visiting a brick-and-mortar store you can scan product bar codes to make price comparisons. Then you could decide whether to buy on the spot or simply hit one button to instantly order and pay for the product online — from any e-tailer you chose — for automatic home delivery.

WebPhones will replace cash, checks, debit cards, and credit cards in paying for products and services of all kinds. Diners in restaurants and cafeterias will simply point their WebPhone at the waiter's portable WebPhone-Reader to zap money to the eatery's bank account. The WebPhone — which my 1993 book *The Future Consumer* predicted as a "TeleCom Wallet" and which Bill Gates later proposed in 1996 as a "WalletPC" — will replace everything we now carry in our wallets and purses. As mobile as your watch and as personal as your purse but safer than either of them, your secure WebPhone will require either a fingerprint or a voice print to operate. It will be worthless to a thief and, should it get lost, you'll have a ready backup copy at home.

The WebPhone thus will contain all your personal identification cards and papers such as driving licenses, social security and health information, and credit card data. As well, your WebPhone will store dozens of favorite family photographs and will serve as your passport. Functioning as an electronic wallet, the WebPhone essentially will put your bank account — if not your banker — in your pocket.

> Retailers must think of the mobile phone as a new outlet, right in their customers' pockets.

As bank tellers and banking machines inevitably disappear, you'll download cash wirelessly to your WebPhone at any time no matter where you are; cellphone users in Europe can already do this. As well of course, stockmarket investors and day traders will use their WebPhone to get stock quotes, buy and sell, and generally manage their investment portfolios and retirement plans.

Moving Around in Mobile Media Mode

WebPhones also will be used to help you move around in mobile media mode. You will use your WebPhone to check flight, train and bus schedules, reserving an assigned seat without need of a paper ticket. As you enter the transportation vehicle — without lining up — it will wirelessly read the reservation stored on your WebPhone and direct you to your seat. The same applies to hotel reservations where your WebPhone will know to which room you have been assigned and will serve as a room key, automatically letting you bypass the front desk. And since you'll automatically check out and pay your bill with your WebPhone, you will never need to visit a hotel registration desk again.

Car drivers — and newbie taxi drivers — will get intuitive driving directions and traffic reports downloaded either to their WebPhone or their cars. Of course, you'll never get lost in Web World. Your WebPhone will constantly identify your position anywhere on Earth, thanks to signals from Global Positioning System (GPS) satellites, and will give you spoken and on-screen directions to any destination.

You will be able to program your WebPhone to alert you if anybody on your phone contact list happens to be close by. Or you could tell your phone to watch out for a particular Armani suit at a specified price on sale at any nearby store.

Obviously, these cool WebPhones will be a lot of fun and you naturally will use them for various entertainment needs. Sports fanatics will get news and sports updates, with hot links to extra pages for more information. They also will watch a variety of sporting events on their WebPhone screens, listening in through a discreet wireless earplug. You can also scan the Web for a movie or concert review, then buy tickets for it. Again, as with airline and transit bookings, you will get an assigned seat without a paper ticket. When you show up at the theater or concert hall, the fast-track turnstile will wirelessly read your reservation and admit you without lining up or taking the WebPhone out of your pocket. And, no matter where you are, your "always-on" WebPhone will deliver your favorite music or audio book to your wireless earplug without disturbing anyone.

> Shopping will be the killer app of the mobile Web, bringing m-commerce to the masses.

Thanks to new cellphone software that transfers data at 600 kilobytes per second (KBps), WebPhones already can communicate wirelessly with other nearby WebPhones or networked appliances. WebPhones thus will replace the exchange of business cards. Similarly, you could easily give a client a digital copy of a proposal or an updated pricing schedule simply by pointing your WebPhone at hers and pressing the send button. As well, WebPhones will come with built-in tiny cameras, their lens no larger than a pinhole, so that global videoconferencing will become an everyday activity.

Mobile Web Lifestyles

Clearly, it is time to stop thinking of the telephone as a handset with a keyboard. Your WebPhone puts the Web in your pocket and serves as a personal portal — a genie that's always awaiting your next command. Wherever you go, surrounded by your personal info-spheric bubble, you will be able to talk and walk, listen and watch, compute, surf — and chew gum! — all at the same time.

Indeed, as mentioned, we'll stop browsing the Web. What began with Mosaic in 1993 will come to an end this decade. Browsing was invented for the desktop PC. With a WebPhone you won't click from page to page but will invoke constantly updated, customized content to be always in your presence. Content will be tele-present in eyeglasses — their transparent, tiny EGD (eye-glass display) appearing as big and as vivid as a 17-inch desktop monitor — as well as in wristwatches, lapel pins and brooches, tiny hearing aids, belts and other accessories. Indeed, your WebPhone and related accessories will be discreet fashion statements, identifying you as a Web Lifestyle savant.

Finally, of course, WebPhones will be used for shopping as already described. As the WebPhone takes us to the era of mobile commerce, those who do not go wireless will get whacked. While the wireless Web is not "Nerdville" anymore, Webmasters are far more important than brick-and-mortar store managers and their landlords. And retail merchants need to think of the mobile phone as a new outlet, right in their customers' pockets.

3 WEB ECONOMICS
The Web Billions

The Internet is bringing about the most fundamental change in business I have ever seen.

— Jack Welch, former chairman
General Electric

COMMUNICATIONS AND COMMERCE have always been two sides of the same coin, and faster and better communication have always brought fundamental economic and business changes.

For example, knowledge gathering and communication once made Venice the center of world commerce. Venetian merchants had a basic need for maps for offshore trade and exploration. But that was only the start. The volume of business letters written and sent increased dramatically between 1360 and 1410. European mega-merchant Francesco di Marco Datini alone exchanged 125,000 letters with his Mediterranean agents, reaching 10,000 letters a year at the height of his activities. His agents complained that they spent half their time reading and answering letters. Sounds just like today's e-mail complaint!

In any event, economics is based on the notion of supply and demand for scarce resources. On the Web, precisely the reverse is true. Web resources can be copied and downloaded indefinitely at virtually zero cost. In short supply is the amount of time or attention that users can devote to Internet activities.

Nobel Prize–winning economist Paul Samuelson defined economics in his 1973 book *Economics* as follows:

> *Economics is the study of how men and society end up choosing, with or without the use of money, to employ scarce*

*productive resources that could have alternate uses, to pro-
duce various commodities and distribute them for consumption, now or in the future, among various people and groups
in society. It analyzes the costs and benefits of improving
patterns of resource allocation.*

Contrary to some opinions, the Internet doesn't change this def-
inition one iota. The Webolution, like its Industrial predecessor,
dramatically changes the economic landscape. But it still adheres
to principles that were the basis of Venetian and earlier economics.

The Web is all about users choosing how much time and attention to spend online and at which Web sites. The Web is all about
users producing and distributing items for consumption, now or in
the future. Web economics analyzes the costs and benefits of how
the Web improves patterns of resource allocation.

Network Economics Are Not New

Yes, there are Internet-induced "network economics" of scale and
scope. But these are no different than in earlier times. Consider
water, electricity, railway, airline, and highway networks. The
more people connected to these networks the better they worked
and the more efficient they became.

The size of a network itself is not necessarily important: railway
branch lines became redundant over time because people simply
chose an alternative. True, networks must be of a certain size to
function at all. For example, if there is only one airport, airplanes
have no place to go. The more airports there are, the more valuable the air network becomes to its potential passengers, and
more people will see the advantages of using it.

In turn, the exponential growth in customer activity — not necessarily of the network itself, which can reach saturation point —
expands the economics of the network at lower incremental cost.
The key is customer activity. Once a network and the number of
people on it reach saturation point, further growth can only come
through increased activity. So it is with the Web at large and with
any individual Web site. However, the larger the network, the
greater the number of people using it, and the more often they use
it, then the greater its "network economics."

For example, when steam power was first introduced it was little cheaper than water power and its real price barely changed

between 1790 and 1830. By 1850, however, its price was half that of 1790. Similarly, from 1890 to 1930 the cost of electricity fell by 65 percent as the electricity network expanded and more people used it. In turn, many entrenched methods of doing things were swept away. Electricity made the steam engine obsolete and suppliers of gas lighting went bust. When electricity was fully harnessed in factories after World War I, productivity increased an average of five percent a year.

The same happened with telecommunications. In 1860, a trans-Atlantic telegram cost $1 per word ($60 in today's money), so few businesses, never mind individuals, could afford to send one. Today, a three-minute phone call between New York and London costs about $2 versus $250 in 1930 at comparable prices. Thanks to the Internet, the cost of planet-wide phone calls will plunge to zero, with even a trans-Atlantic video call costing only pennies per hour by 2005.

Network technologies such as the telegraph, telephone, railroads, and highways also converged communities and economies. They enabled more and faster transport and communication for more people over wide areas and created new market opportunities. The faster the river, train, truck or plane, the faster and farther the product could be moved. Today, the faster and farther you move information, the more valuable it becomes.

Centers of commerce sprang up around networks, creating urban centers and the notion of "going to work." Ultimately, a new network becomes the center of commerce in all its aspects. This was the case with commodity exchanges, seaports, railroads stations, highway systems, downtown financial centers, and suburban shopping malls. Like the seaports and railroad towns of old, digital communities will flourish wherever there is a buck to be made from flowing bits — that is, on the Web.

As with water, steam, electricity and phone calls, the cost of computer processing has plunged, more rapidly than any other network technology in history. Between 1951 and 1984, the inflation-adjusted price of computing power fell 19.8 percent annually and by 28.2 percent a year since. A 1975 mainframe computer performed at 10 MIPS (million instructions per second) and cost about $10 million. Today's PCs operate at close to a hundred times that speed at 0.01 percent of the cost. This 99.9 percent decline in the cost of computing will continue to revolutionize life, society, and commerce.

According to the *Wall Street Journal,* U.S. businesses invested more than $2 trillion in computers, software, and related technologies during the 1990s. In 1999 alone, corporate spending on technology grew 22 percent to $510 billion and accounted for more than 40 percent of all business investment. Consequently, productivity is growing by three percent a year and likely will grow by five percent a year this decade.

As observed by Jack Welch, then chairman of General Electric, "the Internet is bringing about the most fundamental change in business I have ever seen." Consider the following facts:

- information technology accounted for 36 percent of U.S. economic growth in 1999;

- more people are employed in America to make PCs than cars;

- PC sales exceeded TV sales in North America in 1994;

- North American e-mail exceeded "snail mail" in 1995;

- about 950 million instant messages are sent over the Web daily;

- telephone data traffic exceeded voice traffic in 1999; and

- data traffic is now doubling every hundred days.

The productivity improvements of the computer itself follow Moore's Law, named after Gordon Moore, the co-founder of Intel, the world's leading chip manufacturer. Moore astutely predicted that the processing power of chips would double about every 18 months or less at the same price point or less. This pattern has held — PC chips went from 4K to 8K, then 16K, 32K, 64K, 128K, 256K, 512K, and 1024K — and Mr. Moore believes the trend will continue for least another decade.

This re-doubling phenomenon is not new to economics. Textile equipment initially started out with two strands of thread but this quickly and repeatedly doubled to 4, 8, 16, 32, 64, 128, 256, and 512 strands. Like the modern-day PC, the "Spinning Jenny" was cheap to construct, easy to operate, and small enough to fit into even the most cramped cottage. Indeed, many houses had two or three machines. They were well suited to the existing home-based economy and they strengthened the family structure. Families pooled their farm and backyard food production with their spinning and weaving profits to create a family income, thus binding themselves together in common economic interest.

The "mule" — a Spinning Jenny combined with a water frame — appeared in 1775 but also was a hand machine that could be worked at home. Even the coming of the steam engine in 1785 and the resultant power loom did not immediately change the structure of work and society. The number of power loom weavers did not exceed that of hand loom weavers until 1843 — three generations later.

Today, we are witnessing a much more rapid shift in occupations. By 2006, the U.S. Department of Commerce forecasts that "50 percent of all American workers will be employed in information technology."

Local Labor and Consumer Markets

Ultimately, of course, steam power and mechanization required so much capital that it finally separated work from home by centralizing it in factories. The family was split up into separate working units. Men started keeping their money to themselves and the loss of the family wage impaired family stability. Women suffered the most. Spinning was the first to be mechanized and the spinster — literally a spinner of yarn — became dependent on her husband whose earnings now depended on a factory-owning employer.

Nevertheless, the village economy and consumer marketplace continued to operate much as before. Working independently or in small teams, workers made "bespoke" goods (that is, ordered in advance), customized to the exact requirements of an individual customer. Most necessities of life were still available locally in the village or nearby town markets that were the hub of society. Even until the early 1800s, most consumer goods were made within the family or were bought from door-to-door peddlers or at the market directly from local producers.

Not until transport networks improved did family and local self-sufficiency decline in favor of brick-and-mortar retailing. There was an enormous growth in the number of shops between 1820 and 1850. This trend separated the producer from the consumer and the growth of giant stores further shifted business to large urban areas, to the detriment of local shopkeepers and markets. This also led to the demise of products previously made at home: jam, pickles, cakes, bread, and dairy products of all kinds, as well as clothing, draperies and simple furniture.

Thus, while the Industrial Revolution changed where and how products were made, distributed, and consumed — and by whom — underlying economic principles did not change. But the factory did dramatically change the costs of production and consumption, changing business models and leading to the rise of industrial capitalists. So it is with the Webolution. The Internet is a new network of opportunity where those who conduct commerce in novel ways will reap huge rewards.

Online Bazaar Drives Down Prices

One example of a new commercial approach is auctions. To have to negotiate the price of everything you buy would not be an effective use of your time. But collectors and bargain-hungry shoppers love flea markets, garage sales and — it seems — online auctions. First launched in 1995, eBay.com racked up $3 billion worth of sales in 1999, everything from Beanie Babies to antique silverware. Shoppers — that is, bidders — name the maximum they will pay and then top each bid by a minimum amount until they either "max out" or other bidders drop out. The Web site has more than two million auctions ongoing at any one time among 30 million registered users. Amazon.com's auction site can't match eBay's size, but it offers money-back guarantees.

Other hagglers go to Priceline.com where you can make an offer for a growing list of products, especially airline tickets. Every day, the airlines take off with 300,000 empty seats. When filled, the airline makes a huge profit on those spare seats because the only cost of filling them is a free beverage, a low-cost meal, a modest insurance fee, and a little more aviation fuel. Customers name their price and Priceline checks to see if the airline will accept their offer for the flight in question.

> The online auction is perhaps the most efficient form of market ever invented.

However, Priceline itself rejects about 40 percent of the bids it receives on airline tickets as being too low to even bother submitting to the airlines. And less than half of the tickets actually under negotiation are accepted by the airlines, leaving nearly 60 percent of customers empty-handed.

Priceline's name-your-own-price model was destined to fail in everything except perhaps the airline travel sector. Even there, the competition from Travelocity and others is overwhelming. By year-end 2000, the company was in disarray and founder Jay Walker had left.

Other bidding schemes are run by Nextag.com and Accompany.com. Nextag.com circulates your bid to participating retailers, each of whom can accept or reject the bid or make a counteroffer. Buyers negotiate in real time, just like in the stockmarket, but can walk away at any time. Accompany uses what it calls "Buy-Cycle" leverage. It is essentially a volume discounter that offers a discount price that has been pre-negotiated with the seller. Customers place their order and name their price, which can be below the discount. The price falls incrementally as other buyers place orders over a pre-set one- or two-day timeframe. The final price at the end of the buying cycle is what all participants pay. Of course, each item has a reserve price below which the vendor will not sell.

These "reverse" auction systems are not e-tailers per se. Rather they are e-community networks, bringing together customers in a facilitated online marketspace. And they seem to work to the satisfaction of a growing number of online shoppers.

Back in the 1950s and 1960s, of course, merchants maintained non-negotiable prices and rarely held sales. In the high-inflation 1970s, discounting and off-price retailing came into vogue and by the 1980s it seemed that there was a sale every day as the department stores struggled to survive. The new game is fair market value, with the Internet allowing instant price comparisons and efficient online auctions. The online auction is perhaps the most efficient form of market ever invented. The concept spread like wildfire, attracting everyone from businesses that use auction sites as their online sales channel to men and women who want to clean out their attics and garages at home.

Web-Driven Super-Boom

As stated, the global economy will re-center on the household during the next two decades. In the process, as predicted in my 1989 book *G-Forces,* the world economy has embarked on a hefty "Super-Boom" that will last until at least 2020. The Webolution will have such a profound economic impact that wealth creation will be unprecedented.

This wave of prosperity is not only due to the productivity gains under Moore's Law but to the networking effects of the Internet as the number of users continues to explode. This growth will be magnified by the number of business-to-business e-commerce and e-consumer shopping transactions over the Web. The compound value of the Web economy is equal to the volume of online shopping transactions times the number of connected consumers, squared ($WebE = TC^2$).

Every newly connected consumer increases the value of transactions that all other connected consumers can process. Collectively, they can do more, learn faster, share ideas, innovate faster, and build economies at compound rates of growth. In an e-cottage economy, every consumer is a producer again. Consumers will not just buy products from traditional merchant Web sites. They also will buy and sell amongst themselves, as the eBay auction model clearly demonstrates, with their own homes as their only brick-and-mortar infrastructure costs.

Again, then, the Industrial Revolution's capital-cost business model is being smashed to bits by the Webolution where intangible assets create more value than physical ones. In the Web economy, the greatest value is created by a combination of

- intellectual capital in the form of creativity and innovation,
- contextual information and knowledge or content,
- customization and personalization,
- customer knowledge and service,
- brand equity and Web site popularity, and
- lifelong customer relationships.

These economic variables are nothing new. However they change the business model dramatically and create a "market value gap" between traditional and new companies. For example, the value created by Dell or Amazon is far greater than that created by Ford or Boeing.

This market value gap is an essential element of any viable Internet business model. Those companies that focus on intangibles will come out on top. They will realize several principles of Web economics:

Reversal: electrified information reverses all processes.

Access: ubiquitous access maximizes customer attention or "share of mind."

Attention: time, being most scarce, creates most value.

Currency: digits, being most current, create commodities.

Speed: the faster you move information, the more valuable it is.

Virtual: digital networks eliminate distance, creating instant reality.

Interaction: cool interactions lead to valuable transactions.

Fusion: information converges product into value added service.

Service: repeat business builds share of customer.

Wealth: information boosts the value of all it touches.

Web: the value chain becomes a value web.

Profit: the Internet is a computerized royalty stream.

Economics of Surfer Time and Attention

Attention is one of the most important of these Web economic principles. The amount of time that any consumer has available is limited to 1,440 minutes per day. It is an ancient truism that time is money. Each day, we have 24 hours of time, all of which gets spent in one way or another, just like money. Wasted time is like a coin lost down a drain, never to be retrieved by anyone.

Therefore, spending time or paying attention becomes critically important in our hyperspeed economy. Of course, some people have more time and money at their disposal than others. The matrix below shows the relationships between time and money. Web site operators should pursue consumers in the top right quadrant; they have the most time and money to spend online. When you surf the Web, every click is a pre-purchase of whatever may attract your attention on the next Web page. That page may or

$ Rich but Time Poor	$ Rich and Time Rich
$ Poor and Time Poor	$ Poor but Time Rich

Money (to the left of the table)

Time

may not turn out to be worth your time and attention. Moreover, in any single day, you can only make "x" number of clicks.

The amount of time spent between clicks — other than idle time — is time spent at a Web site, depending on how well it captures your attention and for how long. In turn, if you find an interesting page of content, you find it worth your time and attention, which you freely spend there. If the experience is sufficiently compelling, you may even spend some real money in buying something from that Web site. And you probably will come back to that Web site again and again.

That is the essence of Web economics and the key to online success. To sell anything online, Web sites must compel consumers to pay attention.

Winner-Take-All Web Site Economics

In parallel, Web sites have similarly unique economics. Consumers are overwhelmed with choice and, as we shall see, they tend to gravitate to a few favorite Web sites. As some sites get bigger, they attract more users, and the more users they attract, the richer and more useful they become, thereby attracting more users in a virtuous cycle of digital capitalism where wealth begets more wealth.

This produces a "winner-take-all" outcome where a few sites attract most business and the remainder get next to nothing. For example, the 32 publicly held e-tailers racked up $4 billion in sales in 1999 and about 75 percent of that went to just five Web sites: Amazon.com, Priceline.com, Egghead.com, Value-America.com, and eBay.com. The other 27 publicly traded sites and another 87 private sites garnered only 25 percent of online sales. That is, only four percent of the sites grabbed 75 percent of the sales.

> It's a "winner-take-all" outcome — a few sites attract most business; the rest get next to nothing.

As in the old economy, digital monopolies seem inevitable because high-traffic Web sites will have few competitors. Hence, in any given business category, one or two players will come to dominate the market. Moreover, the digital race is almost over before it begins. Once a strong leader is established in a category, outside of a big misstep, it will build on its first-mover advantage to gain momentum and amass an insurmountable position.

The Web amplifies the rewards accruing to those who quickly create a major online presence because it connects sellers and buyers more easily and on a scale never before possible. In addition to the category leader, there will be one or two strong but subordinate innovative competitors who specialize in vertical segments within the product category. Leftovers will go to a clutch of low-budget agile companies who opportunistically clone the offerings of the category leaders.

Middlemen: Disintermediated or Re-Mediated?

Many people believe that the Internet will make all middlemen extinct. But e-commerce is merely reminding us of the centuries-old process of how new technology redefines the middleman's role.

Middlemen have never been very popular and perhaps today's most-detested middlemen are the automobile dealer, the insurance broker, and the real estate agent. Most consumers not only dislike dealing with these people but begrudge paying their commissions. With the early success of Internet stockbrokers and travel agents, these real-world middlemen also are fast falling from favor.

To better anticipate the middleman's future role, if any, let's understand exactly what they do. Throughout history, economic intermediaries essentially have performed two services: bringing buyer and seller together through information; and facilitating the distribution of products and services. While both of these functions will remain, the Web will significantly change how they are performed and by whom.

Generally speaking, the biggest Internet threat to any middleman is an online middleman or end customer who can better leverage the Web. For example, travel agents are experts at finding the most convenient flights, car rentals, and hotels at the best possible prices. However, online buyers of airline tickets and vacation packages can access the same information without having to pay a middleman, hence often gaining a better bargain.

By slashing the cost of communication, the Internet thus makes it difficult for knowledge brokers of any kind to hoard information and charge premium prices for it. However, the Internet also provides opportunities for potential new middlemen. The Internet makes it easier for anyone to become the kind of travel agent who, rather than competing on the basis of privileged information about standardized products, will attract customers by adding value in the form of customized vacation packages for those with special interests, such as art or genealogy.

With regard to the distribution role of middlemen, product channels essentially provide easy, convenient, and inexpensive ways to shop. As an electrified distribution network, the Internet truly smoothes the way for the shopper. As more and more people shop online, they have less and less need to visit a physical store. As this happens, customers no longer need retailers to carry large stocks of products; one "touch-and-feel" sample will suffice. The actual distribution of many products will instead go straight from the factory to the customer's home, eliminating many brokers and retailers. However, products still have to reach the home and this requires delivery middlemen to bring those products to the customer's doorstep.

Obviously, then, the threat to middlemen is not clear cut. The best candidates for disintermediation are those industries that became concentrated as a result of the corporate rationalization and streamlining of the 1980s and early 1990s. Well-known examples are Barnes & Noble in the book industry, Home Depot in home hardware, Circuit City in consumer electronics and, of course, Wal-Mart in the household goods sector. These companies and their leading rivals virtually decimated the networks of small retailers and large distributors and brokers in their industries. The Internet will only further reduce the role of middlemen in such concentrated markets.

By contrast, in complex and fragmented markets, the Internet could actually enhance the role of middlemen who bring disparate information into focus for the online shopper. The Internet does not yet portend imminent concentration in industries where the product does not easily lend itself to being purchased sight unseen or to easy home delivery. Obvious examples are household furniture and appliances as well as automobiles. However, even in these sectors, as already discussed, the role of each player in the value chain is likely to change significantly.

Overall, then, the Web will further eliminate middlemen in sectors already partially disintermediated through concentration. For example, Amazon.com is not just redefining the book industry through applied technology, but rather is pulling that industry into the information age and, in the process, concentrating it.

As the Internet juggernaut rolls onwards, it likely will squash whole industries. Many middlemen face a bleak future. Those that remain will continue to earn their living based on how they help customers navigate the breadth and complexity of a transaction. On the Internet, intermediaries who aggregate, streamline and simplify complex commercial transactions will continue to earn a very satisfactory and respectable living.

Increasing Returns

The Webolution also turns the law of diminishing returns on its head. The Web economy is one of increasing returns where, once up-front investments are made, each unit sold costs no more than the last to deliver and, in the case of purely digital products, the costs approach zero.

Consequently, as about 30 percent of retail commerce inexorably moves online by 2010, few big companies will survive this decade. As management guru Peter Drucker has said, "The Fortune 500 is over." He was not suggesting that they would go away entirely but that the advantage of being a big brick-and-mortar business is less and less relevant.

In my view, almost any company that doesn't successfully make the transition to the home-based, customer-centric Web economy will shrivel and die. The silicon solvent of frictionless capital dissolves brick-and-mortar into click streams of digital consumerism. Some day, even automobile fuel will be delivered to the home — in the form of electric power for electric cars.

Consumers are voting, with their mouse clicks and digital wallets, for the Web economy.

Meanwhile, tech-savvy customers will reward tech-savvy companies. About seventy percent of the North American economy involves personal consumption; even if only five percent of that goes online, then a brand-new $200 billion economic sector will be created, transforming the consumer market in its wake. Consumers are voting, not with their feet but with their mouse clicks and digital wallets, for the Web economy. They are happily changing their daily routine to take advantage of the online marketplace.

Mass market companies, where 70 percent of new products fail and only 40 percent of products are profitable, clearly face a dismal future. Simply consider the limited shelf space in a shop.

Amazon.com offers four million book titles that it displays on virtual shelves in a computer server where its 20 million customers can browse at leisure. Amazon's bookshelves are duplicated all over the Internet at zero cost. How can any bookshop — chain or independent — possibly compete with that?

By going online, brick-and-mortar retailers can dramatically improve their performance. They can boost their revenue by embracing the new value proposition of new channels, extended reach, and individualized customer attention. Costs can be slashed through more efficient administration, lower marketing and selling expenses, and a lower cost of goods sold, thus boosting gross profit margins. Gross margin is a critical measure of online success, and leading e-tailers such as eBay and AOL have gross margins exceeding 50 percent. Asset allocation also can be significantly improved by reducing physical infrastructure and increasing working capital turnover.

When an online transition is carried out properly, brick-and-mortar companies typically will boost revenue by 15–25 percent, slash costs by 25–50 percent, and improve asset intensity by 30–70 percent. Indeed, studies show that the best-case gains will be 50, 70, and 90 percent respectively. What are they waiting for?

Homepreneurs:
Independent Internet Business Operators (IiBOs)

The Webolution thus is unwinding everything that the Industrial Revolution put in place. As media guru Marshall McLuhan long ago observed, "with computers we are headed for cottage economics where industrial activities can be carried on in any little shack anywhere on the globe." The concept of cottage economics is entirely appropriate because, after all, the word "economy" derives from the Greek word for household.

The Webolution also is shifting e-commerce directly into the home. Thanks mainly to homepreneurs (home-based entrepreneurs) and telecommuters, the suburbs are changing and North American family life is enjoying a renewal. For the first time in a century, census data show that North America is experiencing a reverse migration from the cities and suburbs to the exurbs and the countryside. By 2020, it is estimated that as much as 50 percent of the American and Canadian population will have relocated to rural areas, throwing the housing market into turmoil.

It's easy to understand why. Just imagine your commute being a 30-second walk from the kitchen to a spare bedroom or a sunny loft. No more boorish bosses, snarky secretaries, conniving colleagues, pointless PowerPoint presentations, or dimwitted distractions. Thanks to the Webolution, there's no need to "go" anywhere, including to work. Work comes to you the moment you switch on your PC.

Of course, skeptics will remind us that way back in 1893 someone predicted that everyone would be working out of their home by 1993. Well, the Webolution now makes that much more likely over the next few decades. Across the continent, tens of millions of people have become determined to "get a life" — a Web Lifestyle at home. Tomorrow's economy will increasingly be based on the productive output of families working and consuming at home.

> By 2020, up to 50% of the population will have relocated to rural areas, throwing housing markets into turmoil.

Again, we can draw striking parallels with the textile revolution. Then, as in today's Web-driven economy, anyone with a modicum of skill and a little money, and who was prepared to take a small risk, faced a broad and bewildering array of opportunities to make money. Even the poorest family saw the value of owning a spinning machine, the cost of which it could easily afford. As the machines became more complex, they did at first become more expensive than earlier models and a machine bought this year could be obsolete the next. Still, the newer machines produced more, and the demands for output were so great that many families owned two or three.

Of course, new technology is a threat to those who lack it. And so it is today with the PC and the Web. Any family that doesn't own at least one PC is in danger of missing out on the biggest income bonanza in history. Revolutionary technologies create dramatic shifts in economic value, shifting producers and consumers in and out of the money stream. Bill Gates thus became the world's first billionaire by writing software code — an intangible product. Simultaneously, however, those who earn their living with computers are the new home-based entrepreneurs of the Webolution. These "Webpreneurs" recognize the PC as a "golden loom" that, connected to the Internet, is capable of weaving an ever-expanding web of wealth for them and their families.

Every seven seconds somebody starts a new home-based business in North America — 12,300 new start-ups daily. Home is where the future is. And if you are seriously considering starting your own home-based business, you're riding the wave of the future. During the 1980s the number of people working at home jumped 56 percent, according to the U.S. Census Bureau, with 3.4 million Americans working at home in 1990, accounting for three percent of the workforce. By 1999, this had jumped to 19.6 million, accounting for 17 percent of the workforce.

According to many other surveys, including our own, these statistics significantly underestimate the number of people working at home. Our surveys show that some 28 percent of the North American workforce already work at or from home — either for themselves or others — and the number is growing at a rapid rate. We expect it to reach at least 40 percent by 2010. As this occurs, the impact on economic production and consumption — particularly online shopping — will be dramatic.

Web Workstyles

About 60 percent of home workers are self-employed. People used to believe that their livelihood depended on living in big cities and working for big corporations. However, 86 percent of home-based business owners are far happier running their own business instead of working for someone else.

In addition, enlightened corporations are making greater use of subcontracted, self-employed workers, bringing in key skills as and when required. These temporary-contract contingency workers could account for another 20 percent of the North American workforce by 2010.

In turn, self-employed professionals find that they can go online to obtain lucrative consulting contracts. These freelancers compete online with each other for work, posting their skills, fees and promised deliverables. They bid for jobs online, download the materials to do them, and get paid online, all without any contact with the client other than by e-mail. Many freelancers work together as virtual teams for a day, a week, a month, or longer, and then disperse and recombine to work on other projects. It is estimated that some 28 million North Americans operate as such self-employed free agents, largely through the Web.

Larger companies also increasingly operate on the fly, with

many people coming together via internal company Intranets to tackle temporary projects. For example, Hollywood studios used to employ people on contract, stabilizing employee incomes and guaranteeing them work. Over time, the studio system broke up. Today, movie making involves assembling a virtual company which temporarily hires a producer, a director, script writers, set and costume designers, the stars and supporting cast, and the entire technical crew.

Nearby Silicon Valley offers another workplace paradigm. It's often said that the creative people working in the Valley switch employers more often than they change parking spots and without even changing car pools. As well, increasing numbers of Valley workers telecommute. As Stan Davis and Christopher Meyer observe in their book *Blur,* the Valley shows that talent is mobile, that companies form around brain-power projects, that job tenures are short, and that employee adaptability and the value added through productivity are high. Workers in the Valley also identify much more strongly with what they do than with their employers. They also tend to live a Web Lifestyle.

> Families will legally incorporate: their pooled money will strengthen them, leading to fewer divorces.

As the world adopts the Internet, people and businesses will adopt Hollywood and Silicon Valley "Web Workstyles" and business-organizing principles. As work returns to the home, marriage and family will be much more of an economic endeavor, so much so that most families will legally incorporate. Their pooled money will strengthen families and lead to many fewer divorces.

Already, an economically focused family values movement is emerging. Family priorities are shifting to provide their own day-care at home, home-based schooling and e-university education, care for aging parents, building a financial base for personal and spousal retirement, and to being fiscally responsible for their local neighborhood and community institutions.

Web family businesses will more readily identify their companies as family businesses. In the past, business owners either failed to recognize that their companies were actually family businesses or they avoided that identity because it projected a "mom and pop" image. But more and more families now see their company as a family business and feel good about it. Society will be strengthened as stronger families spend more time with neighbors and their local community. Indeed, Bill Gates could go down in history as the person who almost single-handedly brought the North American family and neighborhood community back together again.

Webpreneurs: Small Business Goes Online

Even before the impact of the Internet, small businesses accounted for 99.7 percent of all employers, providing jobs to 53 percent of North America's private sector workforce. Even so, 89 percent of small businesses have fewer than 20 employees. About eight percent of businesses are sole proprietorships with no additional employees, and another 52 percent have fewer than five employees.

The small office/home office (SOHO) market is changing the socio-economic landscape. The fastest-growing part of the North American economy, there were 49 million SOHO enterprises at the end of 2000 and the number is growing by about 10,000 a day. At that rate, there will be 100 million SOHO firms by 2010. Indeed, we at Glocal Marketing believe the growth will accelerate and that there will be more than 200 million SOHO firms within the decade.

Savvy home-based entrepreneurs know that e-commerce will play a huge role in the future of their business. About 50 percent of small businesses already have Web sites but they mostly are companies with more than 10 employees. Among smaller firms, Internet presence is only 28 percent. Many small firms wrongly believe the Internet can't help them because their businesses are too localized. Nevertheless, more than 30,000 small businesses with revenues under $10 million already sell online. They realize that they must index their growth to that of the Web.

The Internet opens up the opportunity for desktop retailing to anyone with a Web connection and a reasonable amount of ambition. Many sole proprietors are becoming Webpreneurs, either on their own or through affiliation with a major e-tailer. In 1999, for example, Amazon.com created an instant-store concept called zShops where anyone can sell practically anything through Amazon.com's Web site. Regardless of size, product or location, Webpreneurs can list items for sale for a nominal fee and place them before Amazon's 20 million customers.

Other Webpreneurs affiliate with Amazon.com to sell books, earning a commission on any sale channeled through their Web site. These Webpreneurs set themselves up as one-click linked affiliates of companies such as Amazon.com, thus essentially setting up a virtual bookstore without the need of a brick-and-mortar storefront or warehouse space, and without having to deal with publishers or ship out orders. An affiliate simply embeds hyperlinked references to books carried by Amazon. Any site visitor who clicks on the book is immediately spirited to Amazon's site.

Again, the key to being a successful Webpreneur is to offer content so compelling that surfers not only visit your site but are willing to click through it to buy related products.

This quiet morphing of Web users into Webpreneurs is a major part of the Webolution. By 2005, about one billion people worldwide will be online; by 2010, that will have doubled to two billion, each representing a family economic unit.

Consider, then, two billion family profit centers comprising four or five billion lifelong cyber consumers — all interacting with you through your Web site.

The mind boggles!

PART II

— • —

Who Will Shop Online

Whether keeping in touch with friends and family, getting information to make better buying decisions, or trading stocks, people clearly see everyday tasks as easier and more convenient when done online. And the longer people are online, the more benefits they notice.

— Bob Pittman, president
AOL Time Warner

THE WEBOLUTION IS DISSOLVING the mass market into "markets of one," and so there is less need to appeal to more than one person at a time. Hence, consumer demographics (age, gender, ethnicity, income, location, education level) and psychographics (what makes customers tick) are decreasingly relevant. Instead, e-marketers need to know what makes customers "click"; they need technographic or "webographic" customer profiles.

Yet, to understand the transition from mass-market brick-and-mortar retailing to personalized click-and-order e-tailing, we still need to profile who is now shopping online and who will do so in the future. This section thus reviews traditional as well as new consumer characteristics:

◆ Demographics: "Web-Gen" Kids to "Wired" Seniors
◆ Psychographics: Why They're "Clicking" Online
◆ Webographics: What They Do Online

4 DEMOGRAPHICS
"Web-Gen" Kids to "Wired" Seniors

The Net-Generation has arrived. There is no issue more important to marketers than understanding this new generation.

— Don Tapscott, chair,
Digital4Sight Inc.

THE SHEER OVERALL NUMBER of potential online consumers depends on the growth of the population at large, how fast they get online, and whether they make shopping a regular habit. The U.S. population will grow from 275 million now to 300 million by 2010. Canada's population will grow at the same rate to reach 33 million, bringing North American society to 333 million in 2010.

The Five Web Generations
My 1993 book *The Future Consumer* explained how each generation of people bears a strong imprint of the milieu in which it is born and raised. This is particularly important to consider in a technologically driven, immigrant society like North America. While no generation has precise boundaries, there are discernible 16- to 17-year birth cycles of about one generation in length. At Glocal Marketing, we define five generational types, as follows:

- **"By-the-Book" (born 1911–1928):**
  Telegraph-era great grandparents; six percent of today's market;

- **"By-the-Clock" (born 1929–1945):**
  Radio-era grandparents; 16 percent of the market;

- **"Baby-Boom" (born 1946–1964):**
  TV-era parents; 30 percent of the market;

- **"Gen-X" (born 1965–1982):**
  MTV-era children of the Boomers; 20 percent of the market;

- **"Web-Gen" (born 1983–2000):**
  PC-era children of the Web; 28 percent of the market.

Everybody's Going Online

Regardless of age, everybody's going online and the profile of North America's 167 million Internet users now pretty much mirrors the population at large. Indeed, the following chart shows that as the population ages and more people get PCs and go online, the age profile of online users will broaden out, shifting to the right in the chart.

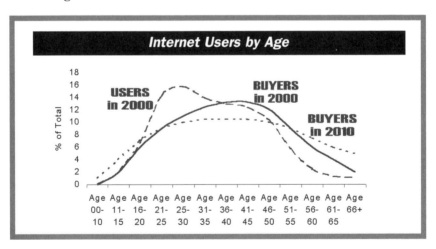

Surfers are Starting to Shop

The profile of online shoppers is now mirroring society at large. Of the online population at the end of 2000, by age group, 19 percent of 16–22 year-olds had shopped online, 24 percent of 23–29 year-olds, 27 percent of 30–44 year-olds, 24 percent of 45–59 year-olds, and seven percent of 60+ year-olds. In sum, apart from seniors, online shopping is going mainstream.

Young people, of course, automatically represent tomorrow's shoppers. Never having known a world without computers and the

Web, they will be the quintessential "future consumer.com." In 1999, there were 10 million North American kids aged five to twelve and another 12 million teenagers (or "screenagers") online. Both these numbers also will double by 2002. Taken together, this group of 60 million young people grew up with PCs and, latterly, the Web. Therefore, we called them the "Web Generation" or "Web-Gen" for short.

These 22 million Web-Gen kids currently spend at least an hour a day online. Any parent who has Web-Gen kids at home will tell you that it is no longer a matter of getting them off the phone but getting them to shut down their PCs. They use the Web not only to play games or research homework but to chat with friends — and to shop.

Web-Gen online shoppers ask their parents for credit card numbers rather than a weekly allowance, and most of them surf the Web unsupervised with permission to buy. At least 75 percent of Web-Gen kids have already shopped online, and they spent about $200 million doing so in 1999 — most of it by the teenage group who spend about $140 billion a year overall on retail goods. Thus, while online purchasing is still a small part of overall spending by young people, the dollar amount is growing rapidly and is expected to top $1.2 billion in 2002 and reach at least $10 billion by 2010. Their most popular purchase, of course, is music (38 percent of buyers), followed by books (28 percent of buyers), electronic equipment, computer games, software, concert tickets, travel, and health and beauty aids.

As the Web goes mainstream, families with kids become a much more important market. Nearly 40 percent of North American households have children. More than 65 percent of those households have at least one PC and most of them go online, doing so for two hours more per week than online households without kids. In turn, about 58 percent of online households with kids are shopping online.

Generally speaking, these families enjoy above-average incomes and have higher education levels, thus constituting a tech-savvy market segment with purchasing power. As might be expected, their favorite online purchase categories are toys, followed by event tickets, sports equipment, and music. These families also are gravitating to the mainline online categories of books, software, airline tickets, and consumer electronics. As e-shopping takes off in parallel with the aging of this tech-savvy generation, the surge of teenage consumers over the next decade will meaningfully expand the viability of many online product categories.

Web-Gen kids congregate less and less at the shopping mall and more and more on the Internet. And just as TV-era Baby Boomers grew up with homogeneity and mass marketing, the Web-Gen medium of choice drives diversity, market fragmentation, individualism, customization and personalization. This is perhaps best illustrated in the music category where Web-Gen fans in small groups can meet, exchange information, listen to sound clips via MP3 downloads, and pen cryptic online reviews.

Web-Gen kids meet less and less at the mall and more and more on the Net.

As this generation ages — about five million new car drivers will come of age annually until 2010 — marketers of every product will have to come to grips with consumer expectations quite different from those of their Baby Boomer parents.

Ethnicity: Globalization of the Web

As well as being multi-generational, North America's online future is decidedly multi-ethnic. People of African, Asian, Hispanic/Latino and Middle Eastern descent are now going online at a faster pace than the overall population. In any event, even though more than 70 percent of the North American population is of European origin, that group will account for only about 25 percent of market growth to 2010. Already, about 40 percent of African-American and Hispanic households are online. But even their online presence is dwarfed by the 76 percent of Asian-American households already on the Web.

Regardless of ethnicity, people of recently immigrated families and related communities enjoy strong ties with one another and with relatives in their homelands. They therefore use the Web to maintain contact through e-mail. However, they also buy products from their homelands, such as movies from India, music from the Middle East, and otherwise hard-to-find food products from Asia. The value of the Internet to these ethnic groups will undoubtedly increase as it becomes widely available in their countries of origin.

While most groups prefer to access Web sites in their native tongue, such as the Chinese-language Sina.com, English sites such as AsianAvenue.com and EverythingBlack.com attract a wide audience. Nevertheless, English will no longer dominate the Internet globally after about 2005, and e-marketers must be responsive to the Web's increasingly ethnic geography.

Geographics: Real and Virtual Communities

Geography on the Web is both real and virtual. In terms of where online users and shoppers actually live, urban dwellers are over-represented. Almost 70 percent of North American Internet users live in the top 50 metropolitan areas versus the 45 percent of the population that actually lives there. Among online shoppers, 51 percent live in big cities, 23 percent live in medium-sized cities and towns, and 23 percent live in city suburbs, but only two percent live right downtown. The remaining one percent of online buyers live in rural areas.

Inner-city residents, tending to have lower incomes, obviously are less likely to own a PC than their suburban and ex-urban counterparts. But they also have access to fewer brick-and-mortar retail stores in their neighborhoods. In Chicago, for example, inner-city retail demand is some 25 percent greater than the supply, leaving the shortfall to be filled from outside. Due to street-safety concerns and transportation hassles, many inner-city residents order products from catalogs but are now switching to online shopping. Hence, many inner-city residents are finding ways to get a cheap PC and to go online. Indeed, some are more inclined to shop online than their wealthier suburban peers, who are slow to break their shopping mall habits.

Internet users also "live" in virtual or online communities. In the real world, many aspects of traditional community life are under threat. As a result, there is a hunger to participate within a virtual community from the safety of home, maintaining real-world ties to family and a few close friends. Many people are finding strong ties online among those with shared interests who are scattered across the world. These "communities of interest" have sprung up in a variety of forms, either on bulletin board systems and forums or through portal frameworks such as GeoCities' "homesteader communities."

Naturally, these communities are attractive to marketers, both because of their content and the way in which they aggregate niches of similar users. Therefore, it is not surprising to see GeoCities build virtual storefronts.

As communities of interest develop e-commerce characteristics, they become e-communities, four types of which are differentiated in the matrix below. E-communities redefine marketplace sources of advantage and undoubtedly will change the way companies interact with customers.

All four basic types of e-community are driven by the experience of community interactions and transactions. To effectively participate in a virtual community, you have to capture its cultural gestalt — its language and customs — just as surely as you must understand the rules, history, personalities and nuances of real-world community.

Community-driven consumers naturally gravitate to those e-communities that offer a wide range of reliable, personally relevant information and product suppliers versus a site of a single merchant. For example, car buyers are less likely to flock to a site that offers only one manufacturer's vehicles. Therefore, e-communities wield much more power than has been seen before in retailing.

While they bring to mind the consumer "co-operative" concept, Web-based communities aggregate buying power so that their members can buy at volume discount prices. The future of these niche e-communities depends on how well the Web continues to pool like-minded buyers from the rising tide of online men and women shoppers.

Types of e-Community

Interest-Based
— Topic Specific
— Interact with Others
— "InfoSpace"
(e.g., gardening; Garden.com)

Transaction-Based
— Product Seeking
— Buy and Sell
— "MarketSpace"
(e.g., auctions; eBay.com)

Relationship-Based
— Experience Sharing
— Support Network
— "ShareSpace"
(e.g., parenting; BabyCenter.com)

Fantasy-Based
— Escape Seeking
— Imagination Exchange
— "DreamSpace"
(e.g., fantasy baseball; ESPN.com)

Gender: "Web Woman" Takes Over

There are now more women online than men — 54 percent at the end of 2000, versus only five percent in 1994. As well, women did 62 percent of online shopping in full-year 2000, with this rising to nearly 74 percent over the year-end holiday season.

Significantly, women either make or influence some 80 percent of all household purchases — equivalent to $1.5 trillion annually. Hence, women will utterly dominate e-shopping during the next decade and they by far represent the best e-marketing opportunity of the Millennium.

Moreover, women have the spending power: more than 75 percent of women deal with household financial matters. Women increasingly are becoming homeowners in their own right and are greatly involved in all aspects of household management, including home-improvement projects and their financing.

As well, the average female surfer earns about $60,000 a year. Indeed, the U.S. Bureau of Labor Statistics reports that 25 percent of women bring home a bigger paycheck than their husbands, up from 17 percent in 1990, and half of working women earn at least half of their household's income. With such purchasing power, the increase in women e-shoppers signals a sea change in what products will sell well online.

Men and women, being quite different, are known to have contrasting shopping styles. While it is risky to generalize, the conventional wisdom is that men quickly spot what they want to buy and buy it; women like to browse and to examine the product before they buy.

Quite naturally, male-female differences also show up among Internet users and online shoppers. While their online habits might seem somewhat opposite to their real-world habits, how men and women approach the Internet actually parallels their offline mindsets. Men tend to use search engines to find information while women tend to have a specific task or objective in mind; they go more directly to Web sites and are more likely to use page links than search engines to gather information.

Being more time-pressured, women focus on fewer Web sites than men and spend less time there. Women bookmark an average of only 10–15 Web sites versus about 50 by men. Hence, a woman's loyalty to the sites on her "favorites" list is very strong.

However, women still browse much longer than men before they buy, spending more time online. In contrast to men, who tend to focus on one area of interest at a time, women also tend to hop around their favorite Web sites during a single online session — among parenting, family, finance, health, lifestyle, and shopping interests.

In terms of content interests, men tend to focus on business news, financial activities, technology, science, and sports. Of course, women are also interested in sports and about 40 percent of online women access sites such as ESPN.com. Women, being more verbal, also use e-mail more often than men, but they are less likely to download files or get stock quotes online.

Women represent the best e-marketing opportunity of the Millennium.

Still, women have a growing interest in financial matters and visit sites in that category. For example, Women.com has an alliance with Bloomberg to provide real-time comprehensive news and analysis on financial markets and portfolio management, as well as family finance tips such as budgeting for baby and childhood education. Women.com is owned by Hearst, the publisher of magazines such as *Cosmopolitan, Redbook,* and *Good Housekeeping.*

The leading women's Web site is iVillage.com, which is organized into more than a dozen branded communities that focus on priority women's interests and provide interactive services, peer support and online access to experts. Content channels include Parent Soup, Better Health, MoneyLife, Career, Work from Home, Relationships, Fitness & Beauty, Travel, Food, and Book Club.

Women thus are turning to the Web not only for the kind of information they traditionally got from magazines but to gain a sense of community — from sites such as iVillage.com — and to shop.

Not surprisingly, men and women also shop for different items on the Web. Despite the fact that the number of women online now outmatches that of men, the latter are still more likely to purchase computer software and hardware. Indeed, the most popular online shopping destinations of adult males over the age of 18 are computer and sports sites. On average, men also still spend more time online than women (about 14 versus 10 hours per month) and spend more money shopping online because they are still the dominant buyers of big-ticket items like computers.

Women, on the other hand, are more likely than men to buy books, music, greeting cards, flowers, groceries, and travel services. In the latter regard, even though a majority of business travelers are still male, women obviously are heavily involved in the purchase of family vacations. In addition, the surge in female Internet use in the late-1990s has made clothing one of the fastest-growing online shopping categories and women already buy clothing online four times as often as men.

The tendency to shop online is strongly related to how long you've been surfing. And it takes two years for women to become comfortable shopping online, compared to 18 months for men. Because they are relatively new to the online world, women still tend to buy in brick-and-mortar stores after having browsed online. However, once they take the plunge and order something online, they buy online just as frequently as men.

Brand awareness is particularly important to women, who look for familiar brick-and-mortar or catalog names online. Indeed, since women do the bulk of household shopping, they are more familiar than men with the Web sites of brick-and-mortar brands but are less familiar with pure e-tailers.

Having now caught up and surpassed the number of male surfers, women have reached the point where they've had time to experiment and are ready to shop. However, because women tend to enjoy traditional shopping more than men, they view e-shopping as a chance to do what they already enjoy, and hence they have quite different online expectations. Women want a different e-shopping experience, just as they do on Main Street or in the mall. They like to browse more graphically oriented Web sites than men and want to be able to communicate with the seller.

More demanding of personal attention, women however are more likely to react positively to gift ideas or suggestions that help them solve problems quickly and seamlessly. Wanting simplicity, service, control, convenience and empowerment in the form of personalization and customization, they also prefer personalized shopping sites and respond better to a personal Web experience.

Women also want relationships with online retailers more than men do. Hence, to make relationship marketing with women truly profitable, e-marketers need to focus on each customer's lifetime value to them. Therefore, one-to-one marketing is highly suitable for these customers who, after all, will strongly influence online shopping in the future. We will return to this point later.

Women love e-mail because they say it helps strengthen ties to family and friends. Using the phone much less and going online, they want to learn "What can this do for my life?" While the Web Lifestyle will be a family affair, clearly it will predominantly be driven by women.

5 PSYCHOGRAPHICS
Why They're Clicking Online

Whether they're buying books, computers, applicances, or groceries, people spend more when they sell products to themselves.

—Alan Webber, founding editor,
FAST Company magazine

N OT TO BE TRIVIAL, but since no one hears you shop online, when you click the "order" button does the cash register ring? Marketers need to know who's clicking online and why. Otherwise, the cash registers will ring on somebody else's Web site.

Generational Milieu: Doing it My Way

At Glocal Marketing we draw on cultural anthropology and social psychiatry to reveal how cross-generational interplay and technological innovation affect buyer behavior. As noted just earlier in the demographic discussion, each generation bears a strong imprint of the milieu into which it is born and raised. Each generation shares a collegial identity and a collective mindset that governs its behavior. In turn, each generation believes its life experience is the norm for everyone and expects others to behave like it. The social milieu changes with the mood of the times, of course, and economic circumstances in particular shape parental attitudes and how they raise the next generation.

Looking towards 2010, the relevant marketplace generations, as identified earlier, are as follows:

• **"By-the-Book" (born 1911–28)**
This generation believes that history moves in orderly straight

lines and, being resistant to change, few of them go online, and probably most never will.

• **"By-the-Clock" (born 1929–45)**
Few of these so-called "Seniors" ever used a PC during their work years. Nevertheless, many of them have Web access, often spending two hours a day online. Other than sending e-mail, they mostly go online for weather reports, health and medicine content, and investment advice.

Half of them buy books and computer software online and some even buy cars online. While they clearly enjoy the convenience of online shopping, many of them have a compulsive obsession with orderliness and seek ease of operation, comfort, efficiency, and practicality. Thus, few of them will go online until Web access becomes both easier and more compelling.

Generally conservative, most of these users are risk averse and less likely to trust the Web enough to buy anything other than simple products online, such as toys for their grandkids.

• **"Baby-Boom" (born 1946–64)**
Every day, some 11,000 Boomers celebrate their 50th birthday, making them eligible for membership in the American Association of Retired Persons (AARP) — something none of them feel ready to belong to. Feeling and acting at least 10 years younger than their own parents at the same age, Baby Boomers are "active adults" — and they are active online. Boomer values were heavily influenced by television but, after becoming computer literate in the workplace, at home they have embraced PCs and cellphones and have gravitated naturally online. Always ready to shift to the latest new thing, they are ditching old media in favor of the empowering Web.

They live active lifestyles and, upon entering middle age, are much concerned with their future health and financial wellbeing. Being skeptical of mass marketing claims and conflicting "expert" views, they eagerly go online to learn for themselves the reality behind product and service claims.

• **"Gen-X" (born 1965–82)**
These somewhat rebellious misfits grew up fast as "latch-key" kids and the children of divorce. Counterculture to the Baby Boomers, they have learned to fend for themselves and are self-sufficient in

almost every way. While they used to frequent shopping malls during their teen years, many of them now reject what they call "mallism." Instead, they "emallgrate" to low-tech, low-info discount warehouses that downplay extravagant consumerism. This trend to escape the mainstream led Gen-X into the PC revolution. Early Web adopters, they often hold a "click out" against Web sites that clearly don't understand youth values.

- **"Web-Gen" (born 1983–2000)**

No member of this generation has known a world without PCs. Like their analog "By-the-Clock" predecessors who built and drove along interstate highways, this digital generation is building the Web and surfing it almost by instinct. Endlessly searching for and adopting new ideas and things, they will travel the world incessantly — in person and virtually. Techno-pioneers, they are the most likely to use PCs, cellphones, and any new e-gadget that comes along. For this generation, e-shopping is the only natural way to shop.

Web World: Super-Cool Always-On Multimedium

Regardless of age, rapid electronic and technical advances are making all consumers more sophisticated and knowledgeable buyers. Their world increasingly defined by immediacy and ubiquity — an "instant-on" pushbutton society, initiated by TVs and built upon by ATMs and cellphones — most consumers simply expect instant access and fast service, anyplace, anytime. As the always-on, wireless, broadband Web becomes widespread, they will become tele-nomadic consumers. It is possible that by 2010 a majority of North Americans will telecommute to everything they do — work, school, and shops — without even thinking about it. As Web culture spreads across society, the majority will live a Web Lifestyle.

What makes shoppers click online? Fast navigation, fast checkout, fast delivery, fast help.

As this "Web World" unfolds, today's prevalent marketing concepts simply will not work. Any consumer born since World War II has grown up in an increasingly visually intensive, multimedia world. People have been desensitized by years of media message bombardment. Consumers armed with online information not only reject but ridicule most advertising, dismissing it as hype and rejecting overstatement or hypocrisy. They rebuff any idea that a salesperson might invade their space, either by knocking on their door, calling on the phone, sending unsolicited junk mail or e-mail "spam," cluttering Web sites with blinking banner ads or, indeed, trying to "sell" them anything. Consequently, it takes a much stronger message to gain consumer attention and, hence, interactive multimedia Web sites will dominate the retail environment.

Of course, a quality product that meets a personal need literally sells itself. Moreover, consumers spend more when they sell products to themselves. And on the Internet they are well equipped to do exactly that. Hence, the entire concept of advertising, promotion and sales is turned on its head by the Web. Any company that fails to understand this is doomed to extinction. The Web is a "cool" medium that will become even "cooler." E-marketers must understand what "super-cool" Web shopping is all about.

Teenagers always offer a glimpse of the future. And today's teens view shopping as an experience not an errand, as an event not a chore. For them, a "cool" brand must exhibit certain characteristics, quality being given. The overriding purchase motivation is simply to have fun. Consequently, e-shopping offers the coolest fun experience. To this generation, the Web is a no-brainer, the only way to "go" anywhere — including shopping.

Gen-X consumers have always sought nontraditional alternatives and Web-Gen consumers are making e-shopping mainstream. Both groups are tech-savvy realists who like things short and simple. For them, life is a matter of "just give me the info" or "just sell me the jeans." Gen-Xers are now buying their first homes, buying their first cars, and having their first children. And, having grown up with the Web — indeed, most Web sites are being created by this group — they are an e-marketer's dream as we enter the new millennium.

Millennium Effect:
"Cool Combo" of Nostalgia and Fast Forward

We are all being influenced both by the Web and the "Millennium Effect" — a sense of newness and starting over that is far more profound than when we enter a new decade. Words such as "first" and "new" will even grab the attention of Seniors and older Baby Boomers who want to experience new firsts: first stock portfolio, first overseas trip, first sports car, first grandchild. Retirement and approaching retirement are times of starting over and new beginnings. Words such as "now," "begin" and "start" reinforce the idea of doing things now, while you still can.

Of course, although words such as "fast" and "instantly" are particularly important concepts for younger generations, they do run slightly counter to the desire of older consumers who prefer to savor the experience of "starting over" at a more reasonable (but not slower) pace of life. These compelling motivators are doubly reinforced by the Millennium Effect of essentially starting over on a clean sheet, a concept that resonates across all generations as we enter the 2000s.

Paradoxically, the Millennium Effect also manifests itself as nostalgia. In a time of turbulent change and newness, people want to feel comfortable and grounded in something solid. They look for reminders of their past and their childhood. Indeed, searching for ancestors is one of the most popular online activities. The nostalgia theme offers a unique advantage to astute millennial marketers. Consider the recent return of these icons: the VW beetle, Colonel Sanders' face on KFC's stores and chicken buckets, Maxwell House's "Good to the last drop" slogan, Coke's contour bottle, and the century-old look of the new Jacobs Field and Camden Yards baseball parks.

These trends show a clear desire to hang onto the past while also embracing and racing into the future. This aspect of the Millennium Effect is yet another form of convergence, in that consumers want a "cool combo" of the old and the new, a hybrid of desirable alternatives. One example is the trade-off between work and leisure, where work and home are blurring. At the same time, people want to be as comfortable at work as they are at home, bringing about major changes in work patterns and dress codes. As I have long told the fashion industry, the business suit and strangling neckties will vanish within a generation.

It's the Service, Stupid!

So what makes "cool combo" shoppers "click" online? By nature, most consumers want things to be simple, easy and fast. And evidence shows that Web users clearly see everyday tasks as easier and more convenient when done online.

Major reasons given by e-consumers for shopping online are

that it saves time, saves driving and parking, the stores never close, and there are no crowds. Indeed, most e-shoppers say that shopping is fun again. They get fast navigation, fast checkout, fast delivery, fast exchanges, and fast help. Not surprisingly, e-shoppers are glad to avoid unattractive brick-and-mortar stores and their product-ignorant, indifferent, and rude sales clerks.

Whether they shop offline or online, consumers are easily "ticked off" or "clicked off" by less than outstanding customer service. Major sources of dissatisfaction in either world are empty shelves and inadequate product info. Of course, the major source of satisfaction for brick-and-mortar shoppers is the immediate gratification that stems from buying an item and then taking it home. However, online shoppers say that they too enjoy immediate purchase gratification thanks to the certain knowledge of next-morning delivery. E-buyers expect convenience, in-depth product info, customized offerings, instant order confirmation, and round-the-clock customer service.

Overall, consumers simply want to do things on their own terms. And the Web's ability to customize and personalize the shopping experience is appealing to customers of all ages and types.

6 WEBOGRAPHICS
What They Do Online

By 2005, people will spend twice as much time with their PCs as with their TVs.

— Andrew Grove, chairman
Intel Corporation

T O UNDERSTAND WHO WILL SHOP ONLINE — plus why and what they will buy — demographic and psychographic profiles are no longer sufficient. Rather than knowing who people are and "what makes them tick," we need to know "what makes them click" on the Web. We need to understand their "webographic" characteristics.

After researching how and why consumers adopt technology since 1985, I began compiling "technographic" profiles in 1991. Since 1995, I have used the term "webographics" to profile human behavior in adopting and learning to use the Web.

Web Adoption Rate
Adoption and use of the Web obviously depends on the ownership of (or access to) a Web access device. By the end of 2000, about 62 percent of U.S. households owned a PC. Today's Web access devices are not necessarily PCs and are even cheaper to buy and easier to use.

Web adoption and usage thus is less dependent on income or education. A more important factor is how digital families take the Internet in stride, going online as a daily habit, as part of a Web Lifestyle. As such Web Lifestyles become commonplace, webographics will become the standard criteria for evaluating and forecasting the future of e-commerce and other Web-based activities.

Internet adoption, as already noted, is happening much faster than with previous media, and some 167 million North Americans were online by the end of 2000. Some argue that it will take much longer for the rest of the population to gain Web access. On the contrary, as the Web gets cheaper and easier to use — and particularly as broadband technology makes the online experience compellingly irresistible — the rest of the population will go online rapidly. We forecast that 79 percent of North American households will enjoy online access by 2010, rising to 89 percent by 2015 and 98 percent by 2020.

About 12 million U.S. households now have broadband Web access and that number, though growing painfully slowly, will continue to expand. Significantly, as anticipated, broadband users spend far more online than those with dial-up modems, and not just because they happen to have higher incomes that allow them to afford broadband. By 2006, Gartner Group estimates that 25 percent of households will have broadband access and these households will spend more than $10,000 per year online.

> Once a PC enters the household, life at home is never the same again.

Once a PC enters the household, life at home is never the same again. Families always adjust their lives around new technology. Most in-home PCs are now bought not for playing games or balancing checkbooks but to go online. Already, some 62 percent of North American homes have at least one PC and more than half of those households are online. In turn, this is changing practically every routine of family life, from TV viewership and reading to making phone calls. People's daily routines are changing, from the moment they get up in the morning until they return home at night. Indeed, more and more people now telecommute rather than suffer the hassle of going to work.

In fact, thanks to the Internet, nobody needs to "go" anywhere. It therefore follows that fewer and fewer people will go shopping. Instead, the shops will come to their desktops or Web access devices. Those who doubt that the Webolution will turn life and commerce upside-down should recall the impact of TV on western society. Now it's the Internet's turn. And learning how the Net will play out is the role of webographic analysis.

Web Optimists and Web Pessimists

Fundamentally, a person's decision to buy a PC and go online depends on whether they can afford to do so. Secondly, their attitude towards technology — which may itself be conditioned by income — will influence their decisions.

Using these two basic variables, the matrix below is based on proprietary research first conducted by the author in 1995 for a major telephone company and since updated every two years. Initially, PC ownership was directly related to income. In 1997, for example, 40 percent of homes with annual incomes of $30–$40,000 had at least one PC; likewise 50 percent of homes with annual incomes of $40–$50,000 had a PC. This ratio of "$10,000 of income = 10 percent PC ownership" applied at any income level, but began to break down as PCs became cheaper.

As PC prices fall and the Web becomes more reliable and useful, people gradually shift into the top-left quadrant. Low-income optimists are basically waiting for the price of PCs to fall further. Most high-income pessimists have a PC but are waiting for easier-to-use applications and services. Low-income pessimists either have no need for a PC or can't afford to buy one.

Lower income groups are closing the so-called "digital divide" and joining the more affluent users online. During 2000, the biggest gain in Web access at home was a 52 percent jump among blue-collar workers, followed by 28 percent growth among retired persons. That compares with a 21 percent growth rate by executives and managerial types.

Web Optimists and Web Pessimists

High-Income Optimists (47%)
- Career-Driven "Fast Forwards"
- Family-Driven "For the Kids"
- Game-Playing "Jockey Junkies"

High-Income Pessimists (16%)
- Intimidated "Slow Learners"
- Indifferent "Know-it-Alls"
- TV-Addicted "Couch Potatoes"

Low-Income Optimists (27%)
- Career-Driven "Stressed Strivers"
- Digital "Price Watchers"
- High-Tech "Toy Buyers"

Low-Income Pessimists (10%)
- Sidelined "Sustainers"
- Analog "Diehards"
- Disinterested "Don't Need It"

(Source: Webographic analysis conducted by the author in 1995, 1997, 1999)

Lower income groups now are gaining access, often in unique ways. For example, in early 2000, Ford Motor Company announced a deal with Hewlett Packard to give home access to its 370,000 employees worldwide. For just $5 a month, any Ford employee can get a Web-connected home PC and color printer. These are powerful 500-mghz machines with four-gigabyte hard drives that employees can upgrade to even more powerful PCs at their expense if they wish. In late 2000, Ford expanded the program to offer a PC and Internet package to some 250,000 employees at its dealerships. Similarly, Delta Airlines is offering Web-access home PCs to its 72,000 employees for $12 a month.

Along with lower PC prices, such innovative programs will rapidly give Web access to the wider population. And as we shall see, once people get a PC and go online, they soon start shopping.

Types of Online Shoppers

Our 1999 online survey of 1,627 users (see Appendix B for more details) discerned five attitudinal types of e-shoppers. The salient characteristics and purchasing habits of these five segments are summarized below. The first three types further explain the two groups of Web Optimists in terms of shopping attitudes. The second two types further explain the shopping attitudes of the Web Pessimists.

Web Optimists (74%)

- *Smart e-Shoppers (31%):* The best-educated consumers, these high-income optimists have been online the longest. Comprising 31 percent of online households, they go online 16 hours a week on average. They prefer e-shopping over brick-and-mortar stores and 64 percent of them have purchased on the Web.

- *Comparison e-Shoppers (21%):* Thriving on the Web, these mid-income optimists hop around the Web unpredictably (often while listening to MTV) but know what they want and how to find it fast. Comprising 21 percent of the market, they also go online about 16 hours a week. About 58 percent have purchased online but they tend to shop on price, frequenting discounters and auction sites.

- *Routine Loyalists (22%):* These lower-income, lower-education consumers comprise 22 percent of the online market and average 14 hours a week surfing. Their buying decisions are heavily influenced by TV ads and water cooler chit-chat. Very brand loyal, they rarely switch products and look for familiar names online. Still happy to shop at the mall, only 28 percent of them have bought anything online.

Web Pessimists (26%)

- *Stodgy e-Skeptics (16%):* Upscale and family oriented, while 72 percent of them have PCs (the majority with Web access), these high-income pessimists sniff at Web Lifestyles and spend little time online. Comprising 16 percent of households, they are focused shoppers who know exactly what they want. But regardless of where they shop, they often are skeptical as to whether they got value for money.

- *Techno Have-Nots (10%):* With below-average education and income, plus kids to support, their available time and money leave them on the other side of the "digital divide." Addicted to TV, these low-income pessimists are negative about new technology and are the least likely to own a PC or have Web access. Comprising only 10 percent of online households, their impact on e-shopping is minimal.

Buyers vs. Browsers

The preference for online shopping clearly improves substantially after the browser has made her first online buy. Indeed, after that first purchase, research shows that customers are at least five times more likely to buy again online than they were before their first purchase.

The earliest Internet users — the so-called "early adopters" — were tech-savvy, intelligent, and curious people who are always the first to try something new. Besides their optimism, the main characteristics of online consumers are as follows:

Confident Buyers

- *Fast Forwards:* want what's new and different, somehow unique, innovative or surprising; look for "cool" Web sites and products.

- *Raging Bulls:* goal-driven achievers who ignore conventional wisdom, despise inconsistency or hype, and buy impulsively.

- *Networkers:* articulate people, plugged in to a network of sources for word-of-modem Web site and product recommendations.

Product Researchers

- *Avid Readers:* cognizant, well-informed, in-the-know people who seek high-value knowledge and products through comprehensive online research.

- *Obsessives:* compulsive, contemplative and intensely involved with career or hobbies, determinedly doing comprehensive pre-purchase research online.

- *Control Freaks:* seek control and privacy through unlisted phone numbers and multiple e-mail addresses; distrust Web sites and order by phone or fax after researching online.

Technology vs. Time Trade-Offs

New household technologies always change household activities. While TV did not kill the movies or radio, consumers certainly reallocated their available time. After all, each of us has but 24 hours a day. Therefore, TV commanded more attention than radio and movies.

The same is happening with Web-linked PCs, which are pushing the TV aside. Heavy Internet users — about 20 percent of the overall population — spend 60 percent less time with television, 34 percent less time with newspapers, work 28 percent more hours at home (and corresponding less time at the office), and spend 24 percent less time in stores. Even the average user watches 32 percent less TV. Today's average adult Internet user will spend about three years of his or her remaining lifespan online. That's a Web Lifestyle!

Of course, not everyone values or allocates their time in the same way. How we trade off our time is influenced by age, personality, culture, and other characteristics. Some of us, either out of choice or because the technology permits it, can combine activities. A common example is driving a car while listening to the radio or an audiotape — or, more riskily, while yacking on a cellphone. Thus, we should not be surprised if, when people go online, they also choose to listen to a radio or the TV soundtrack coming from a nearby set. Indeed, TV is decreasingly used for entertainment and, where that still is the case, the TV often is left on in the background. In other words, rather than watching *Seinfeld* reruns, surfers listen in while they interact online.

Thus, while people are keen to go online via services such as WebTV, the expected PC-TV convergence is not (at least, not yet) occurring in the technology itself but rather in the habits of its users. Besides, with some 280 million analog TVs in North American homes, these non-digital, Web-useless TVs will still likely be around for another decade yet. Hence, people will continue to acquire PCs, WebTVs and other Web appliances as they aspire to the Web Lifestyle. And they will spend increasing amounts of time online.

The 167 million North Americans online at the end of 2000 already were spending 1.5 billion hours a week with their home PCs, three-quarters of it on the Web. At any given moment, there are more than a million people logged onto America Online alone — which many newcomers mistakenly think *is* the Internet itself — and the average AOL user stays online about 30 hours a month. Obviously, they are trading off time that otherwise would be spent elsewhere.

The trade-off between technology usage and time is influenced by the following "TIMES" factors:

Time: available clock time or calendar space;
Information: available knowledge resources and access to them;
Money: available financial resources;
Energy: available mental and physical energy;
Space: available physical space in which to operate.

The Internet, of course, exploits these TIMES factors perfectly: it provides more timely access to more information, using less energy, less money, and less space. Hence, in competing for consumers' precious attention, all products and services should be designed and marketed in ways that boost the consumer's knowledge while saving her time, money, energy, and space.

Time Spent Online: The Propensity to e-Purchase

Experienced online users seek to maximize the TIMES equation for themselves, using the Web to greater advantage as they become more accomplished. The amount of time spent online increases with use. For example, those online more than three years spend about eleven hours a week online compared to just over five hours for newcomers.

Moreover, as online experience increases, users are much more likely to shop online. Online purchasers have about one year more online experience than do non-purchasers. In 1998, for example, 48 percent of North American households had a PC, 25 percent were online, and seven percent shopped online. By 1999, some 52 percent had a PC, 33 percent were online, and 15 percent were e-shopping.

This means that once a PC owner goes online and starts to browse for products, e-marketers need to understand what triggers them to buy. About 50 percent of online consumers have yet to make their first purchase online. Converting browsers to buyers clearly takes time. Households that have been on the Web for less than six months comprise fifteen percent of the online population but account for only five percent of online purchases. Conversely, households that have been online for a least two years comprise 45 percent of the online population, yet account for 65 percent of online purchases.

> As their online experience grows, users are more likely to shop online.

As well, many people actually purchase offline after researching a product online. For every purchase made online, two additional purchases are researched. Of course, as in the brick-and-mortar world, some of these researched purchases are never bought, either online or offline. However, in 1996, for every 10 people who browsed and bought online, another 16 people browsed online and then bought offline. This ratio narrowed to 10:14 in 1997, to 10:13 in 1998 and to 10:11 in 1999. This trend reflects the fact that consumers are gaining confidence in the security of online shopping and are enjoying an improved online experience. Indeed, Web site experiences influence surfers to gravitate to a few favorite sites.

"Favorite" Web Sites

When people first go online, they eagerly try a bunch of new sites and services. But once they've been online for a while, being creatures of habit, people naturally fall into a pattern of checking only a few sites regularly. Such behavior follows other social habits. For example, the average person has a network of about 10 close friends and associates. After all, how many relationships can you meaningfully maintain?

On the Web too, people maintain small networks of relationships through their e-mail address books. And their visits to Web sites follow a similar pattern, with a handful of sites becoming a daily habit. Experienced surfers visit a short list of Web sites that they bookmark onto their favorites list. Indeed, nearly 80 percent of users who've been online for at least two years navigate the Web almost exclusively via their favorites list. And that list constantly gets pruned to keep it manageable.

The critical question thus becomes, how many Web sites are surfers going to bookmark onto their favorites lists? In the offline world, consumers only keep track of two or three brands in any product category. To carry more brand names around in your head is simply too complicated. It therefore is a safe bet that the same behavior will be revealed online.

In fact, about 60 percent of e-shoppers go directly to the Web sites of names they recognize, and most surfers do not keep more than 20 or 30 Web sites on their favorites list. And that includes search engines, genealogy sites, weather sites, stock trading sites, bulletin boards, and so on. Therefore, the number of e-tailers bookmarked onto favorites lists will certainly not be more than 20. Indeed, there may not be more than one or two e-tailers per product category on any one surfer's favorites list. *This key webographic finding is the most important point of this entire book, as it alone will determine who will buy what, and why, from which Web sites.*

Web Site Domination	
% of Sites	**% of Users**
0.1	32
1	56
5	75
10	82
50	95

(Source: L. A. Adamic & B. A. Huberman, The Nature of Markets in the World Wide Web, *parc.xerox.com, May 6, 1999)*

A recent Nielsen/NetRatings survey found that the average number of unique sites visited per month declined from fifteen in 1998 to only nine in 1999. Of course, some sites are visited less frequently than monthly and more than nine sites are on the average favorites list. However, relatively short favorites lists quite simply follow natural economic laws, such as Pareto's 80:20 rule of thumb. In the case of retailing, Pareto's law says that 80 percent of sales will gravitate to 20 percent of the stores and, in turn, that 80 percent of an individual retailer's sales will come from 20 percent of its customers.

The same happens with Web sites. For example, 10 percent of "core visitor" customers at VirtualVineyard.com purchase 80 percent of the wine. Other Web sites report similarly skewed results.

In turn, a few Web sites attract most online traffic. Xerox PaloAlto Research Center recently studied the number of AOL visitors to 120,000 Web sites. The cumulative data in the table above show that the top 0.1 percent of the 120,000 sites — actually only 119 sites! — capture a whopping 32 percent of users. In fact, the top one percent of sites capture 56 percent of users and the top 10 percent of sites attract 82 percent of users.

Clearly, the Web site visitation pattern more than follows the 80:20 Pareto-like character of "winner-take-all" markets. This implies that a small number of retail sites will command the traffic of a large segment of the Web population, capturing the lion's share of online sales. The same 80:20 rule applies to e-shopping.

It is estimated that 87 percent of total online purchasing in 2000 was done by the top 20 percent of online shoppers who each spend at least $1,000 per year online.

In a separate study of 525,000 unique surfers, Xerox researchers also examined how surfers navigate Web sites, including the amount of time spent on each site or at each page. For example, people spend much longer on a Web site when researching a car purchase than when buying a book.

Xerox's study found that inexperienced users click through several pages or links before finding what they are looking for. However, once a surfer finds what they want, they tend to bookmark that page to their favorites list for future use. Then they can easily go directly back to that page next time. For example, rather than going to Amazon.com's home page, my bookmark for Amazon takes me directly to the detailed search page for books.

How Many Will Shop Online in 2010?

Based on these patterns of Web usage and online shopping and the projected number of Web access appliances going into homes, it thus becomes possible to forecast the future of e-shopping. Of 115 million North American households in 2010, we forecast that 83 percent will have at least one PC, that 79 percent will be online, and that 66 percent (or 76 million households) will actively be shopping and buying online.

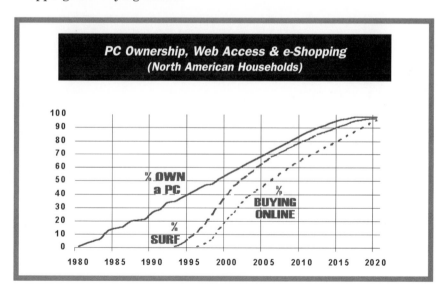

In turn, using webographic profiles, we can reasonably predict how many people will go online and when, how soon they will begin e-shopping, how frequently they will conclude a purchase either online or offline, what kinds of things they will buy and how frequently, and how much they will spend. Those are the subjects of the next part.

PART III

— • —

What They Will Buy

E-commerce is not just about selling books, music, and videos online. That's only the beginning.
— Jeff Bezos, CEO
Amazon.com

THE WEB TAKES SHOPPING OUT OF THE SHOPS. In turn, of course, that takes the shops out of shopping. Instead, the home becomes the shop — a virtual mall showroom for comparison-shopping and a convenience store for buying.

The Web is a shopper's paradise, stocked with everything from vintage wine to brand new cars. By 2010, the Internet will account for about 30 percent of total retail sales. Even if I am half-wrong, the impact on the entire industry will be dramatic. As the Internet gobbles up a huge chunk of their sales, some retail categories will disappear almost entirely from physical stores. As the Web continues to nibble market share away from traditional stores, e-shopping will explode while pure brick-and-mortar retailers get crushed to bits — literally! Retailing will never be the same again.

Most retailers fail to understand that products are merely content. Consequently, most traditional retailers are slow to grasp the reality that shopping is going online. They offer lame excuses for not deploying e-commerce initiatives. In a 1998 survey of old-line retailers — and their attitudes have changed little since then — 47 percent asserted that their product simply was not appropriate for online sales. Another 24 percent did not even see a significant online opportunity for their business. A further 17 percent claimed that it was too costly to go online. In total, 54 percent of retailers said they had no plans whatever to sell any product over the Internet.

There will be significant consolidations and closings within both the department store and specialty retail categories. The most venerable are the most vulnerable. Already we have seen how America's Woolworth, Canada's Eaton's, and Britain's Marks & Spencer struggled for survival during the 1990s. Indeed, Eaton's went bust in 1999, M&S closed all its stores outside Britain in 2000 and is a buy-out candidate. Woolworth's emerged from Chapter 11 bankruptcy as the unknown Venator, only to continue closing stores by the hundreds.

By any measure, the brick-and-mortar shakeout in 2000 was far bigger than the online e-tailer shakeout. The initial damage wrought by the Webolution is evidenced by boarded-up storefronts on streets across North America, and the traditional department stores continued to suffer. In 2000, even Montgomery Ward, a unit of much-admired GE, bit the dust. The firm came out of bankruptcy protection to focus on a niche between a department store and a discount store, only to find that there is no such niche. Out of patience, GE pulled the plug during the normally busy 2000 holiday season and closed the chain's 250 stores. In addition to Montgomery Ward, JC Penney closed 47 stores, Sears closed 89, Lechters 166, and Bradlees closed down entirely.

Department stores only have a future if they come to realize that they are in fact "department" stores and begin to provide a shopping experience that is truly unique. Department stores also must become showrooms where online shoppers can come to touch and feel merchandise which they otherwise will buy online.

— • —

The brick-and-mortar shopping experience is painful: crowded parking lots and shopping aisles, freezing-cold and steamy-hot weather, tired feet and long check-out lines, "out of stock" products and disinterested, discourteous, clueless store clerks. The incentive to escape all that frustration and go online is very strong, regardless of what you are shopping for. Consumers simply have had enough. Online shoppers — who will soon be in the majority — simply don't need stodgy retailers anymore. Growing millions of consumers can now search for and buy goods from a host of merchants through their own computers at any time of day or night. Web shops never close and you have electronic shopping agents at your beck and call.

Following the surge in online shopping that closed out 2000 — online sales for the year topped $40 billion — the debate over whether e-shopping will materialize is over. During the next few years, e-shopping will become as second nature as breathing.

Products Most Suitable for Online Sales

As the 21st century emerges, in almost every product category, Web-only ventures are leading the e-tail revolution — at least thus far. A major reason for their lead is the just-discussed brick-and-mortar retailer skepticism about what will and will not sell online. Many retailers and their landlords still believe online shopping is nothing more than another catalog-like niche segment.

Skepticism about shopping at other than brick-and-mortar stores is not new, as the following quote illustrates:

> *Remote shopping, while entirely feasible, will flop because women like to get out of the house, like to handle the merchandise, like to be able to change their minds.*
>
> — *Time* magazine, 1966

That was then. A decade from now, today's skeptical question of "What will sell online?" will have become "What isn't selling online?"

Beyond what we already know about what's selling online, basic common sense gives a good indication of what kinds of products will be successful online. Based on today's relatively crude level of Internet technology, the suitability of a product or service for online marketing heavily depends on two basic factors:

1. the degree of personal interaction with the product/service and its distribution, i.e., the product's tactile nature and the efficiency of its delivery;

2. the degree of complexity of the product/service and its purchase process, i.e., the info-intensity of the product and its pre-purchase research.

The Internet is an information-intensive, highly efficient, multi-medium — a perfect channel for at least researching, if not buying, a variety of products and services. Of course, products other than purely digitizable ones still must be physically distributed and delivered to the home. As such, some products and services obviously may be more suitably marketed over the Internet than others.

Still, even if you need to buy a pound of nails, on which the shipping costs would be prohibitive, you could still order the nails online, then go to the store and pick them up, perhaps at a drive-through. In fact, any product other than, say, your favorite brand of chewing gum, is more easily located, researched, and bought online.

Many argue, of course, that you need to see, touch, and feel the product before you buy it. That can be true for some grocery items, some clothing, furniture, and perhaps major purchases such as cars and houses. As we shall see, however, not everybody needs to squeeze the tomatoes, try on a new pair of slacks, lie down on a new mattress, test drive a car, or walk through a home before buying it. Today, these products are already being purchased over the Internet sight unseen.

For example, if you do always buy Tom Clancy novels or a certain Nike running shoe, then you can buy them sight unseen. But if you need to try on Armani clothes or test drive a Ford car, even though you are comfortable with their brand name and price, you may still need to see, touch and try them out before you buy. Other products fall somewhere along the continuum between these two extremes. Using these factors to create a matrix (opposite), we therefore can evaluate a variety of products and services as to their basic suitability for online sales. Indeed, as indicated by the bracketed percentages of people buying, all of these products are selling online.

Low information-intensive, minimal need-to-research, light-weight, non-bulky, standardized, personal convenience and replenishment items — on the left side of the matrix — are the easiest to buy online and to deliver to the customer. Conversely, those on the right require much pre-purchase research and, in many cases, are more difficult to deliver. Briefly, the four quadrants can be reviewed as follows:

- **"Convenience" Items:** On the Internet, anything that can be commoditized will be commoditized. The Web simplifies and speeds up the purchase of these "low-involve-

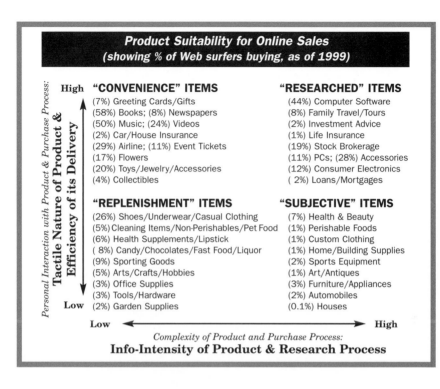

Product Suitability for Online Sales
(showing % of Web surfers buying, as of 1999)

Personal Interaction with Product & Purchase Process:
Tactile Nature of Product &
Efficiency of its Delivery

High

"CONVENIENCE" ITEMS
(7%) Greeting Cards/Gifts
(58%) Books; (8%) Newspapers
(50%) Music; (24%) Videos
(2%) Car/House Insurance
(29%) Airline; (11%) Event Tickets
(17%) Flowers
(20%) Toys/Jewelry/Accessories
(4%) Collectibles

"RESEARCHED" ITEMS
(44%) Computer Software
(8%) Family Travel/Tours
(2%) Investment Advice
(1%) Life Insurance
(19%) Stock Brokerage
(11%) PCs; (28%) Accessories
(12%) Consumer Electronics
(2%) Loans/Mortgages

"REPLENISHMENT" ITEMS
(26%) Shoes/Underwear/Casual Clothing
(5%) Cleaning Items/Non-Perishables/Pet Food
(6%) Health Supplements/Lipstick
(8%) Candy/Chocolates/Fast Food/Liquor
(9%) Sporting Goods
(5%) Arts/Crafts/Hobbies
(3%) Office Supplies
(3%) Tools/Hardware
(2%) Garden Supplies

"SUBJECTIVE" ITEMS
(7%) Health & Beauty
(1%) Perishable Foods
(1%) Custom Clothing
(1%) Home/Building Supplies
(2%) Sports Equipment
(1%) Art/Antiques
(3%) Furniture/Appliances
(2%) Automobiles
(0.1%) Houses

Low

Low ← → High

Complexity of Product and Purchase Process:
Info-Intensity of Product & Research Process

ment," low-research, commodity-like items, particularly those in the top-left quadrant, such as books and music.

- **"Replenishment" Items:** The next easiest products to sell online are replenishment items such as non-perishable food and cleaning products in the bottom-left quadrant. These are bulkier items that thus would incur shipping costs. However, they require no research once the first purchase has been made and you are happy with the product.

- **"Researched" Items:** Slightly more difficult to sell online are the items in the top-right quadrant. Those items are relatively easy to deliver, either digitally online or by parcel post or courier. However, they are information-intensive, complex items that require some consideration. For example, life insurance is less straightforward than car insurance and consumer electronics come in a host of competing choices.

- **"Subjective" Items:** The most difficult items to sell online and deliver to the home are in the bottom-right quadrant of the matrix. These often bulky and heavy products tend to require much research — increasingly now done online — and tend to be bought at brick-and-mortar stores. However, the Web has become a key facilitator in the sale of "high-involvement," research-intensive, subjective product purchases such as automobiles and houses. The power of the Web is to greatly simplify and speed up this time-consuming pre-purchase process. Moreover, every one of the items listed in the bottom-right quadrant is actually being sold online, some of them quite strongly.

Since products in every quadrant of the matrix are selling online, the Web obviously has the ability to converge complex purchase processes with the customer's need to interact with the product.

The Web also converges the otherwise contradictory variables of commoditization and personalization. It drives down the price of similar products, commoditizing them, but allows consumers to buy products more personalized or customized to their tastes and needs. For example, books have been commoditized on the Web, yet the Amazon.com book purchaser can submit their personal preferences of book genres or authors to receive automatic notification of new books or suggested titles of interest.

Of course, skeptics argue that the upsurge in online book sales does not mean that many cars will be sold online. However, the vast majority of consumers simply do not enjoy buying cars from dealerships; many intensely abhor it. For them, the allure of a no-hassle online car purchase, at any time of day or night, is quite compelling.

In any event, the more difficult and time-consuming a purchase, the more likely shoppers are to research it on the Internet before buying it. Hence, the more people browse online, a portion of sales of every product category will inevitably flow to the Web. This will particularly occur as the spread of broadband enhances the Internet experience and the user's ability to buy even "high-involvement" and "touchy-feely" products sight unseen.

Forecasting Online Sales

The two $64-billion-dollar questions are, "How much will be spent online in each category?" and "At which Web sites will it be spent?" The next two sections of this book aim to answer these questions.

The volume of future e-tail sales can be predicted by forecasting five variables. These variables, which compound on each other, are

1. How many people will use the Internet?
2. What percentage of them will buy online?
3. How much will they spend and how frequently?
4. On what items will they spend it?
5. At which Web sites will they spend it?

To answer these five questions, each variable has been forecast by complex computer models and there is no point in spelling out long calculations. In simple terms, however, the forecasting process is summarized in Appendix B.

As explained in the Appendix, the magnitude of future online shopping is much easier to grasp by looking at the percentage of sales rather than their dollar volume. To publish dollar volume forecasts would generate irrelevant argumentative comparisons with other published forecasts, which is not fruitful. Hence, we adopt the simple convention of forecasting the percentage of online sales by category to 2010.

Online Categories

In the end, of course, the best way to identify leading consumer markets and estimate their future is simply to look at what people primarily are already buying online.

To learn what is now selling online and understand what likely will be selling online in 2010, this section reviews a wide-range of products from the earlier matrix, grouped into 12 categories.

We'll proceed in alphabetical order and will forecast "% of total category sales in 2010" in each case as we go:

◆ Apparel and Footwear
◆ Automobiles
◆ Books
◆ Education

◆ Entertainment and Sports

◆ Expressions

◆ Financial Services

◆ Groceries

◆ Health and Beauty

◆ Homes and Home Improvement

◆ Newspapers

◆ General Merchandising

Each category presents an overview of what's happening, including how various players are approaching the online sales environment. At the end of each category, the percentage of online sales in 2010 is forecast, along with a short list of which Web sites we believe will come out the winners.

7 APPAREL AND FOOTWEAR
Virtual "Touch and Try on for Size"

This is a real business.

— Kent Anderson, president
Macys.com

L IMITED CHOICES on nevertheless tightly packed racks, narrow aisles, and cramped and dirty dressing rooms are driving people online. There, they can see dozens of items instantly and customize their own outfits to build a wardrobe with a minimum of hassle.

In the apparel sector, a wide selection of merchandise attracts the most online customers. The current online leaders are catalog companies, e-tailing start-ups, and brick-and-mortar specialist chains — all of which tend to have wide product offerings. Conversely, the traditional department stores and mass merchandisers are very slow to tap the Internet's potential and generally have a small range of product offerings online. Apparel manufacturers are still struggling to understand how the Internet channel is restructuring the industry. Let's review each company type, in reverse order.

Manufacturers Blunder Online
Levi Strauss went online in 1994 and offered customization on its site. But the company essentially admitted failure in 1999 and abruptly decided to stop selling clothes online, claiming that running a world-class e-commerce site was "unaffordable." Levi was never able to decide what to sell online; it wouldn't even offer its

flagship Levi's 501 jeans online, fearing a backlash from European and Asian customers who pay higher prices than Americans. Neither could the company reconcile how to compete alongside retailers that yielded most of its sales. Finally, at the end of 1999, Levi decided to allow Macy's and JCPenney to sell its Levi's and Dockers lines through their Web sites.

Nike has fared little better with its Nike.com site, which laudibly attempted to let buyers customize their own running shoes or cross-training footwear. However, customers were led through a gimmicky shoe-building process in which, for example, they could select the shoe's base and accent colors, and even add a personal I.D. to the product, such as their name or nickname. But overall sales through the site were disappointing and, in late 1999, Nike arranged to sell its products through online start-up FogDog Sports.

Department and "Big Box" Stores Lumber Online

The lumbering department stores are struggling most with the online world. They naively try to simply transfer what they do in the physical world onto the Internet, with predictably mixed results.

Some department stores are trying to differentiate themselves by providing customers with a unique shopping experience. The key is to focus on what the electronic medium does better than the physical world, rather than simply duplicating what the customer has and enjoys in the traditional store. Fast and convenient fulfillment and customer relations are especially important in any online business, especially apparel.

For old-line retailers such as Sears, the Internet provides an opportunity to re-strengthen existing customer relationships while building a new channel that meets the needs of modern consumers. According to Alice Peterson, vice president and general manager of Sears.com, the company found out — albeit far too slowly — that it can do things online that it couldn't do in the physical selling space. The site's crystal-clear menus and well-organized pages give side-by-side comparisons of the Web's largest selection of refrigerators, dishwashers and other appliances. However, as shown earlier, these products are not exactly the most suitable for online sales. Sears is better known for its Craftsman tools and has extended this reputation to the Web site. Hopefully, it will broaden out its offerings from there to include clothing.

Bloomingdale's similarly is trying to extend its fashion reputation to the Internet. If the Federated-controlled company can truly leverage its fashion offices, bridal consultants, and personal shopping services into consumers' homes, then it might be a very effective online player. Bloomingdale's prides itself on fashion trend-spotting and its site offers a "Shop and Trends" search feature. Customers who've heard that lime green is the latest color trend and are looking for a pair of pants can quickly search online and request details of all the lime green pants on offer. The site shows what's available in a much more efficient way than any sales associate ever could in the physical store setting.

Macy's.com is very similar. The site has a "gift-buying wizard" where users enter specific attributes of the person they want to buy for, such as age or gender. It then searches for and provides a list of appropriate gift selections, by price range. The Macy's.com online bridal registry is another feature that adds value to the site.

JCPenney.com has leveraged the company's catalog expertise online to sell everything from toasters to pillows to dresses. The clearly designed Web site groups merchandise in departments for Men, Women, Electronics, and House & Home. Pull-down menus make it easy to buy clothing in the right size. There is a gift registry, special offers, and links to the store's retail hair salons and photography studio.

Nordstrom.com also is a bright, inviting and breezy site, with apparel in categories such as "On the Job," "Off the Clock," and "Comfort Clothes." Nordstrom first entered retailing as a shoe store, and after belatedly opening its suitably elegant Web site in 1998, found that footwear accounted for 30 percent of its online sales compared with 20 percent in its physical stores. So the company promptly created a separate site just for shoes. Dubbed the "World's Biggest Shoe Store," it offers more than 200,000 different shoes including varying sizes of the same style. Mrs. Marcos would love it!

Shoes are easier than clothing to sell online because an adult's shoe size usually never changes and so it is easy to buy shoes sight unseen. Shoe fashion also is fairly stable and many consumers like to buy replacement pairs of what they already own and like. Indeed, most of Nordstrom's online footwear sales are replacement shoes, the best-selling items being women's mule career shoes typically worn with slacks.

More than 1,500 Web sites offer footwear. Online shoe sales in 2000 totaled only $160 million — still less than 0.05 percent of the $40 billion that North Americans spent on footwear. Online shoe sales by 2004 are expected to surpass catalog shoe sales to claim seven percent of all shoe sales. This strong growth is driven by the Internet's ability to offer a wider selection than physical stores, particularly in hard-to-find sizes or specialized styles such as dance shoes.

Specialist Chains Nimble and Quick

During the 1990s, the specialist retail chains in all categories proved themselves much nimbler than department store chains and big box merchandisers. This characteristic is proving even more important in the online world, as the Gap is showing yet again.

The Gap went online in 1996 and has raced ahead, bringing Gap.com, GapKids and GapBaby under one Web roof, and adding its Old Navy and Banana Republic brands in 1999. In that year, the company's online sales topped $100 million, five times the volume of 1998. The merchandise is identical to that in Gap stores and the site is easy to navigate. The company's Web site provides close-up views of buttons and stitching to give you a better idea of what the clothes really look like. Subtleties of color and texture do not come across too well on today's computer screens, but the Gap is ready for the day when they do.

Gap promotes its Web site at every cash register, clerks refer shoppers to the Web site, and splashy window displays urge customers to "surf.shop.ship." The biggest stores also have "Web Lounges" where comfortable couches lure shoppers to use sleek terminals connected to Gap.com. Online customers also can return items purchased on the Web to any Gap store.

Gap's main competitor, Benetton, didn't start selling clothes over the Internet until 2000. Whether the Italian-based company's casual and sportswear lines can catch up with North America's traditional and upstart apparel e-tailers is a big question mark. At least it will enjoy the benefit of lower shipping costs to European online shoppers.

Catalog Retailers' Smooth Transition

Catalog retailers, of course, can exploit the Web faster and almost instantly achieve one hundred percent availability. This is because their products are already photographed and described and so can easily be posted online.

Spiegel's Eddie Bauer clothing chain caught on quickly to the potential of the Internet, launching its EddieBauer.com presence in 1996 with 250 products from its sportswear line. Since then, the online store has expanded to 1,500 unique products from its three divisions (Eddie Bauer Sportswear, AKA Eddie Bauer, and Eddie Bauer Home) and offers close to one hundred percent of the company's catalog product online.

The site is easy to browse, keeping pertinent information on one page, with detailed images alongside each item, and 2-D views of clothing let you see how combinations of clothes might go together. For example, you can click on a banded-collar shirt in any of several colors and drag it over a pair of pants or shoes to see how they match up. An "EB Exclusives" feature lets shoppers store their garment sizes so they can track their wardrobe and add items they might like to receive as a gift. EddieBauer.com has been profitable since 1997 and sales at the site are tripling annually.

Lands' End has unrivaled expertise in providing a human touch for its customers. It was the first company to use an 800 phone number to provide customers with a simple, low-cost way of contacting the company.

More than 90 percent of online customers say they prefer some form of human interaction and LandsEnd.com taps into this desire. The site features real-time human interaction through two features, "Lands' End Live" and "Shop With a Friend." "Lands' End Live" provides an online personalized shopping assistant whom the shopper can question while they browse garments on the site together. The shopping assistant can help mix and match outfits and answer questions via instant chat or over the phone while viewing the same Web pages. "Shop With a Friend" lets two customers meet online from separate locations and then shop the same Web pages together, comparing prices and exchanging opinions via instant chat.

LandsEnd.com has customers in nearly two hundred countries and the Internet has made it easier to reach these customers and expand globally. The site now features a virtual dress-up doll "personal model" that immediately boosted the average order size by about 20 percent. After entering her measurements, a customer can size up a given garment — even a swimsuit — so see how it will look on her.

The company launched its Web site in 1995 with about a hundred products but now offers all its products online. In 1999, its Internet sales grew 340 percent to $61 million, reaching five percent of the company's total sales. Stale product designs led to declining catalog sales in 1999 but fresh lines were introduced. Sales reached $218 million in 2000, with 30 percent of its customers being new buyers who had never bought from the famous catalog. Now generating 16 percent of total company sales from its Web site, LandsEnd.com sells more clothing online than any other company, including the Gap.

Is Apparel Too "Touchy-Feely" to Sell Online?

Stodgy brick-and-mortar retailers sniff, "It's fashion; it won't sell online." True, among Internet users who have yet to buy clothes online, more than 60 percent say they never will, and 40 percent of all Web surfers say they never would do so. Yet, more than 90 percent of those who have already bought clothes online say that they definitely will do so again.

The main reason why people don't want to buy clothing online is an obvious objection and one that isn't easily overcome: they want to see, touch, and try on the merchandise. After all, catalog sales never exceeded seven percent of retail sales, even though LLBean was and still is an expert at using words to describe the "touch and feel" of fabrics. Today, the favorite online clothing purchases are low-cost, low-risk, no-brain, replacement items such as socks, underwear, sweaters and shoes.

Could it be then — as the skeptical old-time retailers claim — that clothing is too "touchy-feely" to sell online? That may be true for now. But as abundant bandwidth becomes available, the Internet will become a "high-touch" medium that will be an excellent tool for selling anything.

Even without bandwidth, the classic apparel retailer Brooks Brothers racks up 25 percent of its online sales in tailored clothing. And software packages such as Snapfashun, which contains 25,000 fashion design details, allow an online shopper to create a custom-fit garment on their own computer screen. After first scanning a full-length photograph of themselves into their PC, users can sketch the garment design over their body image and then experiment by adding details such as color, shape, drape, and pleating of the fabric. In a split second, e-shoppers can change tints, raise or lower the hemline, add pockets or change their shape or style, add and space buttons or zippers, and add, remove, lengthen, shorten, enlarge or tighten sleeves. That gives the online shopper a virtual sample of the garment they are looking for in minutes, precisely customized to their size and fashion preferences.

The Web site Styleclick.com offers a range of top brand-name merchandise products that users can zoom in on to inspect fabric textures, stitching, buttons, and beading. Products can be viewed in high resolution and 3-D rotation, providing visually rich images that allow e-shoppers to make informed decisions. Styleclick.com was the first site to provide side-by-side images of related products from various top name manufacturers so that shoppers may visually compare the look of the items, not just the price.

> As bandwidth expands, the Internet will become "high-touch" — an excellent tool for selling *anything*.

Similarly, by providing the practical and useful information that a woman needs to interpret and develop her own personal style, Shop@AOL's "Chic Simple Wardrobe" helps the online shopper fill her closet. Bloomingdale's uses "Live Picture Zoom" technology, which allows consumers to get a close-up look at fabric and texture.

Already, then, some clothing retailers are trying to overcome the short-term bandwidth bottleneck by providing for "virtual touching." In the near future more sophisticated systems will be commonplace and this will lead to an explosion in online apparel sales.

Forecast of Online Sales to 2010

The overall apparel and footwear market is about $150 billion a year. However, since the big-volume players were slow to move online, only $92 million worth of clothing and footwear was sold over the Web in 1997. Sales grew rapidly to $530 million by 1998 and jumped to $3 billion by 2000, but this still accounted for only two percent of total category sales.

However, the online demand for clothing and shoes is growing rapidly as more women go online and as both men and women become comfortable with e-shopping. About 28 percent of online shoppers already buy apparel and/or footwear online. As a result, online sales are growing fast and some forecasters are predicting about $20 billion by 2003, accounting for seven to nine percent of total retail sales by then.

However, even these forecasts are too conservative. For sure, nearly all catalog and other direct sales of apparel and footwear will gravitate to the online channel very quickly. In addition, as broadband Web access becomes widespread by mid-decade, the ability to virtually "touch and feel" the merchandise will attract a flood of online buyers to this category.

We forecast online apparel and footwear sales, as a percentage of total category sales to 2010, as follows:

Online Apparel and Footwear Sales as % of Total Sales		
2000	*2005*	*2010*
2%	12%	28%

Which Web Sites Will Win

Some 20-odd contenders in this category include Web start-ups, catalogers, and brick-and-mortar retailers.

This decade will see a consolidation and rationalization of the category. No pure e-tail up-start has staked out a big enough first-mover advantage and already many are faltering. No cataloguer is large enough to come out on top. And most brick-and-mortar retailers have been slow to go online; many will lose significant market share. Hence, we are likely to see many alliances, mergers, take-overs — and bankruptcies — in this category, with a handful of dominant players emerging. By 2010, we again forecast this category's "Top 5" Web sites will be

◆ **Gap.com**

◆ **Nordstrom.com**

◆ **JCPenney.com**

◆ **Sears.com**

◆ **Wal-Mart.com**

8 AUTOMOBILES
"Tire Clicking" and Virtual Test Drives

Ford wants to be the leading company; and part of getting there means we have to be the world's leading online provider.

— Jacques Nasser, CEO
Ford Motor Company

THE PROSPECT OF BUYING A CAR over the Web from home is tantalizing when you consider that the typical car buyer tramps from dealer to dealer — only then to be forced to play the all too familiar but frustratingly stupid haggling game. Car buyers, sick and tired of such high-pressure tactics and mysterious price-guessing schemes, are flocking online to get the real scoop.

When you buy a car over the Internet, you don't get pounced on by overly eager sales sharks. A fast and easy way to make contactless price comparisons between dealers, the Web is turning tire kickers into mouse clickers. It is transforming the painful car-buying experience into a low-risk and even fun family activity.

Of course, mouse clicking doesn't yet entirely replace tire kicking — at least not for 98 percent of car buyers. While two percent of car buyers are now buying entirely online, old habits die hard. Still, consumers have never had so many choices when it comes to car shopping. After decades of hustling, in the 1990s car retailing saw wave after wave of new formats hit the market, from car superstores to online referral services to factory-owned showrooms.

Now, tech-savvy car buyers are downloading their dream cars over the Internet. Internet shopping for (i.e., researching) vehicles was up 14 percent in 2000 and more than 60 percent of consumers now use the Web to research their new vehicle purchases. By 2006, according to Forrester Research, more than six percent of total new vehicle sales will be conducted online, compared with less than two percent in 2000. A recent study of auto industry executives by consulting firm A.T. Kearney showed how the industry will radically alter during this decade. By 2010, these executives believe that 29 percent of new vehicles will be bought directly from the manufacturer (either online or through a dealer) and another 21 percent will be made online via Internet-based dealers or referral services. That's 50 percent of sales over the Web.

Dealer Shakeout Imminent

The impact of these changes on the automobile distribution system is already significant. Traditional retailing and distribution costs account for up to 30 percent of a vehicle's price, largely because having a separate store for each brand adds enormous costs and tremendous inefficiency to the value chain. Imagine what a TV would cost if Circuit City had 12 different stores to sell 12 different TV brands. There are simply too many car dealers chasing too few buyers.

We are thus seeing the beginnings of a major rationalization of the automobile value chain and the number of dealerships will decline dramatically over the next decade. In 1952, for example, there were 47,000 new-car dealerships in the United States. By 1972, their number had fallen to 30,000 and by 1992 was down to 23,500 — half the 1952 figure. I predict that at least 50 percent of today's 22,000 remaining dealers will disappear by 2010. As their number gets down to the 10,000 range, the auto retailing model will be dramatically different from today's.

While the industry still moves at the speed of a Model T, Web speed is rapidly redefining its future. As dealer consolidation continues and online shopping gains popularity, small dealers in particular will be squeezed out. In 1979, there were 20,700 dealers selling fewer than 400 new cars per year. By 1999, there were only 10,400 such dealerships. By contrast, the number of dealers selling more than 400 new cars per year rose from 8,800 in 1979 to 12,100 in 1999.

> While the car industry still moves at the speed of a Model T, Web speed is rapidly redefining its future.

Regardless of size, to survive and prosper, every dealership must become a true showroom rather than a sales center — concentrating on the new mobile Web Lifestyle — and a service center to the entire lifelong vehicle ownership experience. Thanks to increases in vehicle durability, people keep their cars longer. Consequently, during the 1990s, auto dealerships got an increasing percentage of their profits from the sale of used cars and from the sale of parts and service. This trend will only continue. As more and more people telecommute, cars will be used less and less and will last longer and longer, further reducing the need for new-car dealerships.

Online Car Sellers: Build-to-Order Next

Meanwhile, the Internet has rapidly opened up automobile sales — new and used — to a range of a new competitors. And the availability of instant pricing has put increasing pressure on the old way of selling cars.

As the Web drives down price, whom you buy from is less important; it doesn't have to be a brand dealer. In fact, the fastest-growing car dealers are companies such as CarsDirect.com, AutoByTel.com, AutoNation, and Microsoft's CarPoint web site. Moreover, perhaps facing up to the inevitable, more than half the traditional dealerships subscribe to one or more of such third-party Internet shopping services.

CarsDirect.com lets buyers see in seconds the manufacturer's retail price, the invoice and, most important, the price that can be had. Once the consumer wants to buy, it takes almost no interaction with a dealer to close the transaction. CarsDirect.com's site offers more than 2,500 different models and lets you choose colors and options, displaying prices in real-time. When you settle on the price, you fill out online forms to apply for financing and insurance. The car is then delivered to your home or office.

CarsDirect.com — in which Dell Computer founder Michael Dell is an investor — not surprisingly emulates Dell's hugely successful "build-to-order, direct-to-customer, discount-price" business model. Car buyers pay CarsDirect.com a credit-card deposit of $250 to begin the ordering process. The company first states a price for the car, based on information extracted from its huge database, then calls several dealers to see who will match it. If no dealer offers a price that low, CarsDirect.com eats the loss and reprices the model for future buyers. Launched in 1999, the company already sells a thousand vehicles a month.

Microsoft's CarPoint site also provides everything you need to buy and pay for a new car. CarPoint creates a no-haggle, no-hassle environment for buyers, one where dealers are required to offer the most competitive price on their first quote and to do so within two business days. In fact, the usual response time is less than 24 hours, sometimes just a few minutes. The site gives you dealer invoice prices plus all-important details on rebates and current specials. You can configure the precise car you want with options and colors. Financing and insuring the car, at the best possible rates, are simple tasks. You can also set up a personal page on the Web site to get tips and deals for the care and maintenance of your vehicle. This personal auto page is like having a reserved parking spot at the service center; it tracks your car's maintenance and alerts you to needed oil changes or tune-ups.

The Web turns tire kickers into mouse clickers; it makes car-buying fun.

AutoByTel.com pioneered the online automobile sector, basically operating as a middleman, referring customers to some 3,000 dealerships. Its Web site sells some 50,000 new and used cars per month, also arranging their financing and repair. You can register your vehicles with "My Service" in the "Car Repair" section, and AutoByTel will send you checkup reminders as well as any recall or technical-service bulletins. In 1999, the company acquired CarSmart.com and also began testing a direct-sales model in a few markets. In early 2000, it began acting as a broker between car buyers and dealers online, handling the purchase and financing arrangements.

AutoNation, the Florida-based dealership consolidator that owns about 400 dealer franchises across the United States, in 1999 linked its individual dealer sites through an umbrella site called AutoNationDirect, making it easier for car shoppers to buy online. By the end of 1999, the company was selling nearly 5,000 cars a month and, having forged an alliance with AOL that will reach 80 percent of potential online car buyers, expects to sell $3 billion worth of automobiles online in 2001.

Manufacturers Stuck in First Gear

Against this background, the major automobile companies have been surprisingly slow to respond to the car retailing revolution. After all, during the past century General Motors has made countless innovations since being the first to counter Ford's lead and offer cars in a color other than black. More recently, in a 1996 response to the initial Internet buzz, GM launched the world's largest automotive Web site with links to each of its divisions, dumping more than 16,000 pages of information online. But the company had more than 150 different sites globally, with no common navigation process.

In 1999, going beyond this info-overload "brochure ware," GM launched its national online service GMBuyPower.com, which was getting 650,000 visitors a month by year-end. This Web site, recently linked to AOL, gives customers access to every vehicle on dealers' lots, plus independent data about competing models.

But this site is no more revolutionary than those set up by GM's competitors. Yes, shoppers can configure the car they desire and conduct an electronic search of dealer inventories to track it down. The site also lets you see third-party price comparisons of GM vehicles versus similarly equipped vehicles from other manufacturers. And, of course, you can apply for GMAC financing online.

Yet even this rather tepid, dealer-based system sent shock waves through GM's network of 8,000 dealers who failed to see its advantage in providing hot customer leads. While it costs about $1,270 to sell the average car, online systems slash that to as little as $150 to $300 per car by eliminating advertising and salespeople. For the auto industry in total, the potential saving at today's prices is a staggering $50 billion a year due to reduced inventory, order-processing, marketing and sales costs.

In the United Kingdom, GM's Vauxhall unit began selling new cars over the Internet in late 1999, delivering the car to the buyer's doorstep within a week of placing an order. Using the Web site, customers can get the trade-in value of their old vehicle, arrange a new car test drive and initiate its financing. The service began with six special "dot-com" cars, two from each of the company's Corsa, Astra, and Vectra brands, with more models added in 2000.

Until recently, the Ford site at Ford.com was tough to navigate, taking 11 mouse clicks to reach a dealer. Recently streamlined to the ideal three-click maximum, the site lets users search for a specific model and put down a deposit for a vehicle. FordDirect.com, an online joint venture between Ford and its dealers, is gradually being rolled out state-wide as antiquated state laws get modified to allow the automakers to get closer to the retail end of the business. Ford ultimately will give consumers an "e-price" rather than a manufacturer's suggested retail price (MSRP), and will let customers configure and finance their vehicles online.

Ford has a joint venture with Microsoft's CarPoint to help consumers find the specific car they want from dealer inventory — or to have it quickly built to order, in the same way that you can buy a PC from Dell online.

Customize-My-Car, Online

In the real world, less than 10 percent of today's new cars are built to order. Most automobile companies build and equip cars in standard configurations and push them through the dealer network. As a result, few people get the car they truly want. Building cars based on Internet orders is something that most manufacturers are working on. In addition to GM's Vauxhall initiative and Ford, Honda also has launched a system that lets consumers configure cars online and arrange for pre-approved financing and service packages.

As customized car buying increasingly becomes the norm, the Internet will become a battle zone for driver mind share. In the future, almost everyone will use the Web to research their car purchases. In 1997, only 16 percent of online users even visited a car-buying site. That percentage rose steadily to 25 percent in 1998, 40 percent in 1999, and more than 60 percent in 2000. Usage is projected to climb to 75 percent in 2002 and 88 percent in 2003. Soon thereafter, buying a car will be like ordering a PC from Dell. Most of us will research, buy, insure, and finance our new vehicles entirely on the Web and the car will be delivered to our homes within three business days.

Of course, diehards in the automobile industry — both in the car companies and the dealerships — still have their heads in the sand on this. They claim that an automobile is much different than a PC; that the buyer needs to touch, feel, smell, and test drive the new vehicle before making up their minds. In reality, of course, tomorrow's computers will bring all these sensations over the

Internet in such a way that it will be almost impossible not to feel as if you're actually sitting in the automobile and test driving it.

As it is, today's better-educated shoppers buy faster, thereby helping to reduce dealer costs and sell more cars. As well, customers will pay more for a car if it has got everything they want, as opposed to the traditional pick-one-off-the-lot compromise. They also don't mind driving up to one hundred miles to get the car they truly want. As the number of such buyers inevitably increases over the next decade, so will the number of cars sold online.

Forecast of Online Sales to 2010

The total automobile market is approaching $800 billion a year, with about forty-five percent being new vehicles. Of these total sales, however, less than two percent occurred online in 2000. Still, almost sixty-eight percent of new car purchases now are researched on the Web and General Motors alone expects to sell two percent of its vehicles online in 2001, doubling that annually thereafter. Some forecasts call for six percent of cars to be sold online in 2004.

These forecasts nevertheless underestimate the potential of this category. A large percentage of car owners are brand loyal and tend to buy or lease the latest version of the same model car as a "replenishment" item. They know what they want. With the advent of virtual test drives, the transition from "research online/ buy-offline" to "click-and-deliver-it-to-my-home" will become increasingly commonplace. In 2010, five million cars will be bought completely online in North America.

Consequently, our forecasts of online automobile sales, as a percentage of total category sales to 2010, are as follows:

Online Automobile Sales as % of Total Sales		
2000	*2005*	*2010*
2%	9%	19%

Which Web Sites Will Win

Today's leading auto sector Web sites are the likes of AutoByTel, GMBuyPower, and the new Ford/Microsoft Carpoint alliance. There will be many more alliances in this category and it is hard to imagine how any upstart can out-compete the major manufac-turers online. By 2010, we again forecast this category's "Top 5" Web sites will be

- ◆ **GMBuyPower.com**

- ◆ **Ford/CarPoint.com**

- ◆ **AutoByTel.com**

- ◆ **AutoNationDirect.com**

- ◆ **CarsDirect.com**

9 BOOKS
Digitized Downloads to Digital Paper

E-commerce is not just about selling books, music, and videos online. That's only the beginning.

— Steve Riggio, vice-chairman
Barnes & Noble

PROVIDERS OF ANY AND EVERY KIND OF CONTENT face an inescapable law of the Internet: anything that can been digitized will be digitized and downloadable. After the first copy is digitized, the cost of electronic distribution is next to zero.

That's why, in 1997, a team of monks at the Haeinsa Temple in South Korea encrypted and digitized 15 million words of Buddhist texts so that the ancient words and teachings of Buddha will live on in CD-ROM format. If monks — the original content scribes — understand the information revolution, how come other content providers still don't "get it"?

The immutable law of digitization will ultimately apply to at least the following categories of content:

- **Words:** *Spoken* (conversations, public address announcements, conferences, radio broadcasts);
  Printed (correspondence, newsletters, newspapers, magazines/journals, books, directories, brochures, printed advertisements, instructions, directions, warranties, contracts).

- **Images:** *Still* (drawings, sketches, paintings, designs, maps, photographs, x-rays);
  Moving (television, movies, videos).

• **Music:** sheet music, songs, audio tapes, CDs, concerts.

Of course, not all of these content categories constitute a retail purchase by consumer households, the main focus of this book. While the list illustrates the wide digital sweep of the Webolution, we will review books here, and newspapers, movies and music in later sections.

e-Books and Digital Paper

The English word "book" is ancient, originating in Old English, German and Norse. Some scholars believe the word comes from names for the beech tree — from beech bark, beech tablets, and beech sticks used in monasteries for the writing and binding of early books.

Actually, the first "writing" was not for text but for accounting, which began with the Sumerians around 4000 BC. It took them another thousand years to begin recording stories, which only became possible with the invention of cuneiform script. The first books appeared in the 15th century but were handwritten, barely legible, difficult to carry, and chained down. Sounds just like our early computers, which also were first used for number-crunching and then word processing.

Today, of course, computers are multimedia voice-activated portable appliances. The book you are now holding was not typed but dictated into a computer, spell/grammar-checked by software, and printed digitally on a computer-controlled press. Despite this high-tech progress, books are technically obsolete — at least as we have come to know and love them — and new technology is about to make the ink-squirted-onto-pulped-trees medium disappear.

Conclusive proof of this came in March 2000, when Stephen King's short story, "Riding the Bullet," was published only in electronic form. Within just two days of its release, more than 500,000 people downloaded the e-story, making it the most successful "book launch" in history. This stunning demand blows away any doubts about whether an audience exists for e-books.

State-of-the-art e-book (electronic book) technology is now coming available on all Windows-based PCs, laptops, and handheld devices — some 210 million new appliances a year worldwide! The driving force behind this reading revolution is Microsoft's new Reader typeface software. The on-screen results of this software rival printed paper in legibility: a clean, crisp, eyeball-friendly, full-page display that provides a truly comfortable, "immersive" reading experience. Moreover, you can highlight text, make margin notes, turn the pages instead of scrolling, and bookmark innumerable places. You can search for words and phrases, look them up in a built-in dictionary, and instantly resize the typeface to your preference. You can even have the text spoken out loud to you if you prefer.

In the United States, Microsoft has teamed with Barnes & Noble to make e-books widely available in its stores. Microsoft also is working with publishers such as Penguin and printers such as R.R. Donnelley to make e-books available. Donnelley and its publishing partners are converting print titles into e-books and will store and manage these titles in electronic form. Similarly, the French publishing company Havas, a unit of Vivendi, is digitizing its entire publishing line. Havas will continue issuing 99 percent of its books in paper format until 2002 but expects e-book versions eventually to take over the market. Meanwhile, the company will re-issue out-of-print books online through its new ePocket division rather than do new print runs.

Bertelsmann, the German media giant, has begun storing new books, as well as much of its Random House unit's 20,000-volume backlist, as digital files. They can be printed on demand or downloaded to e-books. The company aims to market books online in perpetuity, mainly through BarnesandNoble.com, which is 40 percent owned by Bertelsmann.

Microsoft's vice-president of technology development, Dick Brass, expects e-book sales to reach $1 billion in three to four years and says that, by 2020 "50 percent of everything we read will be in electronic form." Indeed, Microsoft researchers and developers familiar with the history of e-publishing and the company's own future plans have developed a timeline for the e-book revolution, partially re-tabulated here:

2001 — e-textbooks appear

2002 — screen displays better than printed paper

2003 — e-book devices weigh one pound, cost $100

2004 — tablet PCs with handwriting input

2005 — e-book/magazine/newspaper sales top $1 billion

2009 — e-books outsell paper books

2010 — e-books weigh ½ lb., hold 1 million titles

2018 — last paper editions of newspapers published

2020 — 90 percent of titles now sold in e-format

Today's e-book appliances do not impair but rather enhance the reading experience. Even with a slow modem, a 300-page book can be downloaded in 30 seconds to an appliance whose weight, appearance and operation is so like a real book that, once immersed in what you are reading, you soon forget about the high-tech medium held in your hand. The screen is the size of a paperback and, even without Reader software, is as clear as newsprint or paperback text. The unit has simple "forward" and "back" buttons positioned right under your thumb and you can jump to any point in the text. You can highlight or mark up the text colorfully using a stylus, and when you open the e-book's cover it awakens to the page you were last reading.

> E-books and e-paper will send the publishing industry into a massive reversal.

Three types of digital paper also are under development, both made of material so thin that it can be rolled up without damage. One version, developed by Xerox and just going into production at 3M, is a thin sheet of flexible plastic made of millions of microspheres. Each of these tiny beads is half black, half white, their "face up" color being controlled electrically. IBM has created a similarly thin, transistor-sprayed-on-plastic, flexible sheet that can be a rolled-up screen. Another version is under development by Lucent and E-Ink who make "electronic ink" used in billboards and large signs such as those displaying flight arrivals and departures at airports. This e-paper is composed of millions of tiny electro-charged micro-capsules, filled with a dark dye and a light pigment, which change color to create images. The image stays on screen even after the device is switched off or until replaced with another image.

Supplementing these inventions, in 2001, Israel-based PowerPaper created a printable battery that could lead to flexible displays, e-paper, plastic transistors, and super-smartcards. The circuitry is printed on ordinary sheets of paper, just like postage stamps; the chemical inks act as the anode, cathode, and electrolyte, and can be stamped in any configuration.

Content displayed on e-paper, being digitized, thus can be automatically and continuously updated, starting over with a "clean digital sheet," so to speak. Indeed, the message of this medium is that, in the digital era, content is a fluid resource.

Such inventions will send the entire publishing industry into a massive reversal. Instead of mass production printing, content will be sold first and then printed afterwards on a customer-by-customer, personalized, on-demand basis. As well, content will be repeatedly updated in a series of versions — just like software — so that those who want the latest edition can easily update or upgrade their content.

Digital Directories and Encyclopedias

E-publishing makes all content available to the masses. Just as the printing press made Mona Lisa reproductions commonplace, the virtual PC does the same for all content. Hence, publishers must stop thinking of paper and focus on the digital interface between the digital content and the digital consumer.

Directories of all kinds are a case in point. When you think about it, telephone directories, the Yellow Pages, or encyclopedias are merely compilations of answers to "frequently asked questions" (FAQs). It is therefore inevitable that they are being digitized and that their paper versions will become museum pieces. Even serious content magazines such as *National Geographic,* whose past issues are collectors' items, are forced to change with technology. Hence, in 1998, *National Geographic* released the complete content of 108 years of its magazines, including 180,000 photographs, on a handful of digital video disks (DVDs).

The saga of *Encyclopaedia Britannica* is testimony to the digital content revolution. Founded in 1778 in Scotland, *Britannica* once was the prized possession of the home library. The company extracted premium prices from guilt-assuaged parents for information that, as the Information Age unfolded, was outdated before it went to press — never mind by the time the slick door-to-door salesman took your order and the hefty, multi-volume set arrived several weeks later. The old way to land a customer was "tell-sell-hope": tell about the product, sell its benefits, and hope they buy. The new way is to inform qualified buyers in an entertaining way, link them to a virtual store, and draw them into a relationship where they will want to come back again. The old model was to close the sale; the new model is all about interactions.

Sales of *Britannica* peaked in 1989 when the company had 7,500 salesmen worldwide. The technology then changed and school kids much preferred getting their homework information from a CD-ROM or, later on, over the Web. Britannica stupidly rejected Microsoft's offer to place the content on CD-ROM, whereupon Microsoft launched its own hugely successful, colorful, multimedia *Expedia* CD-ROM that soon out-sold *Britannica*. *Expedia* cost about $100 versus a whopping $1,250 for Britannica's out-of-date, non-user-friendly, 32-volume set of hefty books. Undaunted, Britannica persevered, launched its own CD-ROM version, made the encyclopedia available online for an $85 subscription fee, and finally dismissed its entire sales force. In 1999, Britannica finally threw in the towel, making the online version entirely free and announcing that "you have to be free to be relevant" in an Internet-dominated market. Precisely!

In late 2000, Britannica edited its content into short paragraphs that easily fit onto small screens and thus became accessible on wireless-modem PDAs and some WebPhones. By early 2001, however, facing hard times, Britannica laid off 31 percent of its workforce and decided after all to ask users to pay for certain content on a subscription basis. The company is emphasizing reference, education, and learning content. One paid service is Britannica-School.com that provides interactive curriculum materials and other tools for the K–12 educational market. So the saga continues.

e-Libraries

Like the encyclopedia before it, the Internet is a universal library, a global information index. If you borrow a book on a favorite topic from your local brick-and-mortar library, other users cannot access it. But a digital resource can be accessed by millions of people simultaneously.

This central feature is being exploited by NetLibrary.com, which buys book rights from publishers, converts them into formats suitable for online reading and then sells them to online libraries and online consumers. Initially, NetLibrary.com had 10,000 e-texts aimed at scholars, students and professionals. But the range of titles expanded rapidly and public-domain books can be downloaded free of charge. Consumers can also access the entire collection for a nominal annual subscription.

Perhaps the most successful e-text publisher is Voyager, whose "karaoke" version of Macbeth lets the reader selectively turn off a character from Shakespeare's play and literally "act the part" themselves from the on-screen text. The text can also be frozen while notes and movie clips are consulted. Such e-texts will soon eliminate the traditional book in specialized areas such as reference works and academic publications.

These new formats also permit interactivity between reader and author, thus opening up new avenues for creative writers. And anyone who goes online can, of course, become an instant author accessible to a global readership. Already, budding authors can gain a legitimate profile through FatBrain.com, a vanity press where published and unpublished authors alike sell works that might otherwise be ignored by the hide-bound publishing industry. FatBrain.com focuses on shortish documents of 10 to 150 pages, calling them eMatter. For a listing fee of $1 per month, authors upload their content, set its price, post a brief description of it, and slot it into thousands of subject categories. Instead of the usual 10 percent royalty, FatBrain gives its authors 50 percent on all sales.

While this model could create a virtual literary explosion — perhaps even another Renaissance — it could doom most mainstream publishers. Each business day in North America, 250 new consumer book titles are published — a staggering 93 percent of which lose money. Indeed, many of the relatively few best-sellers come from smaller publishers who are fleeter of foot and better focused on modern-day consumer marketing.

All publishers are saddled with huge fixed and variable costs: editors, copy editors, administrators, paper and raw materials, warehousing, shipping, unsold returns. They also lack marketing expertise, both in selecting marketable titles and in getting the books sold. So they play the law of averages: publish enough books and a few of them will turn out to be winners, keeping the company at least marginally profitable. Such practices are unsustainable against the Internet juggernaut.

Booksellers: Bricks or Bits?

Where then does this leave the booksellers, whether they are brick-and-mortar, click-and-order, or brick-and-click hybrid? Their fate rests on the future of the book format itself. A book is a medium, a container of content. As the technology of the content changes, so does the nature of the medium containing it. The "message" of the Internet interactive multimedium is that bound books will get "unbound" by the Web. Hence, conventional bound-book publishing and bound-book retailing are doomed. So it doesn't matter whether you are a corner bookstore, an online bookstore like Amazon.com, or a hybrid like Barnes & Noble — all of them are retailing a product that will stop being produced in material form. Therefore, they too must change. They must start making their own product obsolete and create additional value by making electronic books.

Of course, Amazon.com has expanded beyond its original book selling mandate to offer music, videos, toys, electronic games, greeting cards, and auctions — even online groceries. The Canadian counterpart to Amazon, Chapters.ca — which was Canada's only online success story in any product category worth writing about — also branched out into other products, including gardening supplies, but that site has closed.

In terms of books, however, it will soon become irrelevant how many titles are available on Amazon.com's Web site. As conventional books stop being produced in material form, out-of-print titles will become much more sought-after as collectors' items. Hence, Amazon.com is fortunate to have acquired Bibliofind.com, a search engine that finds used and rare books, pointing you to the site of the independent bookseller who has a particular title available for sale. In turn, of course, used rather than new books presage the future of independent booksellers.

Barnes & Noble faces the same situation as Amazon. The largest brick-and-mortar book chain was so slow to go online that Amazon.com grabbed a huge lead in book e-tailing, which it has maintained — for whatever that may be worth over the long run. Any bookstore that does not have a Web presence is driving away customers and sealing its own fate. In April 2001, Borders, the second-largest U.S. bookstore chain, turned over its entire online bookselling efforts to Amazon through a co-branded Web site. Amazon will provide content inventory, order fulfillment, and customer service, while Borders will handle in-store pick-up of online orders.

Already, an online book buyer purchases five to ten times as many books as an offline book buyer. Book e-tailers clearly are skimming off the top customers, leaving less and less opportunity for brick-and-mortar stores. With more than 10,000 bookstores in the U.S., it is self-evident that the vast majority will go the way of the linotype operator and the printing press.

Forecast of Online Sales to 2010

The book category in total is only a $15-billion-a-year business. However, books were one of the first products to catch on with online consumers, more than half of whom now buy books fairly regularly online. Book sales at online pioneer Amazon.com were $676 million in 1999, and it now has an annualized run rate of $1.2 billion. The company's customer base reached 20 million at the end of 2000, 73 percent of whom were repeat buyers.

Overall book sales on the Web topped $2 billion in 2000, accounting for 14 percent of the market, and some forecasts put 2003 online sales at $4 billion, grabbing 20 percent of the category. However, these forecasts are far too conservative. With mass merchandisers such as Wal-Mart moving aggressively online, online book sales will continue to grow rapidly. As well, of course, more and more books will be downloaded to e-books, perhaps replacing bound books in many genres as the decade proceeds. Many such books likely will not be sold by booksellers at all but by their publishers or authors via direct download.

Regardless of who is the seller, our forecasts of online bound and e-book sales combined, as a percentage of total category sales to 2010, are as follows:

Online Book Sales as % of Total Sales		
2000	*2005*	*2010*
14%	30%	70%

Which Web Sites Will Win

Bookstore chains presently account for about 22 percent of total category sales and independent stores sell another 16 percent. After the 14 percent of books sold online, the remaining 48 percent is sold by mass merchandisers, discount stores, book clubs, and mail order sellers. The last two channels likely will be totally replaced by online sales. Independent booksellers inevitably will end up in specialist niche markets, if they survive at all. There will be a huge shakeout in this category, with few survivors.

Amazon.com is by far the category's giant. There are more than 20 competitors, including Barnes & Noble and the German company Bertelsmann. Online book buyers shop at Amazon about 80 percent of the time, with its nearest competitor, BN.com, attracting less than 40 percent of book buyers. Few of the others will survive. By 2010, we again forecast this category's "Top 5" Web sites will be

- ◆ **Amazon.com**

- ◆ **BN.com**

- ◆ **Bertelsmann**

- ◆ **Wal-Mart.com**

- ◆ **Borders.com (partner of Amazon)**

10 EDUCATION
Taking Schooling Out of the Schools

The big move toward using the Internet and home school-
ing is happening because people are dissatisfied with
our failed public schools.

— Dr. Tim Draper, member
California Board of Education

THE VAST MAJORITY of today's computer-literate kids learned to use a computer at home, not at school. The Web takes schooling out of the school. And I firmly believe that most of the next generation's learning will take place at home, not school.

George Washington Didn't Go to School

Home schooling is not new. In the Agricultural Age, the farmhouse kitchen was the classroom and mother was the teacher. While some grammar schools and universities were founded in the Middle Ages, the vast majority of children still learned at home from their parents and, for the well-to-do, from a hired tutor or governess. Early American presidents such as George Washington, James Madison, and John Quincy Adams never went to school. Not until after the Civil War did "little red schoolhouse" learning become the North American norm.

Distance education began in 18th-century Europe, where students mailed written exercises to their professors who, in turn, graded and sent the exercises back to the students by mail. In 1840, Sir Isaac Pitman taught secretarial skills by having students translate the Bible into shorthand, mailing their squiggles back to him for grading. Even as late as 1924, the number of people taking correspondence courses with private firms outnumbered those in college, universities and professional schools by four to one.

Factory schooling then brought public education to the masses. The problem with factory schools is that they force everyone to learn at the same pace, virtually killing most learning before it happens. The computer offers a chance to move everyone to a model of individualized learning. As well, of course, today's complex world of constant change makes knowledge obsolete very quickly. Education can no longer be acquired from out-of-date textbooks during youth and then be expected to serve for an entire lifetime. Rather, learning must be a continuous process culled from constantly updated content.

Mass education will be replaced by individualized learning at home.

Fortunately, the Web offers a new form of interactive learning that allows almost anyone to learn virtually anything, anywhere, at any time. The future requires just-in-time learning where students can "dial a teacher" anywhere in cyberspace. Mass education cannot compete with that and inevitably will be replaced by individualized, lifelong e-learning at home via the Internet.

e-Learning is Fun

At the age of two, my daughter learned to maneuver a mouse as handily as a crayon in two minutes. It is easier for a Web-Gen kid to install software and surf the Web than to open a pencil box and scribble down notes from a screeching-chalk-on-faded-gray blackboard.

North American "screenagers" live in homes with PCs and use them eagerly. Indeed, 92 percent of them used a PC before their eighth birthday and they all now rate themselves as expert users. They find Web surfing as easy as TV channel surfing and say it is a more natural thing to do. Of the time they spend online, two-thirds of it comes from TV watching and another third from playing video games. They say the Web is "more fun" than TV and, more important, that it is "the most fun" way to learn.

Interestingly, the word "school" comes from "skol" which means "fun." With PCs, homework is not hard work; it's fun. In PC households, the average amount of time spent on homework increases by more than two hours a week. Learning is most effective when it's most fun, when the content is most captivating and engaging. Multimedia PCs captivate the imagination: they show live events, animatedly illustrate concepts, and provide meaning and emotion through words and music — all in engagingly interactive ways that challenge, entice, and excite eager minds.

For example, much to the chagrin of literature teachers, you can even study Shakespeare much better by computer. Teachers forget that Shakespeare wrote his plays to be performed live on stage, not to be read from books. In fact, most people in Shakespeare's day couldn't read. Students thus can view an e-text of *Hamlet* or *Richard III* alongside a windowed movie version. They can zoom in for close-ups, do camera pans, and search the text for words and character names, pop up a dictionary explaining obscure words, or click on tutorials about the plot and characters.

Not surprisingly, 93 percent of parents say a PC is the most beneficial product they can buy for their children. A similar percentage of PC owners cite their children's education as the main reason for buying, ahead of work-at-home and financial applications. Parents who once said, "Turn off the TV and do your homework!" now say, "Turn on your PC and do your homework!" In many homes, the PC has already displaced encyclopedias, dictionaries and books as the premier learning resource. And various surveys find that students with PCs get better grades.

Kids and keyboards are a natural fit. Students take notes on laptops, their clicking keyboards a constant companion to the teacher's lecture. Indeed, Web sites such as StudentU.com, Versity.com and Study24-7.com hire university students to take lecture notes and then post them online within 24 hours for free download. Inevitably, this will lead to a drop in attendance at class. Ultimately, there may be nobody there except the prof and the note taker! Long before that happens, of course, the profs will smarten up and place their own notes online for an e-university that also "got the message" and went virtual.

In any event, the majority of students who use the Web for online research feel more confident about their assignments. Two-thirds of children with a PC at home use it to do homework and 85 percent of them complete assignments with information found online. The Web is fantastic for letting people go out and explore things on their own. It can turn every home into a living classroom.

e-Learning vs. Brick-and-Mortar Schools

Whether there ever will be a PC on every classroom desk is not worth considering. The educational Webolution is already taking place in the home. The home PC is changing the way we write, compute, communicate and learn. It has whetted the appetite for individual educational experiences that mass education can never achieve. To put PCs in schools and connect them to the Internet is to perpetuate a failed system. Since the Web takes schooling out of the school, we need to do exactly the opposite and take learning to the learner, at home.

Therefore, rather than putting schools online, we should use the Web to replace schools with "Webucation." In North American schools in 2000 there still were 12 students for every Internet-connected PC. Connecting all schools to the Internet is costing about $15 billion. To provide one PC for every five students by 2005 will cost $65 billion. It would be much cheaper for the U.S. and Canadian governments to give a free PC to each household that doesn't now have one and then switch all schooling to in-home study. In turn, they could close down the schools and save at least $1 trillion a year in school budgets. For a fraction of that sum, they could provide constantly updated e-learning materials and online tutoring to every student from age two through PhD.

Education is becoming prohibitively expensive, both to the individual student and the tax payer. The cost of conventional classroom instruction is about $80 an hour and full-week programs cost up to $5,000. Web-based training cuts these costs in half. Money is being spent in all the wrong places: in brick-and-mortar buildings and libraries that sit unused for months on end. Instead, we should be creating electronic campuses. For example, 200 million pages of books and other reference materials can be accessed from a cabinet-sized 200-terabit server that could replace thousands of schools.

Moreover, Web training serves up instruction anywhere, around the clock, and without commuting or travel costs. Each online course saves at least 20 hours in commuting time. Students could "attend" class according to their own schedule and could pick and choose among courses offered by a wide variety of schools world-wide, seeking out the planet's best instructors. The high costs of education would drop at least ten-fold if education were digitized.

Online education thus is a "killer application" that will radically shrink the centuries-old brick-and-mortar model, starting first at the ossified, mortar-board, ivory-tower level and working its way down through the system. Education fails to see that it is in the knowledge business, developing intellectual capital. Educators are entrepreneurs of knowledge. Yet few business schools seem to know how to exploit this opportunity; only a fraction of schools let you actually earn a degree online.

The Interactive, Immersive Edge

Of course, the resistance to change in academia is enormous. Many universities are proud of the fact that they are among the oldest, most stable, and most unchanged institutions in the world. One distinguished Harvard business professor recently said, "The Harvard experience cannot be duplicated online." What arrogant ignorance! If Harvard Business School is as good as it claims, then it should realize that a business case can't be made for continuing its own outmoded teaching model.

As for North America's public school system, it has more than three million teachers, the majority of whom have never used the Internet. Indeed, most teachers don't have a phone, let alone a PC in their classrooms. Students have access to more technology in their bedrooms than in their classrooms. As a result, students often are teaching their teachers about the Web and digital technology.

Technology needs to be where the learner is and where most learning takes place; today, that is in the home. Those who argue that nothing can replace classroom interaction obviously have never been online. Today's virtual professors post their assignments to electronic bulletin boards and send graded papers across the Web. They find that online students can learn just as well if not better than those forced to sit in banked lecture halls. Online students cannot sit passively in the back row twiddling their thumbs. They must think and communicate with a virtual professor who can pose a question at any moment and, within 30 seconds get responses from every student — and know immediately who has and hasn't replied. This creates a learning experience where everyone is in the virtual front row.

As Plato knew, education is independent of time and place, and is individual; it occurs not on a campus but in a student's mind. Today's education centers on absorbing knowledge and facts. Future education will center on how you express yourself and how your senses learn. Consequently, the conventional division of the curriculum into subjects is outdated. Any subject taken in depth at once relates to other subjects. Hence, by immersing the senses, the Internet is the perfect vehicle for multidisciplinary learning.

The Coming Privatization of Education

Apart from the Web's interactive nature, online education can provide millions of people with learning opportunities they may not otherwise obtain — all in a highly efficient, cost-effective and more businesslike manner. Online learning won't just replace schools but will render them irrelevant. The public education system is in catastrophic need of change, higher education is becoming fossilized, and management guru Peter Drucker predicts that university campuses will stand empty before 2020. Indeed, it is now highly probable that a new online education industry will supplant schools and universities.

Harbingers of this coming upheaval are the for-profit school management companies now running publicly funded schools. The leading company is Edison Schools, with 65,000 students at 120 schools. By 2005, it aims to be managing 400 schools with 260,000 students. By 2010, for-profit schools could capture as much as 16 percent of today's $400 billion K–12 schooling pie, in the process slashing admin costs from twenty-seven percent to eight percent of the total budget.

Starting in third grade, Edison gives students a PC to take home so they can use its "The Common" intranet, giving them access to a virtual library and other learning resources. The next obvious step is to do more schooling in the home. In any event, as public schools continue to lose students to for-profit and purely private schools, this will force other public systems to adapt to parents' needs. In turn, the idea will continue to catch on, school district by school district, reshaping education as we know it.

Some education institutions, recognizing the threat and the opportunity, are attempting to go online. University of Maryland has 10,000 students taking online courses in almost every subject. The State University of New York offers a thousand courses online. Stanford has long offered televised engineering courses to technology companies and now offers a Web-based Master's degree. The University of Maine even offers online biology: students are sent fetal pigs to dissect!

The Apollo Group's for-profit University of Phoenix, at UoPhx.edu, teaches more than 20,000 students everything from nursing to computer science and is growing by 40 percent a year, double the rate of its brick-and-mortar campus, with a 40 percent profit margin. Classes are limited to online teams of 12 students who are each taught by 1,700 part-time teachers.

In the future, students will be able to get a degree without ever leaving their home or car, tuning in wherever they are and at any time, and will have a university education at their beck and call. The University of Twente in Holland is a virtual and mobile university. Its Web-based software lets students follow courses, pick up and turn in assignments, and communicate with professors and fellow students online — via either PCs, PDAs or WebPhones — all without ever going to the campus. Nobody in North America is doing this yet. However, Westview High School, opening in Poway, CA, in 2002, will have a wireless network so that students can access the Web from anywhere on campus and log on to virtual classrooms for assignments. With such a system, one teacher can press a single button to send a message to an entire class or even the entire school. Parents will be able to log on from home to see what their kids are — and are not — learning.

> Online learning won't just replace schools — it will render them irrelevant.

A few schools promise diplomas and degrees to students who combine a smorgasbord of online courses from separate institutions. Columbia University, for example, has created a for-profit arm called Fathom Knowledge Network. Fathom offers for-fee online courses aimed at the lifelong learner via links to Columbia and other schools. Surfers can follow "knowledge trail" links on topics such as architecture, business and finance, or science and engineering. Fathom has 75,000 registered users but the actual number of paying students is less than a thousand. It is aiming for 200,000 users by the end of 2002, 10 percent of whom will be fee-paying students.

There is a growing number of North American private sector online education initiatives. Here are just two examples: Jones International University, the first accredited Web-only private university, has 6,000 students enrolled in business programs, one-third of them at the Master's level, with each course taught by adjunct rather than tenured professors. Kaplan Educational Centers, owned by the Washington Post, operates Kaplan College. It offers an online law degree through its Concord University School of Law under the slogan, "The ivory tower built in your kitchen." Kaplan also offers five hundred online courses across nine professions such as criminal justice, legal nurse consulting and paralegal studies. Kaplan.com is the leader in computerized text preparation for some 30 standardized tests and entrance exams at Kaptest.com. In addition, through Kaplan.com, students can access affordable financial aid to meet many educational goals.

Other start-ups, such as the Milken-funded UNext.com, are collaborating with traditional institutions to create cyber-courses aimed at working adults. UNext.com has assembled a roster of Nobel laureates as board members and partnered with academic heavyweights such as Columbia and Stanford. Video-streaming its lectures from star professors across the Web, UNext.com uses software to detect whether students are learning faster through formulas or video presentations and then tailors the coursework to each student. UNext.com owns Cardean University which offers an online MBA comprising course work developed with faculty from Columbia, Stanford, Carnegie Mellon, and other universities. Cardean, with about 3,000 students and some 400 part-time faculty, woos Fortune 1000 companies with courses designed to improve corporate efficiency.

These innovative schools are often decried by academia as "digital diploma mills." Stodgy professors had better look in the mirror: their ivory towers are brick-and-mortar diploma factories. And they are about to be digitized out of existence by private-sector online education.

Forecast of Online Sales to 2010

North American education is estimated to be a $800 billion market, of which K–12 schooling is worth $400 billion a year on a privatized basis. The leading private school manager is Edison Schools, which aims to be managing 400 schools by 2005. However, its ultimate success will depend not on its ability to manage brick-and-mortar schools but to deliver education online as a consumer product.

Globally, some two million students took educational courses at a distance, most of them online, in 2000. That number should double in 2001 and could double annually thereafter. With broadband access, by 2005 and certainly by 2010, online education could rival the entertainment industry in size.

Our forecasts for online education sales, as a percentage of total category sales to 2010:

Online Education Sales as % of Total Sales		
2000	*2005*	*2010*
2%	8%	16%

Which Web Sites Will Win

The leading online initiatives are in higher education. Examples are Apollo Group's University of Phoenix at UoPhx.edu, Jones International University, and UNext.com. While the latter is allied with Columbia and Stanford, today's big name universities are notably absent from the Web in terms of education delivery.

By 2010, we forecast this category's "Top 5" Web sites will be

- ◆ **UoPhx.edu**

- ◆ **UNext.com**

- ◆ **JonesUniversity.edu**

- ◆ **EdisonSchools.com**

- ◆ **Kaplan.com**

11 ENTERTAINMENT AND SPORTS
Fant@stic Experiences

The Internet is going to effect the most profound change on the entertainment industries combined.

— Steven Spielberg, movie director

HOME-BASED SELF-EMPLOYMENT AND SELF-EDUCATION through the Internet will change attitudes about leisure and entertainment. The rigid Monday-to-Friday, 9–5 work schedule will break down; work hours will depend on workloads and there will be more time for leisure.

Tele-Cottage Leisure Time

In the textile era, where the demand for output was huge, most domestic spinners and weavers were relatively free to set their own hours of work. They worked on set jobs and pieces of cloth. Indeed, that's where the idea of piece work originated. Even though public holidays were numerous and long weekends were frequent, many cottage weavers often devoted Sunday, Monday, and sometimes Tuesday to idleness and sport — working long into the night during the rest of the week to allow them to do so. A British government Textile Commission report confirmed that "at any moment, they can throw down the shuttle and convert the rest of the day into a holiday." As a result, British shops were closed on Tuesdays and still practiced "half-day-closing" on Tuesdays until the 1970s — some still follow the practice.

So it will be in the tele-cottage era. Brick-and-mortar shopping will be less frequent as a Webucopia of games, sports, entertainment, information, and related interactive services funnel into the home.

In some ways, it's the 1950s all over again. In 1948, there were only one million televisions in North American homes, and radio was still king of the airwaves. By 1953, the new medium had submerged the old and the world was permanently different. North Americans gathered around neighborhood TV sets to watch Elizabeth II crowned queen. New celebrities, new brands and new fortunes emerged. Families and society changed.

The same is happening with the Internet. Lacking software, the TV is a dumb appliance: you switch it on and off, flip from one channel of fixed content to another, all broadcast at you according to the time-frame and program content decided upon by faceless producers. Aimed at a mass audience, TV content is so general that couch potatoes surf frantically through a myriad of channels to find something — anything! — of personal relevance.

Up until the Internet, all content media except the telephone — books, magazines, newspapers, radio, TV, music, movies and videos — were essentially desocializing. You read, listen, or watch alone, regardless of how many people are around you. The so-called television "hearth" was a nonsensical concept: the only family conversation while watching TV is to argue over which channel to watch.

At first glance, the Internet also is desocializing — we talk of geek zombies glued to their keyboards. But the Web is like the telephone; it extends human reach globally. As media guru Marshall McLuhan observed back in 1962, all media are extensions of our self. Just as the hammer is an extension of our arms — which is why weapons are called "arms" — the telephone is an extension of our ears and mouth. The World Wide Web of interconnected computers is the most far-reaching intelligence framework ever conceived and, as such, envelops all previously disparate media and converges them into a global multimedium. This multimedium extends all of our senses — our entire consciousness — into cyberspace. Conversely, it also funnels a "communicopia" of infotainment and interactive services into our home and into our brain-mind.

The Web literally "amplifies" all it touches, and nowhere is this clearer than in entertainment. For online entertainment seekers, slow modems don't stop them flocking to the compelling interactive nature of the Web. Already, about 62 million North American adults retrieve content in at least four online entertainment categories: music, games, movies, and sports.

Music: e-Rhythmic Downloads

In 1878, Thomas Edison spun a metal cylinder and spoke the words, "Mary had a little lamb," and the contraption recorded and replayed his voice. In 1999, Shawn Fanning wrote the software called Napster that allowed free downloads of music over the Web and sent the music industry into a CD-like head spin.

As asserted earlier, everything that can be digitized will be digitized and downloadable. Napster.com revolutionized the music scene and fans of every taste have made online music a huge success — much to the bewilderment of many in the recording industry. Rightfully scared silly that free downloads would suck the industry dry, it launched a collective effort aimed at creating standards for secure online music using the Secure Digital Music Initiative (SDMI). But progress was so slow that, while companies such as BMG and Universal did try to set up their own online standard, MP3 format became the de facto standard.

MP3 stands for "mpeg layer 3," a process developed by the movie industry to compress movie files that makes songs readily available online. Previously, just one minute of sound needed a huge 10-megabyte file. Using MP3, the same file takes but one megabyte. It still takes several minutes to download the file but, once downloaded, the file takes little disk space and can be played like a CD track.

The music studios have belatedly seen that old media such as CDs — as with cassette tapes and vinyl records before them — are obsolete, spun to bits by the Web. EMI and Sony were the first to start encoding their music libraries for Internet delivery, and others quickly followed suit. Yet they still fret that music downloads will reduce in-store sales. But that's precisely the point — the music industry should be trying to eliminate today's inefficient distribution system in favor of wider audience exposure on the Internet. Brick-and-mortar sales losses will be more than offset by a greater number of fans. Hence, the old way of gaining exposure via free play on the radio is being replaced by free downloads over the Web to build a cyber-surfing fan base.

The whole Napster craze was misinterpreted: it proved, much to the music industry's chagrin, that people really like getting music online. They like the choice, convenience, and flexibility of downloading and listening to single tracks, almost instantly. That they were doing so freely is beside the point; most say they would happily pay a subscription fee for customized music. Hence the industry needs to unbundle the record album and offer customized subscription downloads.

Three of the world's largest record companies — AOL Time Warner, Bertelsmann, and EMI — are backing a new online music subscription service called MusicNet with RealNetworks, through which they will license their music catalogs in partnership with Napster. As well, Sony and Vivendi allied to form PressPlay in a similar venture.

The latest consumer version of Windows software lets users watch TV on their PCs. Windows XP also incorporates a music format called Windows Media Audio that sounds clearer than MP3 files and requires less storage space on your PC. Microsoft also launched a free Web-based MSN Music service in 2001 that lets users hear a stream of songs that resemble a customized radio channel.

A similar fate awaits radio broadcasting. One radio disk jockey recently bemoaned MP3, waxing about how "people who buy music the old-fashioned way from stores still vastly outnumber those who download," and that the Web is "too slow and unreliable," and, anyway, "you can't beat being able to hold a CD in your hands and read the liner notes." What utter balderdash! This doomed platter-spinner is like the village blacksmith scratching his head as the first horseless carriage sputters past, dismissing any thought that such a contraption could ever change his life.

Meanwhile, there already are some two thousand radio stations available on the Web — though one wonders why more than one radio station is necessary in a world where each surfer can custom disk-jockey their own content, including background music. Merely broadcasting a local station on the global Web does little for its audience or commercial reach. After all, the business purpose of conventional media has been to aggregate an audience and sell that audience to advertisers.

PC Swallows TV

As mass advertising evaporates, however, the television industry also is going to change dramatically. Again, as with radio, television's underlying revenue model will be based more on e-commerce than advertising sales within five to ten years.

TV commercials simply are less and less effective because fewer and fewer people are forced to watch them, even if they do select to view TV programming. Once TV becomes truly interactive — that is, streams through the "always-on" Web — then TV companies will have their chance to actually sell things rather than dubiously claim that they help advertisers sell things. Tomorrow's television will get paid for concrete commercial results, sharing the e-commerce revenue stream it generates. In other words, a commercial will become a true commercial.

Consequently, TV content is in for a major shake-up. In contrast to broadcasting, the Internet does not set the available content. It is an infotainment utility where consumers go for what they know they want when they want it, not on some preset take-it-or-leave-it schedule. This will become more obvious as broadband becomes widely available. When broadband reaches critical mass, Web surfers will want to do much more than send e-mail, chat online, or shop. They will insist upon compelling, immersive infotainment.

But they can't get that over a dumb analog TV. The TV has always been a time-wasting device. Its job has been to entertain rather than help you get things done. As I dictate this into my PC, my friends are watching the Super Bowl on their TVs. I'm also watching the game on a two-inch window on my PC screen.

PCs are time-saving "golden looms" that let you get things done and be entertained at the same time. Just as TV took movies out of the movie theaters — their number plunging from 18,500 in 1948 to 8,000 in 1963 — the Web-linked PC is taking TV programs out of the TV. By 2005, more people will interact with PCs than watch TVs and we will — contrary to conventional wisdom — sit down as a nation for a collective "Web Super Bowl" experience.

Streaming Video-on-Demand (VOD)

To broadcast original streaming content online, Time Warner launched its Entertaindom.com Web site at the end of 1999. The site features entertainment news and information, entertainment services such as locations where movies are playing, and programming such as cartoons and feature films. This is just one of several sites for the growing online video entertainment market. Other sites are for news, information, personal finance, and sports, among others.

Now, AOL Time Warner's AOL-TV will take television online. AOL's long-stated mission is "to build a global medium as central to people's lives as the telephone or television . . . and even more valuable." Beyond Time Warner's video content — everything from CNN to *Friends* — AOL will invest heavily in interactive content. For example, a CNNfn user could execute a stock trade when a company is mentioned on the air. Indeed, many day-traders now have CNNfn on in the background while they trade stocks on their PCs. The AOL Time Warner merger will converge this activity onto the desktop. Similarly, *Survivor* addicts will chat online with buddies during the program or will call up a synopsis of the last program that they might have missed.

> As everything gets digitized, video rental stores will go out of business.

The convergence of movies and the Internet will dramatically slash the cost of movie production and distribution — including actor salaries — while increasing audience reach. Already, it is possible to produce a full-length movie on a PC — everything from scripting, set design, sound tracks, special effects, and the characters themselves — all with equal or better quality than today's films, and then deliver the movie to millions of people globally in their homes.

As everything gets digitized, video rental stores will go out of business. You will download whatever movie you are interested in from an online library of every movie ever made. Your WebPCTV will know what each member of the family likes to watch and will alert you to new releases that you will be most interested in. No more driving to the video store to search a limited selection and then having to drive the tape back again next day.

By 2003, there will be about 10 million people subscribing to video on demand (VOD). VOD over the Web will redefine what it means to be entertained and will take at least half the market away from the brick-and-mortar video stores within five years. Yet companies such as Blockbuster are in denial. Its chairman once said unlimited VOD was still "far from ready" and defiantly proclaimed that "we survived pay-per-view and we'll survive video-on-demand." But then the video-store chain tried to team up with the utility Enron to provide VOD services but Enron backed out of the deal because Blockbuster — perhaps predictably — couldn't get movies from Hollywood studios fast enough.

Blockbuster's bravado misses the crux of what's happening: broadband isn't about being able to download; it's the consumer experience, stupid! Online entertainment will tap into the right-brain emotion of consumers who, in turn, will redefine what it means to be entertained and will demand entirely new forms of programming, such as Digital Video Discs (DVDs). DVDs are starting to take off, reaching 3,871 titles in 2000, up from 2,876 titles in 1999, and sales followed suit. Meanwhile, sales of CDs leveled off in 2000 and likely will start to decline as DVD takes over.

In the future, however, we won't go to movie theaters or even watch DVDs on TV. Rather we'll meet friends on the Web and create our own customizable, interactive theater. We'll take on the roles of movie characters and determine the plot outcome. So much for television studios.

Webertainment e-Commerce Networks

Twenty-first-century entertainment will bridge the gap between fun and commerce via communications media. Sony's So-Net is a sign of things to come. On this fast-growing online service, Japanese kids swap information, buy snacks for their electronic PostPet critters, and browse the shopping mall. Sony is bridging the gap between its core electronics business of TVs, stereos and the like, with the content that gets played on those gadgets — music, movies, games, and even financial services — by providing interactive downloadable content.

Aiming to solidify its lead in "digital lifestyles," Sony launched SonyStyle.com in late 2000. The Web site, which ties in with Sony's quarterly *SonyStyle* magazine published for it by AOL Time Warner, features hundreds of Sony consumer electronic products, dealer location information, and exclusive downloadable content from Sony's music, movie, and games businesses. Sony's visionary chairman and CEO, Nobuyuki Idei, talks of a "Sony Dream World" where a vast array of content is available on a variety of devices, all networked together "to provide new forms of entertainment lifestyles for the broadband age." Sony's upcoming VOD service, MovieFly, is designed to pre-empt the "Napsterization" of movies. It will let users choose from titles that never go out of stock, download them to their hard drive, and then view them repeatedly through a PC or via a wireless link to their TV.

The number of people who play online games is expected to increase to about 160 million by 2003, most of them casual gamers who play about half an hour a week. But the number of gamers and the time they play are both increasing, leading to ramped-up revenue streams. Sony already pulls in nearly $4 million a month from subscribers who play just the single game "Everquest" online. For all games, the subscriber revenue base clearly has huge potential.

The latest video games add more realism to character design, movement, dialog, and interaction. They also allow you to create your own adventures. Sony's new PlayStation 2 is much more than a game machine. Coming with a DVD player for viewing full-length movies, and multiple ports for easy Internet access and add-ons such as a hard drive, PlayStation 2 rivals the PC. It can be hooked to a VCR, cable TV, keyboard, mouse and printer, and can be used to send e-mail via So-Net and to edit video recordings. Game titles are almost incidental.

All Sony's core operations are being converged into network businesses. Sony Online Entertainment, for example, combines Sony Online Ventures and Sony Pictures Entertainment. Sony's new online network, The Station, at Station.Sony.com, is geared toward games and game shows, drawing on its extensive library to provide interactive and multi-player versions of *Jeopardy!* and *Wheel of Fortune* — to be followed soon by *The Dating Game*.

In 2002, Sony is launching a high-speed Internet entertainment service called Screenblast that is a combination movie/music studio for home users. It includes editing tools and clips from Sony movies like *Men in Black* and soundtracks from Sony artists. Users can remix the audio, mix-n-match movie scenes, add visual effects, select soundtrack options, and then play back their own creations.

Interactive Gaming

Even gambling is up for grabs. Despite great skepticism — and much spluttering from holier-than-thou politicians who want to prevent it — online gaming is booming. From the Super Bowl, World Cup soccer and PGA golf to casino-type games such as slot machines, blackjack and video poker, gaming is big business on the Web and getting bigger.

According to a study by RiverCityGroup.com, there are more than 700 gaming Web sites operated either by private competitors or government agencies. Some service providers even alert bettors on their cellphones when their favorite horse is running in a specific race so that they can place an instant online wager. While obviously difficult to estimate, some have pegged worldwide online gaming revenue to top $2.5 billion this year and double that in 2002. By 2010, as much as $20 billion could be wagered online.

The consumer base for online gaming is far smaller than that for sports, movies, music or video games. But the market is also undeveloped in that, other than for lotteries, there are few places where consumers can actually play the slots. A trip to Vegas is not cheap. Indeed, the market would become much larger if major brick-and-mortar brands such as Caesar's Palace overcame their narrow-minded fear of cannibalizing their market and went online. The corporate graveyard is full of companies that failed to embrace the new business model. Casinos that go online will outperform those that stick their heads in Nevada's desert sand.

In mid-2001, however, the state of Nevada woke up and approved a law that paves the way to legalize Internet gambling, currently a $2 billion-a-year business that is largely conducted by offshore companies. You can already play blackjack tables at Yahoo and MSN for fun but these pseudo-gambling programs require only a software upgrade to let you play for money. So the stage is set, and the major casinos, though late to the party, are ready. In 2000, Harrah's Entertainment, a major Las Vegas–based casino, took a minority stake in iWin.com (an online gaming venture owned by Vivendi), and the Bellagio casino has a Web site where you can play Keno and poker.

Sports: Fant@sy Future

The TV has taken sports out of the stadium and trivialized it. Watching any team action sport on TV has become much like a video game. Everything is contrived and artificial — from the turf on up — and fantasy sports abound, both online and off.

Sports provide the number one content on the Internet and on TV. And they drive an insatiable fan base that is anxious for new and improved delivery systems. When the Web and TV converge, there will be at least 100 million sports fans online. But "couch potatoes" will become "mouse potatoes," abandoning TV in favor of a Web-full of offerings: instant chat and one-click-away video clips, player stats and profiles, articles — and sports paraphernalia for instant sale and overnight delivery.

Relatedly, Disney's ESPN operates a 42,000-square-foot restaurant in New York's Times Square, where TVs as big as movie screens and celebrity memorabilia entertain people while they eat. ESPN Zone's themed restaurants give diners the experience of state-of-the-art virtual reality and video games, with a year-round variety of sports programming and sports updates.

Sports sites have an advantage over television because they can deliver information much more effectively to the individual fan hungry for scores and related trivia. Online fans no longer wait for evening sportscasts. Instead, they listen to the game while surfing or watch a play-by-play "gamecast" on a small ESPN.com in-screen window. ESPN.com also is launching an online spin-off of Sports Center called MySportsCenter that will deliver an online package of the day's sports highlights customized to each user's interests and favorite teams. ESPN.com has the best sports reporting, feature stories and analysis on the Web, truly living up to its slogan, "the worldwide leader in sports" and drawing a huge audience. The site's "Play at Home" feature lets *Monday Night Football* fans compete with each other by guessing who will carry the ball, how many yards will be gained, and so on. A feature that illustrates game action in a video-game-like format ranks among the site's top 25 pages each day.

> Soon it will be possible to re-create several live sporting events simultaneously on a home PC.

In the near future, it will be possible to remotely recreate or simulate the experience of several live sporting events simultaneously on a home PC. In most sports, the athletes have become merely actors anyway, animated characters twirling on an avidly watched swath of green plastic carpet or polished oak floor. Game tactics are relayed over ear-pieces and the play-by-play is determined by the commercial interests of the advertiser. Time outs are no different from slugging another quarter into an arcade game. Sport has been commoditized by TV into content designed to fill screens. And teams unable to attract media dollars are doomed — News Corp's Fox Sports network surely can't afford to buy them all.

It would be foolhardy to do so in any case, because human professional sports teams are slowly being replaced by Internet-based fantasy teams. Already, some 12 million people globally spend nearly $860 million a year on fantasy leagues. Sport is becoming fantasy entertainment and is as close to being as scripted as "professional" wrestling. What a joke! When things become ridiculous, they inevitably change. And professional sport is heading for a major shake-up. Indeed, as fantasy replaces reality, the fans ultimately will take back virtual ownership of the real-world teams.

People identify as much with individual athletes as with their team or even the sport they play. TV already has eliminated distance, allowing fans to follow teams thousands of miles from home, and the Web merely exaggerates that phenomenon. As well, of course, many fans immediately switch allegiance to a new team whenever their favorite player gets traded — an increasingly frequent occurrence. The Web's interactivity will only enhance the bonds between fans and individual athletes.

Virtual Champions

We are not far away from a virtual 3D online wide world of CD-ROM/Web hybrid sports applications. For example, a baseball CD will contain 3D renderings of all the players — in any team uniform — along with their movements in exactly replicated ball parks, complete with sound effects. PC users thus will be able to experience a fully animated live game, with the CD-ROM being automatically updated online via Web connection to the real ball park. The same process could be applied to any game, including individual sports such as PGA golf tournaments. Can 3D virtual baseball cards be far away? Already, the trading card company Topps offers limited-issue "Initial Player Offering" baseball cards that can be traded on eBay's online auction site. Football, hockey and basketball cards are also in the offing.

Of course, consumers will still spend money on live sports and entertainment, or a blend of the two. In fact, as we head into an increasingly home-centered leisure society, consumers will have more time and disposable income for sports and recreation. But more and more, they will spend that time and money on their own and their kids' participation in sports. The aging population — aided by the unfolding Tiger Woods phenomenon — almost ensures that golf will be the big sport of the next decade. But the next big North American sporting boom will be soccer, with the United States almost certain to re-host — and win! — the World Cup within the next 20 years.

While the major U.S. sport leagues run their own Web sites, don't be surprised to see the major leagues go global, with a few truly professional national touring teams in each sport. The rest of sports will be pure fantasy and speculative gaming. The Internet is made for gaming. If you don't believe that, then just consider how CNBC's trade-by-trade coverage has transformed investing into a spectator sport. Stock investing has become another version of Vegas. Indeed, most so-called "investors" don't invest at all; they merely speculate on a momentary whim or fancy.

Convergence is blurring the distinction between the real and the virtual. For example, information has already blurred advertising into advertorials and infomercials, entertainment into infotainment, and education into infotorials and edutainment. Due to the telecom-driven info-revolution, the media, entertainment, advertising, and education sectors are being converged into a new industry that we can call the "Experience" industry. Simultaneously, the Experience phenomenon impacts every economic sector, especially — as we shall see — the entire retail industry.

Equally important, this convergence reverses all previous processes. As the Internet reaches critical mass, the entire content and entertainment sectors will converge and then diverge in a rapid reversal that drives out those chasing fool's gold and brings us all back down to earth again. Until that happens, probably in about 20 years, this sector will continue to grow dramatically, especially online.

Forecast of Online Sales to 2010

Throughout the 1990s, North American consumer spending on entertainment grew at a compound annual rate of about nine percent, and the average household spends about nine percent of its disposable income in this category.

Today's combined entertainment and sports market — excluding pornography — is estimated at about $570 billion a year. Already, about 62 million North American adults go online for music, games, movies, and sports. These audiences are doubling and, by 2010, will range from 180 million for games to 280 million for music.

Thanks to the MP3 music breakthrough, music is the leading sub-category, with more than half of online consumers already buying it. More than 30 percent of online shoppers buy videos online and this category will explode as VOD and DVDs become commonplace. Music and video sales over the Web topped $1.5 billion in 2000, accounting for about 12 percent of combined sales in those two categories. Those sales are forecast to double to 24 percent of total sales by 2005. By 2010, all music and video will be digitized and downloaded on demand, driving music and video stores out of business.

In sports and gaming, the audience will gradually shift online as the PC slowly swallows up the TV, the casino and the stadium. Professional team sports is being digitized and fantasized to such an extent that the most natural way to enjoy all these products will be to purchase them online.

Our forecasts for online entertainment and sports sales, as a percentage of total category sales to 2010:

Online Entertainment & Sports Sales as % of Total Sales		
2000	*2005*	*2010*
12%	24%	55%

Which Web Sites Will Win

Most of today's online upstarts — music sellers such as CDNow and video e-tailer Reel.com — as well as brick-and-mortar dinosaurs such as Blockbuster Video, will fade from this category. Only the very biggest players will prevail.

By 2010, we forecast this category's "Top 5" Web sites will be

◆ **AOL Time Warner**

◆ **Disney/ESPN**

◆ **Sony.com**

◆ **Amazon.com**

◆ **NewsCorp/Fox**

12 EXPRESSIONS
Cards, Gifts, Toys, Trips ... and Pets

Flowers, like no other form of communication, are a hyperlink to our emotions.

— Jim McCann, president
1-800-Flowers

ANY GIFT SENT OVER THE INTERNET is a unique high-tech/high-touch form of social expression — a personal hyperlink to the recipient's emotions.

As such, many companies in the "social expression" business — greeting cards, flowers, anything to do with gardening, jewelry, and toys — rightfully fear that the Internet will endanger their livelihood. In this section we also look at pets and travel. While these might appear not to fit their category, they are in fact expressive gifts to ourselves and our families.

Electronic Greetings

AmericanGreetings.com is much more than a card shop. You can stock up on a year's worth of cards and personalize each one with a customized greeting and an additional personal message, as well as a photograph and a signature. Members can maintain an online address book that saves your recipients' information for future use. The company will address, stamp, and mail your cards to arrive on time for birthdays and anniversaries so that you never again have to send belated greetings. The Web site also offers a large selection of gifts, chocolates and gift baskets. AmericanGreetings.com acquired its major competitor, eGreetings.com, in early 2001.

The other competitor is BlueMountainArts.com, renowned for

letting people create and send customized cards online, all free of charge. As the use of e-mail expands and people become more comfortable in communicating online, so will the demand for electronic greeting cards. At the end of 2000, there were 320 million e-mail users; this number is expected to grow rapidly during this decade as the Web becomes an everyday habit. In turn, electronic greeting cards will become an extremely popular service. The habit of going to the card store will weaken considerably. Ultimately, greeting cards will become museum curiosities.

Greeting cards will become museum curiosities.

Online Blooms

Long before anybody had heard of the Web, 1-800-Flowers launched its first online service with CompuServe in 1992 and has since built an e-market stronghold. Yet the floral industry comprises more than 40,000 stores, with total annual sales of $8 billion, and shows no sign of waning. Hence, in this category at least, the Web so far is increasing, not diminishing, the potential market for social-expression products.

Nevertheless, the evolution of 1-800-Flowers shows how consumers gradually switch to more convenient channels. The company was first established in the 1980s when few people made purchases by calling an 800 number and giving out their credit card number over the phone. It took time before consumers gradually got used to the idea. After going online with CompuServe, 1-800-Flowers launched its first Web site in 1995 via Netscape, at which time it was the only stand-alone shopping site running on Netscape's server.

The Web site has hundreds of floral arrangements and gift items, all clearly laid out with large images and detailed descriptions. A floral reference section and the *Fresh Thoughts* e-zine provides floral factoids and flower arrangement tips. There's a calendar that highlights flower-giving occasions and a Gift Reminder service that alerts customers five days before a bouquet-sending date. Online ordering is easy and those received before 1:00 P.M. are guaranteed same-day delivery anywhere in the United States and Canada.

Gardening Escapes

Like sending flowers, gardening has become a widespread form of social expression. Whether gardeners are made or born is irrelevant online: nobody needs a "green thumb," as there is a virtual cornucopia of gardening information online. There are arboretums, botanical gardens, wildlife preserves — in fact, dig around online and you'll find everything you need to know about gardening. You can shop for seeds, get advice and information about the joys of gardening, or send seeds to those of your friends who love to plant.

By far the best gardening site, Garden Escape's Garden.com, closed down in 2000. A stylish catalog, e-zine, chat forum, and gift registry all in one, it divided gardening needs into categories such as perennials, roses, bulbs, lilies, and the like, all of which were subdivided into common and botanical varieties and then divided again into more specific groupings. The Web site's photographs were large and detailed and the links to companion plants were a handy and clever e-tailing stroke.

Garden.com gained 1.5 million customers and sold thousands of garden tools, plants, and accessories through its Web site and catalog, but it wasn't profitable. Wal-Mart bought the Web site content. The Web site name and customer list was acquired by the garden-supply retailer W. Atlee Burpee, which wanted the younger customer base that the old-line retailer otherwise couldn't attract. Let's hope they revive and make profitable what was far and away the top site for seed and plant shopping on the entire Web.

Surfing for Gold Trinkets

Contrary to many forecasts, luxury goods are selling very well online. Neiman Marcus has revamped its successful site to include more than a hundred boutiques. Nordstrom has skillfully integrated its catalog and Web operations. Saks Fifth Avenue also has gone online.

The Web also is an excellent place to buy fine jewelry and watches. While jewelry is normally thought of as a gift bought by men for women, more than half of online jewelry shoppers are women buying for themselves. As with jewelry, watches are a perfect online product: thousands of stock-keeping units, high profit margins, and low shipping costs.

In comparison with the Internet, jewelry stores offer a poor selection of merchandise. Yet watches and jewelry are perfect for cross-selling and up-selling customers into emotive big-ticket items and fashion accessories. For example, NeimanMarcus.com carries more than 500 accessories from top-of-the-line designers such as Gucci and Donna Karan. Live customer service is available on the site to help shoppers match clothes and accessories.

In late 1999, Amazon.com added online watch retailer Ashford.com to its basket of online portfolio offerings. Ashford.com sells 10,000 styles of watches, designer jewelry, fragrances, leather accessories, sunglasses and writing instruments, including brand names such as Rolex and Cartier.

Ashford.com added its own upscale Ashford Collection of pens, scarves, and leather goods in 2000. Such private-label efforts yield higher profit margins and better inventory control. As a result, Ashford.com's gross profit margin is 18 percent and climbing away from the typically slim online margin towards the 30 percent range common among luxury Main Street retailers.

Clearly then, luxury items can be sold online, especially when the e-tailer has a solid reputation and guarantees every item as authentic.

e-Toys "R" Online

There are compelling reasons for consumers to abandon brick-and-mortar toy stores: the self-service model of "big box" stores such as Toys 'R' Us offer no sales support and have surprisingly limited choice. Worst of all, structurally they are not designed for kids!

Shopping at home after the kids have gone to bed is a no-brainer. Kid-free shopping, with no tantrums or meltdowns, an infinite toy selection, and better service in a customized e-store, all combine to make toys an appealing category for online shoppers.

There were too many online toy sellers and most of them blew their budgets on wasted advertising. For example, KBKids.com spent $40–$50 million on advertising in 2000 to generate sales of only $30–$40 million. All three major players — e-Toys, Toys 'R' Us and Amazon — riled customers during the 1999 holiday shopping season by underestimating order volumes and failing to deliver on time.

E-Toys kept the top spot for Web site traffic into 2000 but couldn't survive the 2000 holiday season and went bust. Brick-and-mortar retailer Toys 'R' Us chased hard to catch up but was slow to get online. Their Web site was unappealing and difficult to navigate, much like its dilapidated and crowded stores. The gap between specialists and mass merchandisers is a lot wider online than offline and, in the end, Toys 'R' Us joined forces with Amazon in a hybrid brick-n-click venture. This proved formidable, combining the store's merchandising expertise with Amazon's online savvy, shipping capability, and famous customer service.

Amazon.com always had an extensive toy selection, with all major brands as well as unique items from small, hard-to-find companies. Customer service, of course, is the model of online service: prompt e-mail replies on orders, no-questions-asked cancellations, automatically upgraded shipping at no extra charge.

The Web site has high-quality, high-scale images, with different product views and even audio clips of sound-producing toys. You can search for toys either by toy type or by age on any page. Every item lists the toy's size, age range, and "high-touch" descriptions. As with Amazon's book pages, the toy section includes quality rankings from real customers, many of whom now rate this the best toy site.

Pets: "Bow-Wow" Web

Six out of ten North American households have at least one pet, spending $24 billion a year on food and other supplies to take care of them — quite an expression of love and devotion! As such, we will deal with this category here rather than under the grocery shopping category.

The pet sector had way too many competitors, most of which spent their funding on mega advertising splurges. Besides, how many online pet stores does one need? Pets.com, having failed to garner enough buying customers even by selling products below cost, sold its Web address to the Petsmart brick-and-mortar chain. Petopia, which had the highest traffic of any online pet store and a brick-n-click alliance with Petco, simply took too long to bring its initial public offering (IPO) to market and blew its initial $150 million in venture funding on advertising. Petco finished up acquiring the Web site name. These two sites ought to have been the leaders in this category. Somebody will get it right sooner rather than later, because millions of pet owners sure miss the service and anxiously await its return.

Tripping Online, Virtually Anywhere

"Virtual" will never replace "real" in the things that are deeply important to us. But the Internet does give us the choice to be either "virtually there" or "physically there."

Consider watching a summit meeting or global sports event (as opposed to routine domestic events) on television. You may get close-ups or instant replays, but there is no substitute for actually being there to experience the event. So it is with travel. There is no way you can virtually reproduce the personal experience of actually climbing the Great Wall of China, something my family will never tire of.

Still, one of the many pleasures of surfing the Web is seeing places you've never visited — and may never visit — with a mere mouse click. Travel and tourism is a global industry whose products — tickets and itineraries — are easy to deliver digitally to customers. Planning a trip or a vacation is an information-intensive process that is tailor-made for the Internet. Doing an Internet search on the word "travel" yields hundreds of sites, from car rental agencies to airlines and cruise lines.

Travel and vacation planners not only have access to the giant airline reservation systems, but also to all kinds of hotel and local sightseeing information. As a result, it is truly possible to sample a vacation before actually buying it. Travel sites have become popular Internet destinations and several travel companies are selling airline tickets, car rentals, and hotel reservations online.

Not surprisingly, the biggest online travel site is operated by American Airlines, which started its Sabre Group airline travel service years ago. Its new Internet booking site, Travelocity, offers ticketing and travel-related merchandise such as suitcases, electrical adapters, and videos. Web users also can see airplane seating diagrams, read feature articles written by freelance contributors, and join special chat areas.

Travelocity is by far the easiest site to use and the most comprehensive, providing many travel ideas for the potential vacationer via its Destinations and Interests section. A map of the world lists vacation tour packages and local events — sporting events, exhibits, festivals — taking place worldwide. With this feature, undecided travelers can easily find a number of travel options based on their interests. The Web site also offers common phrases in other languages, currency exchange information, help with passports, and maps. It has the look and feel of a glossy travel magazine that also acts as a travel agent — a winning online combination.

With its 1999 merger with Preview Travel, Travelocity became the third-largest e-commerce site — behind only Amazon.com and eBay — and its membership topped 17 million with sales exceeding $1 billion. The company has a five-year contract with America Online to be its exclusive reservations engine for all travel-related services, plus a contract with Yahoo, which also has invested in Travelocity.

The Future of Travel Agents

Such travel sites are squeezing out the traditional travel agent. After all, when was the last time you called your travel agent or travel department and actually reached someone immediately? How many times does your travel agent have to call you back before they reach you, and how long does that take? And have you ever tried reaching a travel agent at 10 o'clock on a Saturday night to change a flight or ask for information about a dream vacation?

Travel agents that survive and succeed will be those who charge for personalized service in planning detailed vacation itineraries for specialist travelers. Examples would be eco-tours, bicycle tours, operatic tours, art and museum tours, wine-tasting tours, genealogical tours, group adoption trips, and so on.

Nevertheless, online travel bookings still only account for about two percent of total travel revenue. The vast bulk of airline reservations are still done through travel agents. Indeed, fewer than 25 percent of travelers with Internet access actually book travel products online; most of them use the Internet to look up travel schedules and then phone their agent to make the actual reservation. Travelers are slow to learn that online booking is much faster than calling a travel agent, slow to wean themselves from the hand-holding that an agent provides.

While travel agents may well be able to tell you whether your hotel has a restaurant or a pool, they are unlikely to have cultural and political information at their fingertips. By contrast, the Internet has it all: pictures of the hotel, seating charts of the plane, details of vaccination shots that you may need before you can enter a country, visa requirements, language tips, and so on. Moreover, in planning a trip on the Internet, you decide how much or how little you actually want to do on vacation; you are not limited to the programs that your travel agent may offer.

e-Ticketing Gets You There

The advent of electronic ticketing also pressures the agents. After all, an airline ticket is not something you need to see or touch before you buy it. You only need to know that you are booked on the flight you want. The e-ticket thus completely eliminates the need to deliver a paper ticket by mail or courier. Instead, the traveler merely shows a photo ID at the airport, gets a boarding pass/receipt with a seat number printed on it, and boards the plane.

Paper tickets were first eliminated by America West airlines in 1996, but e-tickets have been slow to take off. Now, however, the major airlines are setting up e-ticketing/boarding pass machines in the busiest airports. Frequent flyers can simply pass their airline frequent flyer card through an electronic reader on the machine to receive a voucher showing the gate number of their departing flight, its boarding time, and their seat number. Frequent flyer mileage points are automatically credited to their account.

The Web is also being used to keep travelers apprised of flight changes. For example, GetThere.com, formerly Internet Travel Network (ITN), operates the ITN.net Web site and notifies travelers when their flight has been canceled or offers them a new flight itinerary based on stored customer profiles. It also sends an automatic notification to the customer's hotel, alerting the hotel that the incoming guest's travel plans have changed. A similar advisory can be sent to the traveler's home to alert his or her family of a change in plans or a different arrive-home time.

Forecast of Online Sales to 2010

The expressions market is a complex one, containing many apparently disparate but actually related products and services.

One of the earliest online sub-categories, flowers, now are bought by 21 percent of online shoppers and toys and games are bought by 15 percent. Toys are a $25 billion a year business but overall sales are growing by less that two percent a year. Online toy sales, however, are growing fast and are now forecast to reach 25 percent of that category's total sales by 2010. Most other categories are widely forecast to account for 20 to 30 percent of sales by 2005.

Pet food is a huge retail market in North America. If only a small fraction of sales in this category goes online, it will become a sizable one. However, there were too many players in this category and only one or two brick-and-click vendors will prevail.

Travel is bought by more than 30 percent of online shoppers and alone is the largest e-tail category. Larger than books, music and electronics combined, travel racked up online sales of $10 billion in 2000. While this was only a fraction of the $550 billion total U.S. travel spending, online sales are widely forecast to reach $60 billion by 2005, accounting for 11 percent of all travel sales.

However, these forecasts vastly underestimate the surging online popularity of these categories, which we expect to more than double by 2005 and again by 2010. Overall, our forecasts for online expressions sales, as a percentage of total category sales to 2010, are

Online Expressions Sales as % of Total Sales		
2000	*2005*	*2010*
13%	26%	55%

Which Web Sites Will Win

Since merging with Preview Travel, Travelocity is the third-largest e-commerce site among all categories and, thanks to the size of the travel market, is sure to dominate this category, along with Expedia. Web sites in smaller categories such as flowers and gifts may dominate their niches but they never will be big enough to rate in the overall ranking. Wal-Mart will be a major player in all sub-categories of this product group.

By 2010, we forecast this category's "Top 5" Web sites will be

◆ **Travelocity.com**

◆ **Expedia.com**

◆ **Wal-Mart.com**

◆ **Toys 'R' Us (Amazon partner)**

◆ **Amazon.com**

13 FINANCIAL SERVICES
Put Your Bank(er) in Your Pocket

Some day, we'll all trade this way.

— E*Trade advertising slogan

I N 1998, the vice-chairman of Merrill Lynch, John Steffens, denounced the Internet as a "serious threat to Americans' financial lives." Within weeks, the company woke up to reality and did an about-face, posting all its research free of charge on its Web site. In truth, of course, digits have become the planet's common currency and financial services will never be the same.

Future Money: Seashells to Silicon

Throughout history, as I learned from my bank qualifying exams many years ago, money has always changed with the underlying technology. Seashells, pebbles and grains of rice were among the earliest forms of money. The metal age brought coins around 700 BC and, although China invented paper in the ninth century, paper money did not reach the West until the seventeenth century. IOUs, bank drafts and check forms soon followed. The petroleum age naturally brought plastic credit cards.

Thanks to the Internet, however, credit cards, debit cards, preloaded telephone calling cards, and re-loadable smartcards will become as obsolete as all previous forms of money. Whatever is the most current always becomes society's currency. Today, what is most current is the flow of digital information. Now, money is purely digital — information on the move. Electronic blips representing trillions of dollars flow through electronic networks as easily as a coin drops into a parking meter. Money is going digital.

As money gets digitized, the world's major cellphone and software companies are scrambling to produce the next generation of personal digital assistant that, in my 1993 book *The Future Consumer*, I called a "TeleCom Wallet." The TeleCom Wallet will be a combination cellphone and palmtop computer — similar to the Nokia 9000 introduced in 1997 and the later Nokia 9100, except much more advanced and not much larger than a credit card. I now call this appliance a "WebPhone."

Your WebPhone will replace everything you now carry in your wallet or purse. Everything! No more coins, cash, checks, or bulky credit cards — just a wireless, cardless digital multimedia appliance you will use to shop and pay for everything you buy. It will keep track of all your financial affairs and automatically file your tax returns. You will even be able to transfer money from your WebPhone to someone else's as simply as you now give spending money to your kids or hand over a quarter to a panhandler, who in the future may well ask, "Brother, can you spare some digits?"

Digital Wallets and Online Cash

Companies such as IBM and Microsoft have introduced software that generically is called a "digital wallet." IBM's Consumer Wallet lets Web shoppers enter their credit card information once and store it securely in a "wallet" icon on their desktop. This feature eliminates the repetitious need to enter your name, address, and credit card information when filling out online order forms. Microsoft's version also carries universal log-in features so users can sign on once to access multiple Web sites. Soon such software will automatically be contained in computer operating systems such as Windows or Linux and in WebPhones.

There also have been attempts to introduce new forms of purely digital cash for use on the Internet, either by loading the cash onto a smartcard or directly onto the hard drive of the user's PC. So far, these innovations have failed and are likely to be unsuccessful because it is perfectly natural for consumers to use the familiar credit card online. Indeed, the credit card itself is essentially a digital currency medium. PayPal.com, for example, is a peer-to-peer (P2P) payment system for online adults without credit cards or those afraid to send their card number over the Web. It lets users send and receive money from other users and is growing in popularity. But it will never approach the dominant scale of the credit card companies for online settlement; they account for about 98 percent of all online payment transactions — in contrast to some 24 percent of offline consumption expenditures.

Credit cards are becoming smartcards. Smartcards are "smart" because of a computer chip embedded in the plastic card; the chip holds much more information than does the black magnetic stripe on the back of standard cards. Smartcards are very popular in Europe and will increasingly be used worldwide. Consumers in Europe and Japan can now pay for taxi rides, car washes, and other routine purchases through WebPhones that contain a smartcard-like chip. In Finland, for example, point a Nokia WebPhone at a vending machine and a can of Coke tumbles out; the price is added to the phone bill. You can also download cash from your bank account, just as if you were at an automated teller machine (ATM), through the airwaves and into a Nokia phone for later use.

In North America in 1999, American Express launched its Blue smartcard that can be used both in stores and while shopping online. The card stores personal information such as shipping addresses and account data. The cardholder can also enter relevant personal purchasing information into a companion online digital wallet similar to that of IBM and Microsoft. In addition, at a related Blue card Web site, customers can pay bills online, download personal financial information, and use online financial tools to calculate cash flow and retirement planning goals.

In 2002, the Target discount store chain, with nearly a thousand stores and more than 36 million customer accounts, will become the first major U.S. retailer to issue a smartcard. Also a co-branded VISA credit card that replaces the existing Target Guest Card, you can use it either in the store or at home. Target supplies a free card-reading device for home PCs so that consumers can shop online and even download an electronic coupon onto the card.

Webifying the Bank

Against this background, everybody in the money business is really in the business of information about money; they are infomediaries. The clearest example of this is the now-commonplace banking machine. When you visit a banking machine you do not visit a machine, you do not visit a branch, you do not visit a bank; you visit a digital information network and conduct an electronic transaction in real time. Hence, a bank is an information network. And that network is gradually taking over the handling of all previous brick-and-mortar transactions.

Introduced in about 1972, by 1997 North America's ATMs were handling 51 percent of all over-the-counter retail banking transactions. It will not take another 25 years to eliminate the remaining 50 percent of such transactions. Internet banking will do it much faster than banking machines have. Consequently, I safely predict that there will not be a single bank teller left in North America by 2020, probably much before then.

The ATM has been training bank customers to handle their financial affairs electronically. This has not occurred faster due to the age of the banking population and the only recent introduction of more sophisticated online banking. It very often takes at least one generation before technology becomes widely accepted in society.

For example, my dear mother will not use an ATM — it took years before she would leave a message on my telephone answering machine. She is simply uncomfortable with technology. I have used a banking machine ever since 1972 and, consequently, my daughters naturally think the banking machine *is* the bank. It is perfectly normal for them, having grown up with this technology, to think of it as the natural way of doing things. So it will be with the Internet for every type of financial service, not just bank deposits and withdrawals.

> Web pages will become personalized "money dashboards" that constantly update customers' financial affairs.

These tips of the digital money iceberg are a loud wake-up siren for everyone in the financial services industry. Many financial products and services simply do not require a physical point of contact for sales or customer service. Mutual funds, stocks and bonds, insurance, credit cards, bill payment, mortgages, and installment credit are all currently being sold and serviced by mail, telephone, kiosk, PC, cellphone and — very soon — mobile pocket-sized WebPhones. When that occurs, you literally will have your banker in your pocket.

In the future, online financial service providers will deliver Web pages in real time to desktops, laptops and WebPhones. These Web pages will serve as a personalized "money dashboard" that constantly updates a customer's complete financial affairs. Intuit's Quicken service already allows consumers to handle virtually all their financial information online, including credit card, bank account, and brokerage accounts. You can handle your tax payments, buy insurance or a home, and plan your child's college education or your own retirement.

In the future, such services will alert you to bills requiring payment, dividends coming due, and so on, along with a complete balance sheet and earnings statement with projected future cash flows. They will alert you to investment opportunities such as the chance to rewrite a mortgage on better terms. You also will be offered pre-approved mortgage refinancing and other loans, based on the updated strength of your net financial position and projected future prospects. Quicken is rolling out stock portfolio and tax advisory tools that will offer "vignettes" or scenarios of your financial potential based on your current situation and particular financial goals.

Blurring Industry Boundaries

This unfolding revolution in financial services is already blurring the lines between various sectors of the industry, with banks, stockbrokers and insurers all getting into each other's business. The trend will now speed up, thanks both to the Internet itself and to the recent repeal of the Glass-Steagall Act, which prevented the various players from venturing into each other's territory.

As well, some players in this industry are venturing into other aspects of retailing. At American Express, of course, you can not only pay your credit card bill but trade stocks and buy airline tickets. At E*Trade you can not only trade stocks but do your banking and get a discount on perfume. Merrill Lynch — whose vice-chairman, you will recall, in 1998 called the Internet a serious threat to our financial lives — has even run an auction for diamond earrings!

Financial service companies have long wanted to transform themselves into giant money supermarkets. The Internet now makes this strategy much more attainable for those companies that are ready to radically change how they market their services. As things now stand, less than 20 percent of customers are willing to keep all their assets in a single financial institution. And, in the

Web's frictionless environment, consumers can click their money around at will from one company to another.

Thus, while many customers may prefer to consolidate the money side of their Web Lifestyle with one institution, they will still shop around for competing products. As already happened in online brokerage, service charges will be pushed down dramatically and companies will have to compete on something other than price. And that means value added forms of financial consolidation, which won't necessarily come from traditional players.

While generic "banking" of some kind is essential to any modern economy, a traditional bank, stockbroker, or insurance company is not. In addition to many Internet start-up financial services, some non-financial companies are entering the industry. For example, Sony Corp. is re-focusing its core businesses into what it calls network services, shifting emphasis from pure hardware to the delivery of financial services. Sony thus aims to converge entertainment and finance into a new So-Net network service, including banking and insurance. The company also will be launching an e-money service using special card readers and contactless smartcards via So-Net.

Following Sony's lead, Softbank, the Japanese-based Internet investment conglomerate, is about to open an online bank as the centerpiece of an online financial services mall. Softbank's portfolio of more than one hundred Internet-related holdings already includes a stake in the online broker E*Trade as well as InsWeb, the U.S. online insurance Web site.

Meanwhile, traditional banks the world over continue to tiptoe around the edges of the Web. Despite their obvious ability to dominate the new digital financial services industry should they so decide, they are in great danger of being pushed aside. On the other hand, with their millions of customers and established brands, the big banks could come to dominate many aspects of e-commerce.

For example, Chase Manhattan is launching a business-to-business purchasing service where business customers can both buy directly from vendors, such as office supply companies, and sell their own goods over the Internet. Wells Fargo, which had nearly four million online banking customers at the end of 2000, also is testing a service that lets bank customers buy products from an electronic catalog. WellsFargo.com customers, whose number is expanding by about 100,000 a month, already can access mortgages, check account balances, make payment transfers, and trade stocks. The number of U.S. households banking online is expected to triple in the next five years, from 15 million today to about 46 million by the end of 2005.

e-Bulls and e-Bears

The stock market, of course, is an absurd anachronism. In the electronic age, it is a time warp to watch frenzied traders scurrying around the New York exchange, barking into hard-wired phones and scribbling trades on scraps of paper. As with bank tellers, it is safe to predict the elimination of all floor traders, not just by 2020 but by 2010.

Charles Schwab is the vanguard of financial services and remains the best-positioned online brokerage. It has nearly $1 trillion in assets under management in eight million active investor accounts, 40 to 50 percent of which are online.

Since the entry of Schwab into online trading, competition has become fierce, and intensified competition from inside and outside the financial services industry will create a truly electronic stock market like the Nasdaq, driving transaction costs down below one dollar per trade, if not making them entirely free. About 85 percent of Charles Schwab's trades already are done over the Web by some 2.5 million online customers. This compares with only 42 percent of trades by all brokers.

Floor trading will be eliminated by 2010

So it is only a matter of time before the entire industry follows the Schwab model. Already, e-brokerages hold about $5 trillion in assets belonging to 40 million U.S. households, accounting for about one-fifth of total invested assets. Schwab boasts that its employees see themselves as "the custodians of our customers' financial dreams." When was the last time your banker had such a thought?

Schwab's main rival, E*Trade, is expanding rapidly internationally and acquired the online Telebank in mid-1999. In response, Schwab joined with two other e-brokerages, Ameritrade and TD-Waterhouse, to form an online investment bank. The three brokerages combined have five million online customers already. In an attempt to attract more female clients, E*Trade has begun opening brick-and-mortar offices called E*Trade Zones in Super-Target discount stores. It also installed a network of some 10,000 E*Trade ATMs at gas stations, drugstores and supermarkets to give one-stop access to brokerage and bank accounts.

With such rapid growth in e-brokerage, it is not surprising that 42 percent of all trades at the end of 2000 were done online. Investors who trade through the Internet tend to have 20 percent more financial assets than those who use traditional stockbrokers and trade three times as frequently. Again, this is not surprising in that higher-income households were the first to buy computers and the first to go online.

Insurance Won't Risk the Web

Affluent consumers also tend to buy more insurance. However, while forty-two percent of stock trades are placed online, less than two percent of insurance policies are bought that way.

Apart from the rigid conservatism and sleepy culture of the industry, this is mainly because most insurance companies tend to think that their customers are the agents who sell the policies, not the end consumers who actually buy them. The industry is an agent- and renewal-driven business where personal contact between agent and customer is viewed as the best way to explain and sell often-complex policies. In reality, the industry is afraid to offend its agents by axing them. The Internet, of course, places much information right onto a customer's PC screen. Still, reluctant to upset their agents, most insurance companies ignore the Web.

A few insurers are experimenting with referral sites that provide information and quotations while keeping the agent involved for the final sale. One such side is InsWeb.com, partially owned by Softbank as noted above, which has a few dozen insurance companies in its network and is the Web's leading insurance site. The service is now helping about three million insurance shoppers a year, most of whom are looking for automobile, health, term life, homeowners' and renters' insurance coverage.

Some sites function as an insurance agent, allowing consumers to sign up online. For example, customers of Quicken's Insure-Market.com can pay for policies online with their credit card. Quicken's average term life insurance policy sale is more than $400,000 — five times that sold by a traditional agent.

Perhaps the most natural insurance to gravitate online will be commodity-type policies such as home and automobile insurance. Yet, only 22 percent of such sites offer online quotes, and only half of those allow users to buy policies online. Industry leader State Farm has no plans for an Internet sales program.

By contrast, Progressive Corp. lets car owners pay for insurance electronically, with premiums based on mileage. Normally, automobile insurance premiums are based on risk factors such as the driver's age and driving record, marital status, and the age and model of the vehicle. The company sensibly believes these factors are less important than how much the car is used and when and where it is driven. The company thus monitors the miles and routes of drivers via a tracking box affixed to the car, capturing that data via cellphone and satellite. As a result, insurance premiums have dropped by an average of 25 percent.

More complicated policies such as health insurance also might be a natural for the Web. Most health insurance is carried privately in the United States and research shows that the vast majority of U.S. Internet users who have health insurance would prefer to manage their coverage online. This preference reflects a deep frustration with healthcare red tape and bureaucracy in the U.S.A. and represents a big opportunity for insurers and benefits management in general. American International Group (AIG) processes about 500,000 claims by phone, fax, or mail. By putting self-serve claim features on the Web, AIG lets customers enter their own data and view their companies' claims history online. This saves time and money, averts errors, and reduces frustration by giving the customer a claim number instantly.

Insurance agents are in great danger of extinction.

Matters would be greatly simplified for most users if they could go online to check their coverage, file claims and check their status, find a doctor or a hospital when they move house, look up information on other plans, and enroll at the outset. Yet nobody in the industry has taken any significant steps to grasp this opportunity.

One is only left to wonder why insurers are so afraid of the Internet when they are, after all, in the business of covering fear of the unknown. As a result, the entire $300 billion that North Americans spend annually to insure their cars, homes, health, and lives is up for grabs. And the industry's two million insurance agents, who presently skim off an average 20 to 30 percent of premium dollars in commission, are in great danger of extinction.

Virtual Loans: Name-Your-Own Mortgage Rates

Mortgage brokers and lenders face similar challenges. The conventional wisdom is that mortgage brokers are a crucial party to the home purchase and ownership business because mortgages are so complex and the system for approving them is so arcane that customers need an adviser.

These days the quickest and easiest way to finance a home is to get a mortgage over the Internet. There are more than a hundred mortgage-related Web sites. These sites help you decide whether you should rent or buy, just how much home you can really afford, and how tax breaks will play out. Most sites let you configure the impact of a 15 to 30-year loan, at a variety of interest rates, while taking into account factors such as bank fees.

The dominant online lender, E-Loan, has been a mortgage broker and lender on the Web since 1997. It already generates billions in annual mortgage originations and their business model saves consumers as much as 80 percent on loan fees. E-Loan also offers all types of loans, from fixed and adjustable rate mortgages to auto loans and credit cards. It even provides relocation services if you move residence more than one hundred miles away.

After failing to acquire E-Loan in 1998, Intuit bought mortgage lender Rock Financial, thus making Quicken Mortgage competitive with E-Loan and going a step further by giving online pre-approvals and locked-in interest rates. In early 2000, General Electric quietly launched a consumer financial Web site called GE Financial Network at GEFN.com to offer a slew of converged financial services: banking and bill payment; mortgages, equity loans, and credit cards; auto, life, home, or long care insurance; or GE mutual funds and, coming soon, stock brokerage.

"You've Got e-Bills!"

GE Capital, one of the biggest providers of private-brand credit cards for more than 300 retailers — including Exxon, Wal-Mart, JCPenney, Toys 'R' Us, Disney, and Home Depot — now issues credit card bills online. That way, consumers can make their monthly card payments over the Web instead of by a check sent by mail. American Express and VISA already provide similar online services to millions of accounts, and GE Capital's move thus accelerates the trend to online bill payment.

It is estimated that more than 22 billion monthly and other periodic bills are mailed to North American consumers annually. Clearly, this is a major economic inefficiency that presents a huge opportunity for Internet financial service providers. E-billing is perhaps the next "killer application" on the Web and is certain to capture the vast majority of household bills by 2010. While only 200 billers account for 70 percent of the bills, only one percent of consumer bill payments is made online. If these billers "webify" themselves and only five percent of billing is done online by 2005, this will be enough to grow the service from about $50 billion today to $350 billion. Far more likely is that the Web will capture at least 25 percent of e-billings by 2005 for a total of $1.8 trillion.

The total amount of e-billing will grow rapidly as yet more players enter this market. At the end of 1999, AOL's Netscape unit joined with Sun Microsystems and three of the biggest U.S. banks — Chase Manhattan, First Union, and Wells Fargo — in a consortium known as Spectrum to simplify e-bill payment. AOL also made a five-year pact with Quicken to allow AOL's 30 million users to receive, view, track, and pay both electronic and paper-based bills online. In the future, when AOL users log on they may hear two welcoming phrases: "You've Got Mail!" and "You've Got e-Bills!"

Meanwhile, Microsoft's MoneyCentral joined with Citibank and First Data Corp., the dominant financial transaction processor, to form the TransPoint bill payment service. Not to be outdone, Yahoo partnered with the CheckFree electronic billing company to launch Yahoo! Bill Pay on its Web site.

The cost of printing and mailing a bill is between 50 cents and $2.00 in paper, labor, and postage. In addition, of course, the customer has to write a check, on which a service charge is applied, and then affix a postage stamp to the return envelope. Virtually all of these costs will be eliminated when the bill is presented and paid online.

More important, e-billing is a unique service in that the active customer will return to the Web site several times a month just to attend to their bill payments. This creates an excellent opportunity for e-billers to communicate frequently and one-to-one with their customers, perhaps cross-selling additional products or services to them. As e-shopping continues to explode, it is natural that e-bill payment will follow.

Indeed, e-billing may be crucial to creating a critical mass of consumers who use online financial services in general. The more bills people receive and pay electronically, then the more likely they are to bank and conduct other financial transactions online.

Forecast of Online Sales to 2010

In 1995, only two million users went online for any kind of financial service — most of them to balance checkbooks with Intuit's Quicken accounting software. By 1997, 22 million people were managing their money online, with 14 million of those engaged in online investing. At century's end, 30 million were investing online (representing 42 percent of stock trades), another 15 million were banking online, and 10 million were buying insurance. After eliminating overlaps, some 48 million were buying financial services online.

In 1999, about $5 billion in mortgages were originated online. This will skyrocket to $250 billion by 2005, accounting for a third of all new mortgages. In addition, by 2003, most forecasters expect at least 15 percent of credit card applications and 10 percent of personal loans will be applied for and approved online. The next online killer application will be bill payment, with 25 percent of household bills being paid online by 2005 and 70 percent of them paid that way by decade's end.

By 2010, about 92 million North American households will bank online, 58 million of those will trade stocks and mutual funds, and 44 million of them will buy insurance of some kind. The stodgy insurance industry is painfully slow to go online and is ripe for "Amazonization." As this occurs, it will further boost online sales of this overall category. Some $10 billion of automobile insurance alone will be sold online by 2005 and, by 2010, virtually all auto and home insurance will be sold on the Web.

Overall, our forecasts for online financial service sales, as a percentage of total category sales to 2010, are

Online Financial Services Sales as % of Total Sales		
2000	*2005*	*2010*
7%	21%	39%

Which Web Sites Will Win

The convergence of the finance industry in general and the Web's commoditization of financial transactions in particular will squeeze out stock, insurance and mortgage brokers. Of today's top 10 financial Web sites, there is but one traditional bank (Wells Fargo), no full-service stockbroker, and no insurer. While start-ups such as Schwab, E*Trade, and First Virtual Bank revolutionized the industry, they will be unable to compete as the big banks and brokerage houses inevitably lumber online. By 2010, this sector's "Top 5" Web sites will be

- ◆ **Citicorp/Travelers**

- ◆ **Wells Fargo**

- ◆ **Fannie Mae**

- ◆ **Intuit/Quicken**

- ◆ **Morgan Stanley Dean Witter**

14 GROCERIES
No Need to Squeeze the Tomatoes

We clearly see online grocery shopping having explosive growth.

— Chuck Tyson, director of e-Business
Pillsbury

MOST PEOPLE CONSIDER grocery shopping a chore. Out of 22 household tasks, one study found that grocery shopping came in next to last, just ahead of cleaning. Shoppers simply don't enjoy it.

By contrast, 23 percent of online consumers have already bought groceries online. And 94 percent of them say not only do they enjoy it but they are absolutely delighted with the service and are dismayed when their provider has had to shut down or pull out of their market area.

For them, two hours a week of supermarket hell have been transformed into a click-happy ten minutes on the Web. In short, supermarkets are a huge waste of a person's time and tech-savvy grocery shoppers simply don't feel compelled to squeeze the tomatoes. A majority of all households say there is nothing they would not order online from a supermarket. As such, most consumers seem to be waiting for their trusted grocery store to offer online shopping and delivery. They aim to win back their grocery shopping time and spend it with their families.

To understand the future of grocery shopping we first need to look back 50 years to when supermarkets began replacing the corner store, the grocery delivery van and the milkman. The Internet is unwinding those 50 years, once again making the delivery person both economically viable and customer-desirable.

The End of Supermarkets as We Knew Them

As this unwinding occurs, supermarkets will vanish. They will be replaced by superstores that serve those still without Web access, by doorstep delivery vans coming from grocery e-tailers' warehouses, and by local grocery counters that cater to last-minute needs.

In 1998, Microsoft chairman Bill Gates semi-startled a group of top food retailers when he predicted that one-third of food sales would be sold electronically by 2005. Nevertheless, the stodgy grocery industry has done little to heed this challenge and is highly vulnerable, for at least three big reasons:

1. Supermarkets sell replenishment, commodity items, ideally suited to e-tailing. The average price of supermarket products is only $2, the average check-out tab is only $23, and weekly sales per square foot are only $11 — this according to survey data from the Food Marketing Institute (FMI) in 2000, the industry's own trade association. As a result, the net after-tax profit of supermarkets is only one percent. Hence, if they lose five to ten percent of topline sales, they cannot hope to earn a profit. The most popular e-grocery items (so far) are dry goods (65 percent of buyers), health and beauty (53 percent), vitamins (43 percent), cleaning stuff (38 percent), and pet supplies (35 percent). Even frozen foods and meat (33 percent each) and fresh product (27 percent) are popular items. Every sale made online is coming out of the supermarket's slim profit margin. The handwriting is clearly written, on an invisible digital sign hanging over the supermarket check-out line.

2. Supermarkets are digitally challenged. The same FMI survey shows that only 46 percent of supermarkets are even able to scan bar-coded cases of product, only 30 percent use computer scheduling of employee shifts, only 20 percent use electronic data interchange (EDI) to any meaningful extent, only five percent use cross-docking to move shipments faster through distribution centers, and a mere one percent use customer self-check-out systems. In other words, the entire value chain of the supermarket distribution system is way behind the times, causing gross operating inefficiencies. No wonder they can't earn more than one percent on their investment. Supermarkets would earn more money for their shareholders by selling out and putting their capital in a certificate of deposit.

3. Supermarkets are ignorant — and arrogant — about what shoppers want and need. Only 14 percent of supermarkets think that home delivery is important and only 20 percent are in the least bit concerned about online competition. As a result, only one in four supermarkets offer any kind of home shopping or home delivery program. On the other hand, the FMI study shows that 60 percent of supermarket executives think the Internet will indeed impact consumer shopping in the next five years. Yet their inaction implies that the Web won't affect them. What makes them so blind? Other research shows that 72 percent of online grocery shoppers say their service is excellent or very good and about 94 percent say their orders are correct, fresh, undamaged, and on time.

While the U.S. supermarket chains are painfully slow to respond to the evident demand, by contrast the U.K.-based Tesco chain is a roaring online success, grabbing about 80 percent of Britain's online grocery market. Tesco's Web site features include "Express Shopper" (searches for items on your shopping list), "Recipe Collection"(automatically puts ingredients for pre-selected recipes straight into your shopping cart), and "Favorites" (regular items you usually buy). Tesco picks and packs the orders from its existing stores but is planning to build Webvan-like distribution centers once its business grows. So far, it has 500,000 online customers and about $310 million in annual sales, making it not only profitable but the world's largest e-grocer.

While online fulfillment costs can be greater (since in-store shoppers pick and pack for themselves), Tesco finds that online shoppers order more items as well as more profitable ones. As a result, the average online shopping order is at least three percentage points more profitable than the average in-store order. For a business that normally has a slim net profit of less than two percent, that represents a huge gain — a gain that the dinosaurial U.S. chains seem willing to forego.

To be fair, Albertson's has offered an online service in Seattle since 1999, Publix is launching a service in Atlanta, Foodland lets Hawaiian shoppers pick up online orders at a drive-thru, and Safeway has acquired 50 percent of GroceryWorks.com which serves three Texas cities as well as Phoenix and Columbus, Ohio. Dutch chain Royal Ahold, which owns the Stop & Shop convenience chain in the U.S., also acquired the U.S. dot-com start-up

Peapod.com (serving the North Eastern region) and is piloting a Tesco-like program at some of its thousand supermarkets in various parts of the world.

The brick-and-mortar supermarkets that survive will be destinations for those few perishables and ready-to-eat meals that consumers may decline to buy online. The survivors will reinvent themselves as convenience outlets for "meal solutions."

An excellent example is Wegman's supermarket in Syracuse, New York. This mammoth store offers freshly prepared foods either to eat in the store at its Market Cafe restaurant or to take home and reheat. It also offers uncooked dishes that can be finished at home, as well as pizzas, pastas and grilled sandwiches cooked to order in the Cafe's open kitchen that you can take out or eat in. There also is a vast fish department of nearly a hundred varieties, many flown in from around the world, that are cooked to taste at no extra charge. Shoppers also can drop off their dry cleaning, have a facial at the make-up counter, fill prescriptions, pick up videos, drop off film, buy flowers, or eat lunch — and can do so 24 hours a day. The entire place is exactly what supermarkets should have become 20 years ago.

Another important trend affecting this industry is the aging population, implying a drop in the food consumption as calorie needs decrease with age. There also has been a major shift in eating habits, with time-pressured households moving away from traditional meals. Indeed, supermarket sales per square foot have already plunged 46 percent between 1970 and 2000, a trend which obviously will continue until the industry rationalizes its distribution system. Supermarkets face tremendous industry overcapacity and fail to recognize that they no longer exist in an isolated segment. Rather, they must compete for "share of stomach" with all supermarket formats, the entire restaurant industry and, now, online grocery e-tailers.

Online Grocery Doorstep Delivery Services

Everybody agrees that home delivery of non-perishables such as laundry detergent is a no-brainer; its shelf-life is seven years! But convincing consumers that they can buy perishables sight unseen is the major challenge now being tackled by grocery e-tailers. The success of online grocery retailing depends on super-quality products and extra-careful handling. Vegetables and fruit can be stored in chilled warehouses and delivered in climate-controlled trucks — without ever being picked over or dropped as they inevitably are in the supermarket. Grocery e-tailing will not only prove more efficient but will result in higher-quality, fresher produce that hasn't sat on shelves for several days. In short, online grocers will see their service as a medium for delivering satisfaction, not as a shopping service that delivers groceries. And, thus far, they've had mixed success.

Operating from a warehouse in Boston with a fleet of delivery trucks, Streamline.com made grocery deliveries to "Streamline Box" units placed in customers' garages. The unit had three sections: a refrigerator, a freezer, and shelving for dry goods. A Streamline field agent, equipped with a bar-code scanner, first would visit the home and record what the customer already had in the fridge, pantry, and medicine cabinet. The agent then created the customer's initial "personal shopping list" and posted it to the Web site where the customer could edit it and place orders from more than 10,000 grocery items. Customers could also order prepared meals, arrange for dry cleaning, buy flowers, rent videos, get shoes repaired, and ship courier packages. Customers placed orders about once a week and spent around $100 each time. Streamline shut down in 2000 after selling out to PeaPod.

The PeaPod.com online grocery-shopping service began making deliveries in 1990 in Chicago, later expanding to San Francisco and Boston. At first, the company hired "shoppers" to fill online orders by picking groceries from individual supermarket shelves. Then it rolled out a warehouse-based national model where online shoppers can browse whole categories, much as in a supermarket, or jump straight to their customized personal shopping list. Items are broken down by cost per ounce, making it easy to comparison-shop. The Web site also provides nutrition facts for just about everything, including fresh fruit, and shopping lists can be sorted in more than a dozen ways, including by fat or carbohydrate content.

Shoppers can add comments to their orders such as "only ripe tomatoes" or "four green and two ripe bananas" and indicate whether they will accept substitutes. They see a running tally of their bill as they compile their shopping list. Once the order is complete, shoppers select a next-day delivery time and Peapod zaps the order to its nearest warehouse. More than 60 percent of Peapod's customers are two-income families with children and average household earnings of more than $60,000. Peapod retains more than 80 percent of the customers who try the service, company revenue has doubled annually, and it now serves most major U.S. cities. However, struggling financially, it was acquired by the giant Dutch supermarket chain, Ahold, in 2001.

EthnicGrocer.com has carved out a successful niche in hard-to-find ethnic foods, sales of which are growing seven times as fast as traditional supermarket fare. They primarily serve the Asian-Indian, Chinese, and Latin American immigrant consumer segments in North America, as well as gourmet cooks interested in all types of cuisine. It has expanded beyond groceries to include apparel, jewelry, hair oils, music, DVDs, religious ornaments, cookbooks, recipes, pre-paid AT&T phone cards for international calls, and even an e-money transfer service for sending funds "back home."

Webvan Ran Out of Gas

Launched in 1999, Webvan.com began with grocery deliveries in the San Francisco Bay Area where it had 50,000 active customers who spent more than $80 per order. The company began expanding to 26 new markets and was investing $1 billion in a national network of automated distribution centers and a huge fleet of delivery trucks. The company's stock went public in late 1999 to wide acclaim, with the first day's trading giving Webvan a total market value in excess of $8 billion. The company also formed marketing alliances with food manufacturers such as Pillsbury, Quaker Oats, Nestle, General Mills, and Kellogg.

Then everything started to go bad. The company's stock price collapsed along with those of other dot-coms. The company was forced to retrench, operating only in the San Francisco Bay Area where it began. Though still not profitable even there, it was quite successful and customers loved it. Even though it was forced to close down in 2001, Webvan at least proved that there is a demand for online grocery shopping. And, given time, I am sure that somebody else will make it work as a profitable and successful business.

Webvan offered more than 18,000 items and allowed customers to schedule next-day shipments within any 30-minute timeframe of their choosing. High-tech tracking systems monitored orders from the moment they were placed on the Web site. At the distribution center, pickers placed the orders in plastic tote boxes color-coded for refrigerated, frozen, or dry items. Each picker walked no more than 19 feet in any one direction to reach 8,000 bins of goods that were brought to the picker on rotating carousels. The tote then went by conveyor belt to adjacent areas for the rest of the order.

Once the orders were complete, the totes were loaded onto refrigerated trucks and taken to docking stations strategically located around urban markets. There, the totes were moved onto small vans for direct delivery to customers' homes. No local delivery van traveled more than 10 miles in any direction so that the uniformed driver arrived at the customer's doorstep within their pre-selected 30-minute time window. The drivers, known for their helpful courtesy, unpacked the order for the customer. Less than two percent of orders ever arrived late.

Webvan leveraged technology to not only reinvent the grocery business but to boost grocery margins significantly. In so doing, it changed the rules of one of the largest consumer sectors and revamped the grocery value chain into a wider value web. Webvan transformed the main elements of the grocery product — necessity, frequency, and reliability — into a home-centered relationship with consumers. Webvan simplified people's lives by taking the groceries out of the supermarket, putting them virtually onto the shopper's desktop, and then delivering them to the kitchen countertop. Why didn't the supermarkets think of that? Why don't they do so now that Webvan has run out of gas?

Let Your Digital Fridge Do the Ordering

Of far greater significance than Webvan could be the digital fridge permanently connected to the Web's grocery suppliers. Frigidaire's online model comes complete with a bar-code scanner with which consumers can re-order a fresh bottle of ketchup, salad dressing, or any other product. You simply scan the almost-empty container across the touch-screen in the fridge's door panel. This panel picks up the bar code and automatically re-orders a fresh supply.

Automatic replenishment of grocery products will have a profound effect on their distribution and marketing. After all, most families spend much of their quality time in the kitchen or the adjoining family room — which is exactly where e-tailers want to reach them. With an online fridge you can send any order to any e-tailer, scan and purchase goods, pay your bills, and send e-mail.

Alternatively, you might use the CMi Advantage 2000, a converged PC/TV designed with grease-proof, shock-proof, washable components built to withstand kitchen use. Developed by CMi Worldwide of Seattle, the system has a Web browser, cable-ready TV, and video and audio CD. The company also has launched the Advantage.net portal with channels covering family, health, home, lifestyle, cooking, chat, e-mail and, of course, shopping.

In Europe, Electrolux partnered with global cellphone maker Ericsson to develop an online fridge that can be accessed wirelessly. Already on the market, this fridge comes equipped with a camera that allows a cellphone user to view exactly what is or is not inside the fridge. This might be a real boon for those still unfortunate commuters who wonder whether they need to stop for milk on their way home.

Online Beverages: e-Pop to Virtual Wine

Even vending machines are going online. Companies such as Coca-Cola and M&M-Mars have networked vending machines that order their own replenishments. Smart vending machines also allow you to pay for the product by smartcard or cellphone. Coke also is testing a vending machine that automatically changes prices based on either the demand at a specific machine during various hours of the day or prevailing weather. In Japan, some vending machines already adjust their prices based on the outside temperature.

We cannot possibly complete a review of food and beverage retailing without considering wine. After all, Virtual Vineyards went online in 1995 and became an immediate hit with wine buyers. Now called Wine.com, the Web site combines product breadth and value with high-touch convenience, providing credible information and an entertaining education in wines. Users learn as they shop, something they can rarely do at their local liquor store.

A key feature is the tasting chart showing the intensity, sweetness, body, acidity, tannin, oak, and complexity for any label in which you are interested. You can also e-mail a staff of experts with queries. Offerings go beyond wines to provide gourmet foods, preserves, detailed menus, recipes, and even napkins for your dinner party table.

Wine.com merged with Amazon-backed WineShopper.com in 2000, only to lay off two-thirds of its employees and then be acquired by eVineyard in early 2001, its future in doubt.

Despite the setbacks, buying family groceries or gourmet wine online is no more futuristic than ordering a book that way. Indeed, online grocery shopping today is roughly the equivalent of buying books online three years ago — something that only a few early adopters were doing. It clearly has a better future.

Forecast of Online Sales to 2010

The total grocery market was about $500 billion in 2000, with less than 0.5 percent of this sold online by a gaggle of more than 30 online grocery delivery companies of various kinds.

Grocery shopping being one of the most detested household chores, it is inevitable that online grocery shopping will take off rapidly during this decade. Yet most forecasters now expect online grocery sales to account for only 1.5 percent of the market by 2003 and perhaps four percent by 2005. These timid forecasts vastly underestimate the pent-up demand for doorstep grocery delivery, as Tesco is showing in Britain and as Webvan proved in San Francisco.

Our forecasts for online grocery sales, as a percentage of total category sales to 2010:

Online Groceries Sales as % of Total Sales		
2000	*2005*	*2010*
1%	12%	27%

Which Web Sites Will Win

To survive the coming supermarket upheaval, major brick-and-mortar chains such as Kroger and Safeway have no choice but to go online and eliminate many of their stand-alone sales outlets. If they successfully make the transition online, they will dominate this category. If not, they are history. Giving them at least some benefit of the doubt, by 2010, we forecast this category's "Top 5" Web sites will be

- **Safeway.com**

- **Kroger.com**

- **Quixtar.com**

- **Wal-Mart.com**

- **PeaPod.com (Ahold)**

15 HEALTH AND BEAUTY
e-Prescriptions and Online Make-Overs

Our desired result is to make healthcare more efficient, but also to make it better, to help patients and physicians work together. This is the right idea at the right time.
— Jim Clark, chairman
Healtheon/WebMD

HEALTHCARE IS A LUMBERING BUREAUCRACY full of change-resistant doctors; a system so backward that it is actually dangerous to your health!

Fortunately, the Web is rewriting the implicit contract between doctor and patient. In the future, the patient — not the doctor — drives the system. Tomorrow's patients will routinely go online to download their health information, get e-diagnoses from doctors and other caregivers, review their charts, track their treatment plans — and buy health and beauty products.

Health and beauty supplies are a natural e-tailer category since they are information-intensive products, mostly nonperishable, easy and cheap to ship, and they generate lots of repeat purchases. Indeed, healthcare is a larger online business than books and music, and e-pharmacies carry huge selections of everything from aspirin to zantac. And, unlike at the corner drugstore, when you shop online nobody else sees what you buy.

Web-Informed Patients
Not surprisingly, therefore, about 55 percent of North American consumers already search for health information on the Internet — a number that is growing by 30 percent a year — and half of them say they will buy health products online. In 2000, North Americans

spent $220 billion on wellness, from fitness clubs to vitamins. This will reach at least $1 trillion by 2010, and most of that will be sold online. Direct sellers and network marketers such as Quixtar have positioned themselves to become the dominant distributors of wellness and nutritional products that health-conscious and weight-conscious people are using in record numbers.

Most consumers searching for health information online are women because they make most healthcare decisions within a family. More than 60 percent of the health information that users read online is family related, usually for children or aging parents.

In fact, a key factor driving the demand for health information is the aging population. It is well known that older adults use about five times as many drug prescriptions per year as healthy midlife adults. And research shows that Internet users aged 40 and above are at least 50 percent more likely to use the Web for health information than their younger counterparts.

Consumers increasingly show self-reliance in maintaining their physical and mental well-being. Knowledgeable consumers usually make better lifestyle and healthcare decisions and do play a much more active role in their self-care. Anyone with Web access who faces a health crisis can easily find information on procedures, new therapies, and innovative treatments that may not even be covered yet by their health plan. The modern consumer also can conduct a widening array of healthcare transactions online, such as buying prescription drugs, comparing insurance rates, signing up for insurance, and submitting health status updates.

Yet the healthcare industry — as with most other industries — is slow to recognize the Internet's potential business opportunities and threats. In addition, there is strong and irrational Internet resistance from physicians, who control about 80 percent of healthcare resources. Hospitals dedicate only 2.5 percent of their budgets to information technology. In North American healthcare generally, less than a third of physicians use a computer of any sort to access patient information, only 37 percent of doctors use the Internet for anything (mostly e-mail), and 40 percent of critical patient data is missing when doctors need it.

A notable exception is Washington Hospital Center where, for example, digital CAT (computerized axial tomography) scans appear on the neurosurgeon's trauma unit PC faster than the patient is returned from the CAT-scan room. Digital imaging replaces film and allows multiple doctors to view the same image instantly and simultaneously. Digitization converges cumbersome paper medical records and charts into a single electronic patient record. Digital prescriptions and test results cut the number of serious medication errors in half. In non-digital hospitals, it is estimated that physicians waste as much as 60 percent of their day just hunting for data.

HealthSouth is building a prototype medical center of the future — a fully digital hospital where each bed has a Web connection so that doctors and nurses can check and update patient records online. Due to open in late 2003 in Birmingham, Alabama, the hospital will be smaller than usual because less storage space is needed, increasing efficiency and cutting costs by 20 percent or more.

As more and more consumers seek increased control over their own health, the balance of power will continue to shift from doctor to patient. As a result, doctors who fail to provide online access will suffer increased patient turnover in their medical practices. As patients become better informed and more assertive about their care, they will insist upon better service from all their health service providers. Increasingly, this will be done through the Internet, blurring the roles of the various players by giving a distinct advantage to those who build a stronger online presence through superior service and value.

Patient Heal Thyself — Online

Patients — not doctors — are leading the healthcare Webolution by forming their own online self-help communities. Many patients now find more help in cyberspace than in their own doctors' offices. Tech-savvy consumers resist being treated as stereotypical patients with "condition x" and wish to be treated as individuals. Already, about a third of online health users are retrieving doctor-related information. While less than 10 percent of online users are aware of a Web site operated by their own doctor, nearly three-quarters of them say they'd prefer to use one.

Faced with this dilemma, many users go to Web sites such as MediConsult.com where they pay a sizable fee for each online consultation. In response, the American Medical Association (AMA) launched a new company at the end of 1999 called Medem, a name derived from the "medical empowerment" concept. AMA, which together with other groups represents more than 400,000 doctors, has signed up several thousand doctors for a YourMD service on the Medem site. This provides physicians with a customized Web page, secure e-mail connections with patients and colleagues, patient-education materials, and the newest information related to their medical specialties.

In this way, AMA aims to compete not only with MediConsult.com, but also with sites such as WebMD.com and Medscape.com. WebMD.com features online chats with experts, message boards, medical updates, a medical library and drug reference guide, and the ability to customize the site so that you can keep informed on specific illnesses. Medscape.com was set up by doctors for doctors and often suffers from impenetrable medical prose. But the site claims more than 500,000 non-physician visitors and its depth, scope and credibility are unrivaled. Thankfully, however, a companion site at CBS.Medscape.com has been launched for civilians.

Even with these credible sites, the Internet makes it easier than ever to be a hypochondriac. Anxious patients no longer have to trudge to the library to research symptoms in monster directories such as the *Physicians' Desk Reference* or the *Merck Manual*. More than 16,000 health-related Web sites provide an over-abundance of information and misinformation for "cyber-chondriacs." The more they research symptoms, the easier it is to become convinced of their imminent demise.

Fortunately, mental health professionals are also setting up Web sites that let worrywarts test themselves for depression as a first step toward diagnosis and treatment. The National Mental Health Association's site at Depression-Screening.org lets patients answer questions, print out their score, and take it to a therapist. This site is not a diagnostic tool but an online screening device that eases the decision on whether to seek treatment.

At-Home Tele-Medicine

More and more patients are doing their own doctoring as in-home, treat-yourself medical devices proliferate. Asthma patients, for example, can use a pocket-size airway monitor called AirWatch that records breathing. Hooked to a phone line, it sends data to a computer and, within minutes, a report is sent to the doctor for review. Monthly, the doctor and patient both get a report on how the asthma is responding to medication.

Similarly, diabetics can monitor their blood-sugar readings over the Internet. They prick their finger, squeeze a drop of blood onto a glucose meter, connect that to their PC, and zap the reading to their doctor via the DiabetesWell.com site to see if they need to modify their medication.

Some heart pacemaker patients now transmit data over phone lines to their doctors. But heart-device maker Medtronic is setting up a service where, starting in 2002, heart patients with pace-makers, defibrillators and other implanted devices will transmit their up-to-the-minute cardiac data over the Internet to cardiologists. Ultimately the data will be downloaded automatically without the patient having to do anything, even when the patient is asleep. The information could include heart rate, status of the electrical lead connecting the device to the heart, and the status of its battery. The doctor or nurse would be able to reprogram the device by sending directions to the patient's home over the Internet. Or the doctor could arrange changes in the patient's medication regimen and order up a modified prescription.

Even serious wounds can be monitored from a distance. For example, American TeleCare equipment allows a "video visit" evaluation of a patient's condition right in their home. Evaluated visually and verbally, patients are checked out in detail on heart, lung, bowel sounds, and blood pressure. High resolution video allows the clinician to view wounds and dressings, as well as measurements on blood glucose meters, IV pumps, blood oxygen meters, and so on — all in about three minutes. A similar non-video system by HomMed allows the patients to do much of this for themselves, taking just a few keystrokes to download the data, either wirelessly or over the telephone. These remote monitoring devices allow a single nurse to monitor 500 patients from *her* home as opposed to having to visit each one at *their* home.

An online medicine cabinet has been designed that uses face-recognition to identify different household members and their special needs. Sensors on prescription bottles help the cabinet to identify each drug so it can alert patients if they take the wrong bottle — or the right bottle at the wrong time. The cabinet also can monitor vital signs, chart them for the patient, and transmit the data to the doctor's office.

Patients, nurses and doctors routinely interacting with each other online in this way is the real healthcare Webolution. By 2010, tele-medicine will be a routine part of daily life and health maintenance.

e-Charts and Smartcards

Already, healthcare providers are starting to use Internet-linked PC tablets to check patients' lab test results, input vital signs, order medications, and perform other quick transactions. Such electronic pen tablets, with pull-down menus, are replacing charts at the patient's bedside.

In the near future, every patient will carry a smartcard that stores all their medical information — much like a comprehensive medical alert bracelet. The card will store full patient history, current medication, allergies, immunization records, recent hospitalizations or operations, lab results, treatment files, x-rays, HMO and insurance information, blood donor information, chronic illnesses — the list is endless. Indeed, by 2005 or so, your entire medical history, including the sequence of your genome, will be stored on such a card or in your WebPhone.

Thus, upon arriving to pick up a patient, a paramedic will swipe the patient's smartcard through an on-board diagnostic machine that both displays the patient's medical history and downloads it to doctors in the hospital emergency department. The paramedics will video-chat with doctors on call who can see and talk with the patient and the paramedic to administer the most appropriate en route care. Injuries will be x-rayed for instant viewing both in the ambulance and back at the hospital.

Smartcards are also reducing the enormous administrative costs that soak up nearly 30 percent of total annual healthcare budgets in North America. Insurance companies, for example, process nearly five billion claims a year, most of them manually. Paperless systems are starting to reduce this enormous burden. For example, RealMed is giving smartcards to patients and installing software at doctors' offices for a digital network that links patient, practitioner, and insurer. The patient presents the smartcard to the doctor, the system verifies insurance eligibility, and data are automatically sent to the payment center, which then authorizes a transfer of funds. Apart from substantial cost savings, the system slashes the reimbursement time from forty-two days to four minutes.

Health Plans Go Online

Another factor driving online healthcare demand is the shift to managed health plans in the United States and the related transfer of greater responsibility for healthcare to patients themselves.

In the 1990s, many commercial and Blue Cross/Blue Shield health plans began providing Web-based services to their members. Their main incentive was to reduce operating expenses. For example, a routine inquiry handled by a customer service officer costs about $3, while a more complex call can cost $10 or more to resolve. By contrast, an Internet transaction normally costs but a few cents and certainly no more than a dollar.

As a result, health plan Web sites offer benefit plan summaries and eligibility information, claims status updates, physician directories (complete with driving directions), glossaries of medical terms, and answers to FAQs. As well, customers can submit inquiries via e-mail, download printable claim forms, and order replacement ID cards. Blue Shield of California's MyLifePath.com site is just one example of how to leverage the Internet to boost brand equity among existing members and to prospective customers.

WebMD.com brings all healthcare participants — patient, doctor, insurer, medical lab, hospital and pharmacy — into a single Web-based platform that streamlines an entire medical transaction. Doctors can call up patient records and insurance information online, and patients can schedule appointments, see lab results, and renew prescriptions online. The company is the largest electronic processor of medical claims — about two billion annually — over the Internet.

WebMD also partners with HNC Software to link doctors and insurers so they can process workers' compensation and automobile injury claims over the Internet. Most insurers and state workers' compensation funds use HNC's software. WebMD also partners with Medtronic, the world's largest maker of medical devices to provide online healthcare information to consumers.

Still, WebMD failed to recognize that nearly half the doctors work in small practices where the economics of technology is more difficult to establish. But, after acquiring CareInsite and Medical Manager, it formed an alliance with AOL to provide health content via co-branded Web sites where consumers can communicate with their doctors and health plan providers. WebMD's revenue more than doubled in 2000 to $185 million and the venture should be profitable in 2001.

e-Pharmacies: Eliminating Illegible Rx Slips

Chicken-scratch drug prescriptions — more than three billion annually — are also being digitized. The Allscript e-prescription pad lets doctors submit a patient's drug order immediately through a pocket device, either to a local brick-and-mortar pharmacy or an online prescription delivery company.

Of course, consumers have long bought medicines via the mail, and online pharmacies operate in a very similar fashion to their mail service counterparts. They offer the same advantages: convenience, in the form of no waiting at prescription counters plus home delivery; and the privacy of at-home ordering. Yet the almost simultaneous launch of PlanetRx, Drugstore.com (now part of Amazon.com), Soma.com (now part of CVS) and other online pharmacies produced little reaction across the pharmacy industry.

Visitors to PlanetRx find a wide array of health-related products and valuable information. Drugstore.com's clean Web site has well-organized tabs that make it easy to find products, and its "Solutions" tab is especially helpful and informative. The best e-pharmacy set up by a brick-and-mortar drug store is CVS.com (formerly Soma.com). It has the true look and feel of a real-world pharmacy, including a virtual "Pharmacy Counter."

Walgreen.com, the Web site of the largest brick-and-mortar drugstore chain, provides patients across the United States with same-day delivery or pick-up at a local Walgreen store. Prescription insurance programs are accepted online and patients can access their personal prescription history. The site also provides details on potential drug interactions, health and wellness information from the Mayo Clinic, and prescription-order status checks. You get e-mail reminders for new and refill prescriptions and, if you wish, reminders of doctor's appointments. You can also e-mail questions to the "Ask Your Pharmacist" section.

Walgreen's is not afraid of cannibalizing its brick-and-mortar sales. On the contrary, it sees a growing market and plans to expand its 2,800-store chain to 6,000 stores by 2010, many of them with drive-through pharmacy windows.

Finally, if all else fails . . . yes, you can even plan your funeral on the Web. In 1999, almost 50,000 coffins were sold over the

Internet out of 1.9 million total casket sales in the United States. Funeral service firms, of course, have long been accused of gouging grief-stricken relatives. Now, however, tech-savvy family members can save 50 percent or more on the right casket.

Virtual Fragrances Waft Online

The cosmetics industry also is getting an online makeover. Online drugstores quite naturally are adding beauty sections to their product lineup in an attempt to capture some of the $12.4 billion that North Americans spent on cosmetics in 2000.

Many in the industry debate whether women will swap the personal attention they get at the cosmetics counter for the click of a mouse. Again, as indeed in all Internet-threatened sectors, claims that "you can't smell anything over the Internet" or that "colors don't look so good on a screen" don't stand scrutiny. True, the cosmetics industry has traditionally relied heavily on the "touchy-feely" aspects of its products, free samples are liberally distributed at cosmetics counters and customers often try the product to get a feel for the colors and textures of each brand. About 15 percent of buyers receive their first contact with a fragrance from the free samples, through friends, or from magazine scent strips.

But industry diehards fail to admit that 70 percent of perfume sales are repeat business: once the customer knows what she likes, she simply buys refills. Generally speaking, cosmetics shoppers buy brand names that they have come to like, and most consumers know exactly what the products are. Moreover, particularly for commodity items such as lipstick and nail polish, most people find one brand and keep on using it. For such products, the Internet is a perfectly natural and ideal sales channel.

Several other factors also contribute to the online beauty boom. Price is one major factor because cosmetics tend to be dominated by big manufacturers such as Elizabeth Arden and Estée Lauder who attempt to limit supplies to sustain higher prices. However, the artificially high price of major cosmetic brands also means that lesser-known brands can easily undersell them. This strategy also plays into the hands of e-tailers who then don't need to discount their product in the same way that "webonomic" forces push e-tailers of many other products to do. In addition, of course, cosmetics weigh but a few ounces and therefore can be shipped at minimal cost.

Mainly however, the online beauty boom will be driven by women — particularly young women — who are flocking to the Internet and now outnumber men both as surfers and online shoppers. Cosmetics sites particularly appeal to a younger, tech-savvy consumer who is pressed for time. She is more likely to shop if she doesn't have to leave her home or office, particularly when she is merely replacing products that otherwise would be a hassle to buy.

As for the need to sniff the product, future technology will waft fragrances out of our computers. Just as today's PC monitors display millions of vibrant color combinations by mixing the three primary colors of red, yellow and blue, future PCs will generate billions of odors by blending different portions of "fragrance primaries" that have been digitized. A company called DigiScents already has a prototype of such a system, with smell samples for many varieties of chocolate, roses, and even the famed "new car" aroma. This technology can define a typical aroma with a mere two kilobytes of data. Future consumers thus will be able to sample the subtle fragrance of flowers and the waft of good perfumes.

Crude fragrance-generating equipment already is used in high-tech entertainment systems at tradeshows, museums, and various family entertainment centers across North America. Made by Digital Tech Frontier, these "virtual scentstations" simulate at least 50 odors, including freshly cut pine trees, peppermint, and cherry Life Saver candies. It is only a matter of time before this technology comes to the Internet. As pleasant, authentic fragrances get digitized and go online, so will aromatherapy and cosmetics sales of all kinds.

Create-It-Yourself Cosmetics

Procter and Gamble (P&G), the world's oldest and largest packaged goods manufacturer and a major player in the fragrance market, has been very slow to go online but clearly smells online profits. A licensee of fashion giant Hugo Boss, P&G is selling Boss men's cologne exclusively via the Internet on the Jasmin.com Web site, bypassing department and cosmetics stores entirely.

P&G also markets create-it-yourself cosmetics and beauty products over its own experimental Reflect.com site. In categories such as cosmetics, skincare and hair care, Reflect.com customers can choose everything from the package to the scent and color of the product, selecting from 50,000 possible packaging and product combinations. In other words, the product lines don't even exist until each customer goes online and customizes them for herself.

Reflect.com also personalizes beauty by providing a service, not just a product. For example, when a woman buys a lipstick, Reflect.com sends her a range of samples in other colors along with her order. If she buys a foundation that she has blended to match her skin type and tone, Reflect.com also sends free samples that are slightly lighter and slightly darker than the one she ordered.

North America's leading mascara manufacturer, Maybelline, was slow to move to the Web. And while its site includes an interactive beauty adviser, a newsletter, and FAQs on numerous beauty concerns, Maybelline.com does not have an electronic shopping capability. The short-sighted parent company, L'Oreal, is apparently reluctant to cannibalize its physical store sales.

By contrast, French cosmetics giant Sephora's online store has 14,000 different kinds of lipstick, eyeliner, blush and perfume — dwarfing any other selection anywhere. Sephora is a division of LVMH Moet Hennessy Louis Vuitton, which racked up more than $250 million in offline sales in 1999. Company chairman Bernard Arnault is a great believer in e-commerce, with personal investments in ventures such as the failed Webvan grocery and the PlanetRx.com pharmaceutical Web site. Sephora.com, with close ties to Guerlain, Shiseido and Christian Dior, is expected to be a strong competitor in this booming product category.

Avon was late to the Web, setting up a site in 1997, and did not pursue an aggressive online strategy. For decades, direct sellers have relied exclusively on the enthusiasm of door-to-door sales reps. But the Web can reach millions of buyers simultaneously. Avon's direct sellers account for 98 percent of company sales. The Web will inevitably wipe out a large portion of Avon's 465,000 U.S. sales reps and will change the role of those who remain with Avon as it makes the transition to online sales.

Avon finally woke up to the Web's potential in late 2000 and is spending $60 million to change how the company does business. Hoping to attract a more tech-savvy group of e-Reps, update Avon's dowdy image, and revive stagnant growth, Avon aims to fight off competition in the cosmetics segment. Today, most reps fill out an antiquated 40-page order form (yes, 40 pages!) in pencil and send them in by mail or fax. The new Web initiative, called MyAvon.com lets e-Reps create a personal Web page that they can use to run their business. The company ships the orders directly to the customers. As well, it is putting boutiques in Sears and JC Penney stores, plus kiosks in shopping malls to drive additional sales.

Avon also is trying to broaden its appeal to become "the source for anything and everything a woman wants to buy," either online, through an e-Rep, or in a store. The company is adding nutritional supplements and vitamins made by Roche to its product line and plans to offer financial services and legal advice targeted toward women.

To ease the shift, Avon has arranged to get discounted deals on PCs and Web access for the reps. Still, some 60 percent of Avon's reps don't have Web access and it clearly will take time for them to get up to Web speed. Once that happens, however, the rep will be able to eliminate most of the admin work that now consumes about 25 percent of their time. Moreover, they will be able to become beauty consultants rather than order takers, allowing them to boost their sales.

Forecast of Online Sales to 2010

The overall healthcare market was about $190 billion in 2000. In addition, another $75 billion was spent on neutraceuticals and vitamins, and health and beauty aids of various kinds.

While online sales were only two percent of the market in 2000, the rapid expansion of upstarts such as WebMD, combined with the aggressive movement online of drugstore chains Walgreen and CVS, will spur sales over the Web. As well, of course, an aging society of health-conscious consumers will drive rapid online sales growth during this decade, particularly in prescription drugs and vitamin supplements. Older people use at least five times as many prescriptions as the average healthy adult, and prescription drug sales will expand dramatically.

Some forecasts call for combined health and beauty sales to top $14 billion by 2005, accounting for five percent of sales. This vastly underestimates the online potential of this combined category by at least half.

Our forecasts for online health and beauty sales, as a percentage of total category sales to 2010:

Online Health and Beauty Sales as % of Total Sales		
2000	*2005*	*2010*
2%	12%	30%

Which Web Sites Will Win

This category should belong to the two major brick-and-mortar chains, Walgreen and CVS. But both have been painfully slow to go online. Indeed, Walgreen plans to rapidly expand its brick-and-mortar presence in the face of a tech-savvy consumer base that wants to buy things online. Why should consumers trudge to the drugstore for a prescription when they can get it delivered within the hour by an online service? With its purchase of Soma.com, CVS has moved aggressively online and could easily overtake Walgreen. Meanwhile, WebMD continues to expand rapidly, Amazon has moved into the category through Drugstore.com, and Quixtar has come online with its vast distribution system for vitamins, cosmetics, and other items in this category. Consequently, Walgreen may turn out to be the biggest casualty.

All considered, by 2010, we forecast this category's "Top 5" Web sites will be

◆ **WebMD.com**

◆ **CVS.com**

◆ **Quixtar.com**

◆ **Walgreen.com**

◆ **Drugstore.com (Amazon)**

16 HOMES AND HOME IMPROVEMENT
Digital Living in Web Style

It's a good thing!

— Martha Stewart

A HOME IS THE MOST INFORMATION-INTENSIVE, complex, important, and expensive purchase any family makes. Is it possible to sell homes online?

e-Listings Are Everything

In residential real estate, "listings" of homes for sale are everything. And thanks to the ease of putting listings online, the conventional multiple listing service (MLS) will not survive. Hence, traditional real estate agents will lose their monopoly on listings, and agents could become obsolete. As the general trend of buyers taking charge of their own transactions online spreads to home buying, traffic on home search and mortgage loan sites already shows that buyers enjoy the online home-buying experience too much to give it up.

In 2000, nearly 40 percent of home buyers — some eight million people — did use the Web as an information source to help them find houses. This percentage would undoubtedly be higher if the best sites had better search tools, less skimpy listings information, and plenty of good visuals.

As a result, online real estate firms are scrambling to build the most comprehensive site with the biggest brand and the most extensive distribution network. In 1996, the National Association of Realtors (NAR) granted access to all of its member listings on its own Web site, Realtor.com — some 1.3 million listings, representing 97 percent of all U.S. homes for sale.

Microsoft's HomeAdvisor site is designed around the entire home purchase event, from the beginning transaction through helping the buyer find a neighborhood, an ideal home there, and the financing to buy it. The site has fantastic local geographic, school and crime data, features that are especially useful for those relocating to unfamiliar places. However, despite it being a Microsoft site, HomeAdvisor has no photographs on half of its listings, virtual tours are non-existent, and homes listings give scant information. But it now does "automated appraisals" online, estimating a home's value without having to send out mortgage appraisers to the home.

Virtual Walk-Through Saves Time

Although few people will ever buy a home unseen, you can save a lot of time, not to mention wear and tear on shoe leather and tires, by first searching electronically. On the Internet, home buyers can search for available homes by price, location, number of bedrooms, and so on, and within minutes a short list of suitable houses becomes available. Without the Internet, home buyers have no choice but to drive around endlessly with their broker exploring neighborhoods and barging through innumerable homes. On average, such home buyers spend 16 weeks visiting 28 homes before reaching a final decision. The average online home researcher visits only seven homes. Hence, there really is no comparison between the old and new ways of home buying. The purchase time is slashed from months to a few hours. So, to move house, use your mouse.

The time saving doesn't end there. Buyers also then can do a virtual walk-through of homes to shorten the "must visit" list even further. New home builders treat potential buyers to a virtual "fly over" of what the finished development will look like. Virtual tours also allow home sellers to expose their properties to a wider audience without the hassle of real home visits. For example, Bamboo.com offers 360-degree virtual tours of homes through AOL, Yahoo, MSN, and other Internet channels. Consequently, Sunday afternoon "open houses" will become a thing of the past.

Facing these trends, real estate agents must re-position themselves as transaction managers. Instead of spending half their time finding houses for buyers, they need to initiate the transaction with a contract, manage it online in a secure way, and assure that all the pieces fit for a seamless online closing. Buying a home is a much more complex transaction than simply closing and financing the deal. Customers view home buying, finance, and ongoing home maintenance as logically related. Yet they are forced to deal separately with real estate agents, banks, mortgage brokers, trades people, contractors, furniture suppliers, decorators — the list goes on.

Smart real estate agents will orchestrate the entire "value web" of the deal so that the various pieces fall together — allowing the client to follow progress in real time. There's a huge opportunity for agents to take the hassle out of moving house. They should expand their service to contact utility companies, clubs, banks, and so on, to change your address details. Realtor sites should include accurate floor plans, clear street maps, area details, transport routes, schools, sample home prices — even accept online offers with credit-card down payments for homes.

Realtors also will have to serve specialized market niches where they can add real value to the transaction — examples are relocating homeowners, seniors, trade-up buyers, and first-time buyers. Realtors cannot merely adapt their existing real-estate model to the Web — which is what most of them are doing.

You also can buy and sell a home online by auction. Homebid.com, the first online real estate auction house, shatters existing property marketing models. In mid-1999, Homebid.com sold a block of 30 homes in the Phoenix area for an average price of $336,000. Earlier in the year, it auctioned off 136 foreclosed homes in Connecticut. Homebid.com now lists individual homes on which buyers can bid and close a transaction without a real estate agent in the middle. In late 1999, luxury homebuilder Shea Homes conducted an experiment to sell one of its newly completed houses online. They sold it within six days for more than its retainer price.

Atlanta-based Beazer Homes lets buyers check the progress of their new home's construction online, with progress photographs, through a password-protected personalized Web page. Home-Builder.com has about 150,000 new homes listed from about 12,000 builders. But five of America's largest new homes builders — Centex, Lennar, Pulte, D.R. Horton, and Kaufman & Broad, which collectively build more than 100,000 homes a year — have enhanced their own Web sites to handle transactions with home buyers, suppliers, and subcontractors and started an online exchange called BuilderHomesite where builders can list their homes. The site offers listings, serial numbers and repair contracts for installed appliances, home security and pest control services, as well as furniture and other home products.

Moving the Furniture Around Online

Furniture hunting in the brick-and-mortar world is tedious, confusing, and time-consuming — not to mention being hassled by tobacco-smelling salesmen in plaid pants. But can bulky, big-ticket, large-consideration, "touchy-feely" items like furniture and appliances be sold online?

The $190 billion a year North American retail furniture industry has shown how *not* to do business on the Web and less than one percent of furniture was bought online in 2000. The industry is fragmented and difficult to manage, yet the basic idea of selling furniture online is valid. Furniture shopping is time-consuming, the selection is confusing, and the tobacco-stinking, plaid-suited salesmen are dreadful to deal with.

A growing number of customers would much rather buy furnishings online. It sure beats spending all weekend trudging your kids around a multitude of football-field-sized showrooms for their home decorating needs. All of it can be done with the click of a mouse, selecting from thousands of styles.

Behind this surge of Web shopping for furniture and appliances are changing lifestyles, work-at-home offices, the concept of "cocooning," and the trend towards extended families where seniors move in with their married children and grandkids. All this means that our homes must serve a greater variety of functions: they must not only be attractive new living arrangements but spaces where we can work, play, learn, and think. To these busy households, Internet shopping is the only way to go.

Again, however, as in other sectors, most furniture manufacturers are afraid to alienate retailers by marketing directly to the public. If they have a Web site at all, they merely tease shoppers with a few online offerings only to direct them to a retailer. As a result, most consumers can only comparison shop online and are still being forced to trek to a local store to buy.

That's the case at Sears, at least for major appliances. As noted earlier, Sears.com has by far the biggest online presence in the home appliance market, with more than 2,000 brand name appliances plus hundreds of smaller items such as vacuums and countertop gadgets. Already, some 20 percent of appliance purchases in Sears stores are influenced by research done online and Sears is positioned to dominate the home appliance market on the Web. The site's Tool Territory section also has more than 3,500 of Sears' own Craftsman handtools, plus 6,500 other brands of various kinds. In addition, Sears has extended its relationship with TV's home improvement expert Bob Vila, going online with the BobVila.com home improvement joint venture.

By far the best online furniture retailer was Furniture.com, featuring 150 manufacturers and more than 50,000 items on its site. The site also had a room planner so you could move furniture around a virtual space to see how you might reconfigure your own home. It had detailed descriptions of each piece's construction, fabric type, and warranties. Fabric swatches — samples of which they mailed out to you — could be enlarged to study their pattern, color, and cloth structure or softness.

However, consumer demand was so strong that Furniture.com and its manufacturers both had delivery problems early on because they didn't expect it. The company promised delivery dates that manufacturers couldn't meet, and it couldn't cope with the resultant volume of customer complaints about delivery, never mind costly and unwieldy product returns. It also spent excessively on marketing and advertising, blowing three times its 1999 sales on unnecessary advertising and, even though sales in 2000 were running one hundred percent above those of a year earlier, the company closed down.

Decorating with Web Style

Homepoint.com operates an integrated network of home furnishing and decorating supersites that form the largest virtual furniture and home decorating showroom on the Web. Originally carrying only furniture, the site expanded in 1999 to include accessories, lighting, and wall art. It carries a huge selection of brand-name furniture such as bedroom sets, sofas, desks, and entertainment centers in various styles and price ranges.

Homepoint exploits the Web's unique ability to enhance the furnishing shopping experience such as virtually trying out various combinations of pieces, layouts, accessories, and decorating advice. Online experts help you decorate your home, answering questions and giving advice on home decorating.

Of course, the maven of household advice is Martha Stewart, and MarthaStewart.com tells you all you need to know about cooking, entertaining, and gardening. Her decorating craft kits would beautify any home. You can schedule Q&A sessions either with Martha herself, with editors of *Martha Stewart Living,* or special guests. All in all, "it's a good thing!"

Another site, DecorateWithStyle.com, offers an even wider range of wallpaper, blinds, and inexpensive artwork, with over a thousand wallpaper choices, including many brand names. The site also makes it easy to calculate how many rolls of paper you require for a particular room. Often lauded for its nationwide referral service for the building trades, Improvenet.com has a huge photo gallery of designer case studies and an Idea File from which you can clip, store, and customize your own ideas.

Home Improvement Goes Online

While the home handyman can buy all his tools from Sears.com, it isn't easy to find a box of nails online because the shipping costs are higher than the price of the product. Cans of paint face the same weighty challenge and paint samples are tough to match online. Similarly, lumber, shingles, gutters, and ladders have yet to find much presence on the Internet.

Home Depot, like big box retailers in other categories, has been slow to go online but its presence will be strongly evident by the time you read this. Having taken the lumber and hardware industry by storm, Home Depot can be expected to be a big winner in cyberspace. The company is an expert at localized marketing and distribution, moving 85 percent of its merchandise directly from manufacturers to the storefront. No products languish in warehouses; rather each store is treated as a distribution center. While it might be more efficient for the company to centralize all its merchandise at headquarters, the company wouldn't be as responsive to local conditions, such as a heavy snowfall in Denver or a new construction boom in Seattle.

This distribution model is ideally suited to reach local consumers via the Internet. Today, store associates walk the aisles to spot goods that need replenishment, entering re-orders into mobile devices that connect instantly to manufacturers. The same system can be extended online. As well, short-term product demand is forecast locally, with more than a year's worth of data held at store level so the manager can adjust for local demand based on buying patterns. When Home Depot goes online in mid-2000, there will be no national price. Rather you will enter your ZIP code and get the inventory and pricing of your nearest store. As well, you will be able to order for pickup or delivery to your home.

The company's Web site, HomeDepot.com, already offers customers project tips and provides them with personal Web pages and a personal project file. In this way, customized information can be sent by e-mail on new products or upcoming in-store project demonstrations. Already, the site's Home Minders feature has some 500,000 subscribers that use the service to receive e-mail reminders about seasonal gardening activities and home improvement tips based on the age of their particular home. Home Depot also offers instructions for more than a hundred project types and provides estimates on the amount of time, materials, and money that they entail.

Computers Direct, Software Downloaded

Home offices are in vogue; computers and related products remain the most-bought product category online, and office products are in demand among Webpreneurs and telecommuters. Yet consumer electronics retailers are ripe for "Dellization."

Dell is the poster boy for direct selling. Now the leading seller of PCs worldwide, since its founding every Dell PC has been sold either online or over the phone. Customers rave about their ability to customize their order online at Dell.com where they can configure, purchase, confirm, arrange next-day shipping, and track their orders. Dell's average customer spends $2,535 per year with Dell.

In addition to Dell, nearly 30 e-tailers offer computer hardware and/or software, with Gateway.com, Buy.com, BestBuy.com, and CompUSA.com being Dell's main contenders. CompUSA.com offers a massive product selection on a really fast-loading, slickly laid-out site that's a breeze to explore. There also is a great section for Web-Gen kids to browse.

Software retailer Egghead closed all its brick-and-mortar stores in 1999 and shifted its entire attention to its Web site, selling about $200 million of software a year online. While that move also may not succeed, this is a harbinger of what's to come for traditional retailers. Certainly, for low-margin products that are easy to buy online, this is the way to go.

Consumer Electronics: Configure Your Gizmo

Likewise, consumer electronics retailers add little value to their products. There is a bewildering array of complex products that are barely differentiated from each other, either in terms of style or features. And in-store service tends to be minimal or non-existent. By comparison, online shopping agents can scurry up product comparisons in seconds, undermining the product confusion deliberately engineered by copy-cat manufacturers with their multiple product numbers.

The major e-tailers are CircuitCity.com, BestBuy.com and CompUSA. These three alone control about 35 percent of the $80 billion consumer electronics market through about a thousand stores — many of which are vulnerable to closure as manufacturers start selling direct to consumers. Sony has begun selling direct to Japanese consumers, eliminating the retailer entirely, instead allowing customers to configure their own PCs, cameras and other gadgets at its Style.com Web site. The company aims to sell 20 percent of its consumer products online within three years and undoubtedly will start doing so in North America also.

Home Office Supplies to Go

In the office supply business, OfficeDepot.com is the place to go. The office supply company integrates e-business technology across all channels, thus increasing customer service while reducing transaction costs.

A case study in how to avoid being "Amazoned," Office Depot is the brick-and-mortar leader in office supplies and equipment, and was one of the first merchandisers to go online. Its Web sites attract business and retail customers alike, letting them place orders for next-day delivery. It has customized Web pages for about 40,000 corporate clients and the Web site already accounts for more than 20 percent of Office Depot's sales to companies.

Customers get real-time order status updates, regardless of whether they were made by phone, fax or online. Users who make frequent purchases can create lists of products they are most likely to buy. These lists appear whenever the user goes to the site.

Office Depot booked $850 million in online sales in 2000, double that of its former rival Staples (which it now owns), and up from $350 million in 1999. Profitable from the get-go, sales for 2001 are expected to double again to $1.7 billion, representing 20 percent of the company's overall sales. More than 40 percent of Office Depot's customers already do some ordering online. About 14,000 items are offered online, twice as many as in stores, and customers can check in-store inventory and either have their order delivered or made ready for drive-by pick-up. Now the company is expanding to offer high-value online services such as tax preparation and bookkeeping for small business.

Forecast of Online Sales to 2010

Excluding home sales, the overall home improvement market — including sales of furniture, appliances, PCs, software, and consumer electronics — was about $724 billion in 2000.

Software is one of today's biggest online shopping categories, with about 64 percent of online shoppers buying it via Web download. By 2010, all software will be downloaded — or rented on a pay-per-use basis — via the "always-on" Web. Online software use will be as cheap as a phone call and we'll never need upgrades; they will occur automatically without our even knowing about it.

As this unfolds, the software business likely will be so commoditized that, monopoly or not, Microsoft's growth rate could slow to a crawl. Indeed, the company could shrink in size. Its decision to focus almost exclusively on software is a big strategic blunder — perhaps bigger than any ever before made in corporate history. It also confirms Microsoft's poor understanding of the Webolution and explains its repeated inability to execute an effective Web strategy. Maybe its new "dot-Net" plan will save the day after all.

Almost all PC hardware and most consumer electronic gizmos will be bought online in the future, with Dell poised to dominate the entire category. Office supplies also will be a big online business, catering to the tens of millions of North American home-based Webpreneurs.

Traditional household appliances and furniture are a fast-growing online category, as is home improvement in general. In addition, of course, more and more homes themselves will be sold online, perhaps accounting for five percent of new home sales by 2005 and ten percent by 2010.

Our overall forecast for homes and home improvement sales, as a percentage of total category sales to 2010:

Online Homes and Home Improvement as % of Total Sales		
2000	*2005*	*2010*
3%	10%	20%

Which Web Sites Will Win

Today's chain-store retailers of PCs and consumer electronics will vanish. As well, a large percentage of appliances and furniture will be sold direct to consumers without them ever having to visit a store. The battle for this overall category will be won by the big players — if they effectively transition online before upstarts gain significant first-mover advantage. That being the case, by 2010, this category's "Top 5" Web sites will be

◆ **HomeDepot.com**

◆ **Realtor.com**

◆ **Dell.com**

◆ **Sears.com**

◆ **OfficeDepot.com**

17 NEWSPAPERS
The "Digital Me"

You can't stand still. We're approaching an inflection point where we'll cannibalize print.

— Neil F. Budde
Wall Street Journal Interactive Edition

MODERN TECHNOLOGY decouples content from the old paper medium. Newspapers cannot possibly survive against 200 million soon-to-be one billion networked PCs and WebPhones.

"Web Kills Press" . . . e-Read All About It!

People have an endless appetite for news and information; they need and use it all the time — but they prefer it fresh. Nowhere is this more evident than in the business world. According to a 1998 survey by Deloitte & Touche, 91 percent of business executives said the Internet would be their primary news source by 2005. Only 50 percent expected to still get any news from daily newspapers, 35 percent from television, 32 percent from magazines, 21 percent from weekly newspapers, and 14 percent from radio. Today in America, there are more people online than had TVs when Armstrong stepped on the moon in 1969. Coincidentally or not, since that year, daily newspaper readership has plunged from 80 percent to 55 percent in 2000.

Newspapers compete for consumer attention. And the major competition for info consumption is now coming not from TV but from the Internet. AOL alone has 30 million paid North American subscribers, at least one million of whom are simultaneously online at any given time of day. Yet America's top 20 daily papers can muster a combined circulation of but 14 million.

Not many years ago, many evening papers became morning papers to avoid being killed by evening prime-time TV. Since 1950, the number of evening papers in the United States has plunged from 1,450 to about half that number by the end of 1999. Today, in turn, the Web is killing prime-time TV. More than 80 percent of online households are on the Web during prime-time hours of 8–11 P.M. Since 1995, when the Net itself became a news story, prime-time TV has dramatically lost adult consumer "mind-share," plunging two percentage points annually to only 36 percent of adults in 2000. And the trend will inevitably continue, perhaps even gaining speed.

Surfing More, Reading Less

The Newspaper Association of America (NAA) stoutly maintains that cable TV, radio and daily newspapers have held their adult audiences. In truth, NAA's aggregate data are quite misleading. In fact, the longer people stay online, their use of print media drops dramatically.

Web surfers tend to be heavy users of all types of media. Those who spend only two hours a week online also spend six hours a week reading newspapers and magazines. But those who are online 10 hours a week spend less than an hour a week with print media. In other words, not only is the number of readers dropping but those that still have newspapers delivered are spending less time reading them.

A major online activity (along with e-mail and financial management) is keeping up with news and current events. Indeed, the online population is a higher income/higher education segment — precisely the same upscale audience as for daily newspapers. Hence, by not going online, a newspaper will lose audience to other Internet news providers — including other "online newspapers."

For starters, newspapers cannot count on today's aging Baby Boomers behaving like their parents, that is, reading more papers as they get older. In fact, many seniors are as "wired" as today's kids. As for the kids, just as fewer of them now toss newspapers onto front porches, fewer of them have grown up with newspapers on their own doorsteps. Most young people sniff that "nobody reads newspapers anymore," because they consider papers old fashioned; reading newspapers simply isn't cool. Today's screenagers say paper is a ridiculously outmoded news vehicle — "as dead as the pulped trees it's printed on." They want scrolling screens, not cumbersome "continued on page B6" broadsheets. And don't underestimate this grossly mislabeled "don't-read" generation; they actually consume far more info than their time-pressured, newspaper-skimming parents.

Not that today's youth are beyond reach. But you've got to go after them with an unbeatable offer. Let's be honest, most newspaper content isn't exactly a killer draw for the youth audience. Yes, several papers now have some youth- and teen-oriented pages. But teens still say newspapers are boring and not relevant to them. Most teens say that youth pages in newspapers are written "for kids," not teens. Hence, 70 percent of teens surf for news. They regularly go online anyway for homework help and, once online, seek out their kind of content: music, entertainment, games, comics, sports. Within 20 years, kids will ask their parents, "Tell me again, when did you stop using newspapers, magazines, and books?"

Co-Existing with the Web

A newspaper's future is not about how it is going to keep selling newspapers; it's about understanding how people will live their lives. People are going to live highly connected lives, largely through the Internet. All of life and commerce is converging on the Internet. And newspapers have to position themselves at the confluence of that convergence.

How will newspapers coexist with the Net? To succeed, a new medium must offer benefits over old media. Newspapers were better than town criers because the information was written down. Magazines were handier and had photos. Radio was live and timely. TV was radio with moving pictures. The Net is "all of the above" as well as storable, customizable, and interactive. People with "always-on" broadband Web access are using the Web differently than dial-up modem users. Broadband changes how people experience their content. Newspapers will truly enter the twilight zone as always-on Internet achieves critical mass. At that point, why would anyone get their news from newspapers?

While some passive media will still be in demand, interactive media will take center stage and users will move smoothly from one to the other. Offline media must blend seamlessly with online multimedia. But newspapers have yet to do a great job of leveraging both media.

We also will see more consolidations in this industry as well as many alliances with players in the online world. In October 1999, I asked an audience of newspaper publishers what they would do if AOL took over a major publisher. Several jaws dropped, some heads shook, but most were unconvinced. Yet this is exactly what happened in January 2000 when AOL took over Time Warner.

The Web dramatically changes the content world. It alters how we access and use information, changing what and how we "read." And while the Net looks to be wide and shallow, it actually is extremely deep. Users want any or all of "breaking news," in-depth analysis, and customized content — and they want it digitally.

In the 1950s, before TV took off, people got breaking news from radio and read about it in tomorrow's paper. Today's printed news has a logical life of the amount of time it takes to skim-read the few pages that interest you. Since CNN recycles news every 30 minutes, few stories live beyond a few hours. Internet news is very short-lived; one online service recycles news every 15 minutes. On my own PC, incoming stories are killed in seconds; my PC scrolls it, grasps it, deletes it, or saves it for later use. Against this background, the very word "newspaper" is absurd, and the term "online newspaper" is as unimaginative as "horseless carriage."

> The term "online newspaper" is as unimaginative as "horseless carriage."

The value of news clearly depends on its delivery mode. TV news is faced by the "two minute" rule: no story can take more than two minutes to tell; viewers will not tolerate more than two minutes of a story they find irrelevant to them. Print news is faced by the limited size of the front page: stories have to be continued inside, which frustrates readers immeasurably. The Internet has an "eight-second, three-click" rule: pages must load within eight seconds and content must be within three clicks or I'm gone.

The Internet thus not only speeds things up but further raises consumer expectations about timeliness and convenience. It particularly speeds up the retrieval and dissemination process. E-mail eliminates the chore of going to the mailbox or waiting in line at the post office. E-news means we don't have to pick soggy papers off our driveways, trek to street-corner vending boxes, or scramble to a newsstand on Sunday lest they sell out.

Increasing millions of people want instant, ubiquitous digital access to digital info. Already, it is estimated that 85 percent of the info produced daily is "born digital" anyway — it never existed on paper. So why not keep it that way? Yes, print media are affordable, portable, easy to read, and generally user-friendly. But imagine an e-display so thin it looks and feels like paper. Something with a built-in microchip into which you can load text/image/sound from any source — a reusable multimedia "news-tablet" that typesets itself upon voice command. As noted, such e-books and e-paper are either already on the market or about to be.

By 2005, I predict that such a "news-tablet" will cost less than $50, will hold more than a year's worth of "papers," and will be easier to read than newsprint. It will have variable type size (for aging eyes) and thumb-touch page forwarding — no more thrashing through broadsheets in search of the rest of the story "Continued on Page B6, Column 5." Content will be downloadable wirelessly, will be able to be read out loud to you, and will be instantly erasable. If you want a hard-copy print-out, zap the story to your home printer — which every home will have. Imagine, every home with its own full-color printing press! Indeed, today's tech-savvy family buys a full-color, high-definition printer for less than $100.

Even today, rather than continuing to squirt ink on paper and then dump it in my driveway, newspapers can zap my customized edition to my always-on printer by 5 A.M. — with an updated version ready for me after supper. Indeed, newspapers could send me a full multimedia update every 10 minutes; if CNN can do it, why can't they?

Right now, I get my favorite global newspapers and magazines sent to my desktop. They're all waiting for me when I log on — and you can't beat the online subscription rate. Low cost and ease of use are attracting consumers online in droves. They are becoming real-time digital consumers who absolutely prefer multimedia over print. Those who "read" their newspapers online say they are better able to find more useful information, in less time, in a conveniently organized fashion. It is therefore no wonder that the online *Wall Street Journal Interactive* has some 500,000 paying subscribers and is profitable.

So why don't newspapers just get rid of their presses and trucks and let the consumer provide the display medium, the printer, the paper, and the ink cartridge? The e-publishing model is entirely different: ink-laden pulp, shipped via diesel-guzzling trucks, is far too capital- and labor-intensive to ever compete with digital downloads that most info-consumers now prefer and will increasingly insist upon.

To survive and prosper, newspapers and magazines have no choice but to go online — as the most successful pioneers are already doing. Digital magazines — exact page-for-page replicas of newsstand versions in downloadable and searchable form — are going online. Ranging from *Harvard Business Review* to *Popular Mechanics,* they are being put out by Qiosk.com's qMags venture, as well as by NewsStand and Zinio.

Knight Ridder, America's second-largest newspaper chain, operates the Real Cities network of local portals and has consolidated all its online properties under KnightRidder.com. The company first went online in 1993 with MercuryCenter, the online extension of Silicon Valley's *Mercury News* and the USA's first full-text online newspaper. Indeed, the company moved its entire head office to Silicon Valley to better understand the future of publishing. The company's online operations now encompass some 50 Web sites and, as I also suggested at the earlier-mentioned newspaper publishers' conference, it intends to pursue e-commerce opportunities by helping local merchants build online stores.

Despite this example, such suggestions usually elicit derisive smiles, scoffing guffaws, brusque dismissals, or reassuring explanations that there really is no threat. For example, in a fairly recent speech, the head of one major newspaper firm — who shall remain nameless — made the dumb assertion that "the job of a newspaper is to sort out items which are relevant to the public's interest over and above those which address purely individual needs," and hence "customized on-line newspapers don't work." He also sought to reassure his audience (and doubtless his own witless self) by saying that "a newspaper in its present form works; it's already wonderfully interactive; the Internet will not draw away our readers." What absurdities!

The "Daily Me"

Newspapers have brainwashed themselves to think of their business as a mass medium. But the era of mass is over, smashed to smithereens by the digital revolution. Today's consumers want customized information. The Internet is a self-segmenting medium that will inevitably speed up the specialization of every kind of content into vertical categories.

Neither is the Internet a mass medium. It is an intensely personal one: Web surfers are as individual as their fingerprints; they interact with the Web in unique ways. Info-consumers want personally relevant content. Newspapers, perhaps more than any other business, ought to understand this because a newspaper also is not a mass medium but a personal one, used differently by each customer. Radio and TV force you to listen and watch on their schedule; print media let you absorb content at your own pace and volition. So does the Internet.

However, this makes the Web a two-edge sword that will either make or break any business. By understanding that the Web is a personal medium, newspapers should be able to adapt to it; but if they don't embrace the Internet, it will defeat them in short order. Clearly, then, the Internet complements a newspaper and lets it reach a broader audience with deeper information in real time. It hugely increases a newspaper's capacity to captivate and aggregate an audience.

Not that newspapers can simply shovel content onto a Web site. Few editors and reporters understand that the Internet multimedium is quite different from the static paper page. You need to let users create their own unique content of personally relevant interest; each user can have a "Daily Me."

As such, content alone is not king! The Internet brings a context-centric era where compelling user experiences command most attention. For example, people are desperately trying to understand today's rapidly changing world and the impact of the Internet on their own lives and society at large.

A newspaper's greatest strength lies in local news. They should leverage that strength and see news as readers see it, by covering more grassroots stories, more neighborhood reports. Consumers want information relevant to their daily lives which revolve around family, neighborhood, work and shopping — around their fast-changing, Web-based, home-centered lifestyles.

To best evaluate societal change, the user must be placed in a future frame of reference that is made personally relevant to them in a compelling way. A newspaper's strength is its ability to analyze and put things in context. The Net expands rather than diminishes the need for depth and interpretation. Why aren't more newspapers capitalizing on that?

Publisher as e-Commerce Mediator

In the end, of course, the bottom-line purpose of a newspaper has not changed: it is to use content as a medium for delivering consumer segments to vendors of products and services. E-commerce is about bringing together buyers and sellers; and a newspaper's future rests on mediating e-commerce to help people complete transactions.

E-commerce is about driving traffic to brick-and-mortar stores. About 80 percent of personal consumption occurs within 50 miles of home. Hybrid "bricks-and-clicks" retailers — national and local — want to drive offline and online sales. Local content providers are the best vehicle for that. Newspapers should become e-commerce gateways to global and local markets on a vertical niche basis, allowing users to search for products by category and keyword, providing tools whereby they can bid on classified listings or compare pricing at retail outlets. A good example is the *Orlando Sentinel*'s ShopNow guide.

As newspapers well know, classified advertising pulls in 25 percent of their revenue and 40 percent of their profits. What they refuse to admit is that every nickel of that is vulnerable. Display ads by big department stores and automobile dealers bring in another 55 percent. And every nickel of that is vulnerable too. Business display and personal classified ads are simply moving to e-channels. Job hunters as well as buyers of cars, real estate, and household products and services of every description are turning to Web sites such as Monster.com, CarPoint, Realtor.com, and Quixtar.com, both for information and to buy. Advertising always goes where the consumers are. And as more and more consumers flock to the Web to conduct their lives, ad money is inevitably following.

As much as 20 percent of U.S. classifieds will have moved online by 2005. This will seriously undermine the economics of many, many newspapers. *Washington Post* and the *Tribune* formed a new company in 1999 called BrassRing to go after the job classifieds. But they are a bit late to the party because the Internet tends to reward those who get there first.

In any event, online classifieds should not only let users do fast, detailed searches but also let them specify sought-after items. Then, as *Orlando Weekly* is doing, the newspaper should notify them by e-mail when a match occurs. Again, newspapers have the local advantage: if a reader lives in Atlanta, the perfect used car he finds online in Denver is of no use to him. But newspapers can't take much comfort from such anomalies. Rather, they must exploit their local advantage online to the greatest extent possible.

Some of a newspaper's biggest advertisers, of course, are supermarkets and general retailers. As this book asserts, supermarkets are about to be severely beaten up by online grocery stores. As grocery shopping goes online, newspaper inserts and fliers will be replaced by e-coupons and individualized online offers. As for general retailers, they all are potential victims of "Amazonization." The smart ones are scrambling to get online, and e-tailing is gathering a strong head of steam. However, if local merchants succumb to online megastores, so will newspapers, so they need to create a local online merchants' portal.

Indeed, most newspaper revenue in future will not come from subscriptions, newsstand sales, or advertising but from mediating e-commerce; from commissions on e-mediated online and offline sales. Newspapers can prevail and succeed in the digital era because they are better than anyone else at collecting, editing, filtering, and presenting locally relevant information and at aggregating the e-commerce purchasing power of local consumers for commercial advertisers. But they must plunge headlong into digital ink, to harness the Internet juggernaut to provide custom content and facilitate e-commerce.

Forecast of Online Sales to 2010

The total value of today's newspaper and magazine market is irrelevant because every cent of it is vulnerable to the Webolution. During this decade, the Web will mercilessly eliminate every form of display, career, real estate and other kinds of classified advertising. Every printed newspaper is vulnerable; all will vanish within a generation, by 2020 or so. To survive, print publications must not only go online but must develop a formula to capture a share of the measurable e-commerce that they are able to facilitate.

Including e-commerce revenue (in lieu of advertising), our forecasts for online newspaper sales, as a percentage of total category sales to 2010:

Online Newspapers as % of Total Sales		
2000	*2005*	*2010*
2%	15%	35%

Which Web Sites Will Win

The Web will squish print media back into pulp. Newspapers and magazines have no choice but to go online to stand any chance of survival, never mind to prosper. Yet, few publishers understand the Internet well enough to start transitioning their newspapers online; most are in pig-headed denial. Surely, the AOL Time Warner merger swept away all doubts.

By 2010, we forecast this category's "Top 5" Web sites will be

- **KnightRidder.com**

- **USAToday.com (Gannett)**

- **WSJ.com (Dow Jones Co.)**

- **WashingtonPost.com**

- **TheNewYorkTimes.com**

18 MASS MERCHANDISERS
The Battle of the "Big 5"

Online, the balance of power shifts from the merchant to the customer. The merchant has to recognize that.

— Jeff Bezos, chairman
Amazon.com

A N INTERESTING BATTLE is likely to emerge among five online giant merchandisers: four up-starts — AOL, Amazon, eBay, and Quixtar — and the brick-and-mortar giant, Wal-Mart. We'll review each in turn, starting with Wal-Mart. (Webvan, on this list in the first edition of this book, has run out of gas.)

Wal-Mart

Wal-Mart sells exactly the kinds of products likely to succeed online. However, after four years of false starts, Wal-Mart continues to struggle with its online operations.

Its Wal-Mart.com site has some 600,000 items in 24 general-merchandise departments plus a Photo Center and a Travel Department. The site also has a fast-growing selection of books, toys and electronics, and also sells airline tickets and travel reservations. An online pharmacy lets shoppers order prescriptions for mailing to their homes or pick-up at a local Wal-Mart. Users also can receive e-mail reminders for refills or basic medical advice. The site also has a "My Wal-Mart" feature where customers can customize their shopping experience by composing a "Wish List," personal shopping lists, and set up a reminder calendar.

Astonishingly, just prior to the year-end 2000 holiday shopping season, Wal-Mart took down its Web site for several weeks to do some upgrades. The stated aim was to make the site less dazzling and more efficient: simpler, faster, easier, they said. Yet when the site came back up, well into the busiest shopping season of the year, it was drab, clumsy, and hard to navigate — and it still is. You have to wade through pages of product categories before you see an image or price of any type of item. It lacks any of the elements that drive online sales.

What is so surprising is that the world's largest retailer — with 90 million weekly shoppers and $500 million a day in sales! — cannot get its online service working properly. Give me 10 percent of $500 million and I'll give Wal-Mart the world's absolute-best Web site within a week, starting from scratch!

Wal-Mart's greatest brick-and-mortar strength is its greatest online weakness. The company is supply-side focused, optimizing inventory and delivery to big box stores, calculating sales and profit margins per square foot. This super-successful single-minded focus is blindfolding Wal-Mart to how the Web works, which is one customer at a time, based on what each customer wants; the Web is demand-driven not supply driven. And Wal-Mart clearly doesn't get it yet. The master brick-and-mortar big-box mass merchandiser simply doesn't know how to sell online.

By the way, Wal-Mart's main big-box rival, K-Mart, is no better. Its BlueLight.com site — a dumb name if ever there was one — is another bumbling Web initiative. BlueLight, named after its Blue Light in-store specials — there's the first mistake! — is supposed to bridge the culture gap between the young, hip, urbane, web-savvy customers and the staid, special-seeking, unwired, in-store shopper. So why the heck do they call it BlueLight? Apart from the lousy name, like Wal-Mart this is K-Mart's third attempt to get up and running online. The best feature was that K-Mart offered free Internet access and signed up several million users.

The question becomes how many of those will struggle to shop at the clunky BlueLight site when they can go to Amazon or Quixtar? Indeed, BlueLight found subscribers spending hundreds of hours a month playing games online or using the service to run their own Web-based businesses; they weren't shopping at BlueLight at all. So BlueLight began charging for unlimited access if users made no purchases online. Guess what? The change succeeded in turning surfers into shoppers. In response, however, Wal-Mart also offers a fee-based unlimited Internet access service called "Wal-Mart Connect" in conjunction with AOL. It thus seems the two big box competitors are determined to bang heads online as much as they do offline. And it appears like a no-win situation for either of them unless they can get their Web strategy working.

Amazon.com

Amazon.com was the very first place most people bought something online. Since opening its virtual doors in mid-1995 as an online bookstore, the Internet retail pioneer already has become the King of e-tailing — a one-stop shopping powerhouse for virtually everything, redefining what commerce is all about.

Amazon sits atop the e-tail world, an icon and a bellwether of e-commerce and, despite what investors think of the stock, Amazon's 30 million customers in 160 countries — not a handful of overpaid stock pundits — will make the company fulfill its promise. Amazon has built a system that is scalable and volume-tested that is very difficult to replicate. Amazon is the pre-eminent e-pioneer that has built a new business model: personalized, data-base-driven revenue generation flowing not from the product per se, but from knowing as much or more about the customer as did the old general storekeeper. It has created and mastered a whole new way of doing business, has built an incredibly powerful and trusted brand, and profits will surge as the company leverages its loyal customer franchise across higher margin profit lines. As recently as 1996, AOL too was the laughingstock of Wall Street but rebounded to stun the world with its take-over of Time Warner, the world's largest media company. As with AOL, Amazon is not a stock but a satisfied customer base.

Any nuanced analysis reveals that Amazon made many good moves in 2000. As a result, it boosted sales some 40 percent over the prior year, selling $1 billion in merchandise during the last quarter alone at a gross margin of 23 percent. The average annual customer sale rose from $108 in 1999 to $134 in early 2001. The company is already profitable on books and CDs/DVDs/videos — it sells an astonishing 52 percent of all CDs/DVDs/videos sold in America — and will be profitable overall going into 2002. Already selling digital cameras, other consumer electronics, and computer accessories, Amazon started selling computers in late 2001. It costs the same to receive, stow, pick, sort, pack, and ship a digital camera as it does a book, making the camera much more profitable in dollar terms. Most PC sales are moving to the Web, climbing 52 percent in the first half of 2001, while in-store sales declined 26 percent in the same period, both year-over-year.

As well, the company's new alliances with Borders, Toys 'R' Us, and Best Buy will boost sales in existing business lines. Brick-and-mortar companies are set up to ship to stores, not individual customers, which Amazon has perfected. So these alliances are a perfect complement of core competencies. Going further, Amazon has launched what essentially is its first non-retail business, a movie service called "In Theaters" that offers local show times, reviews, and paid advertising from big movie studios such as Disney, thereby allowing it to cross-market DVDs and movie soundtracks.

From books to autos, Amazon.com has created an e-commerce portal that anchors the world's biggest shopping mall, the Web. Now offering about 30 million items, its closest online rival is Yahoo, which has 6,000 stores and some eight million items, including most of those offered by Amazon.

Many have asked why the first edition of this book did not include Yahoo, not even in the "Top 50" e-tail Web sites of 2010 (see page 259). I thought then that the pure portal model would not survive and, in any event, that none of the major portals would become an e-tailer of significant size. I still think that to be the case. After all, portals are too broad and shallow; surfers want vertical depth of content to satisfy their specialized interests in sports, news, finance, and so on. Now, Yahoo has been profitable for nearly five years and may well turn out to be different. After all, it no longer is a pure portal, having converted itself from an online "directory" and search engine into a gateway for other Web sites. Of course, many thought that such gateways would be the online equivalent of the TV networks and would garner gobs of advertising dollars — which they did, from free-spending dot-coms, a revenue source that has been commoditized and all but dried up.

Yahoo is by far the dominant gateway portal, twice as big as its nearest competitor, Lycos. But it does not in fact command the biggest gateways to e-commerce because shoppers go directly to their favorite Web site for their needs, whether that be Amazon, Quixtar, or eBay. Indeed, unlike eBay, Yahoo began charging for its auction listings only to see those listings plunge by 80 percent. The problem is that Yahoo and other portals had led customers to expect directories, search engines, or portals to be free. Yahoo has

180 million users worldwide but has not found a way to monetize their affiliation, either through subscriptions or e-commerce mediation, thereby placing it at a huge competitive disadvantage vis-à-vis companies such as AOL Time Warner. By mid-2001, Yahoo's revenue was plunging, management was bailing out, and the company's prospects looked bleak. I doubt it will still be around in 2010. Hence, Yahoo again gets left off the "Top 50" list. At this point, I just don't think it will be a sizable retailer, if it survives at all.

Returning now to Amazon, by competing with major online and offline retailers in so many key product categories, Amazon.com is simply destroying the traditional retailing value chain. In so doing, it has turned competitors' brick-and-mortar assets into liabilities. For example, bookstores and other retail chains must open new stores in new markets if they are to grow sales — a huge cost that Amazon almost completely avoids. Amazon boosts its sales by simply getting more people to visit its single online store and then servicing them through a handful of warehouses. Physical bookstores must stock about five months' inventory versus Amazon's ten days' worth of stock. And being new, Amazon.com's distribution network is designed specifically for e-tailing, allowing it to send out merchandise one item at a time to individual customers. At full capacity, Amazon's new warehouses will be able to ship $10 billion a year in products.

Amazon also is far and away the online leader in the use of technology and digital marketing strategies and techniques. As a result, it has built a huge brand name from scratch to become the Web's leading e-tailer. Selected as *Time* magazine's "Man of the Year" for 1999, company founder Jeff Bezos points out that "Amazon's business is not selling things but helping customers make purchase decisions by helping them sort through the infinite shelf space of the Internet."

AOL Time Warner

AOL is so big that many people think it *is* the Internet. Its 30 million–subscriber base is growing by about one million a month — or one per second! And its members average an astonishing 70 minutes a day online. These 30 million use AOL as their Internet service provider (ISP) and about 50 million more have AOL on their favorites lists, yielding an online audience of 80 million regular visitors. AOL delivers more stock quotes than any newspaper, more mail than the U.S. Postal Service, and some 800 million instant messages fly around AOL daily. It sells a widening array of products — everything from long-distance telephone service to movie tickets — and operates one hundred Internet music channels and publishes 250 Digital City guides. It owns a stake in an Internet telephone company, the number one online travel service Travelocity, an online education firm, PC-maker Gateway, and satellite TV distributor DirecTV.

Time Warner stands out for its content, distribution, global reach, and a huge customer base — 95 million cable subscribers alone. Its brands include Warner Music, Turner cable networks including CNN and HBO, and Time Inc.'s raft of magazines that can be digitized and sold online.

> AOL is so big, many people think it *is* the Internet.

The merged AOL Time Warner is a consumer powerhouse. Their more than 100 million customers can create an interactive, customized webcast, converging columnists from *Time* with video from CNN. AOL Time Warner now enjoys massive cross-marketing opportunities and commercials for AOL are commonplace on CNN and various publications. Conversely, magazine subscription promotions on AOL yielded 500,000 new subscriptions to Time Inc. magazines in 2000.

But that's only the start. AOL Time Warner is positioned to facilitate online shopping in every single product category reviewed in this book: apparel, automobiles, books, education, entertainment and sports, expressions, financial services, groceries, health and beauty, homes and home improvement, and newspapers and magazines. More than 75 percent of AOL members are online shoppers. Indeed, AOL members spent a record $20 billion online during 2000 at various sites including AOL (i.e., not at AOL's site alone) and this accounted for an astonishing 43 percent of all online shopping. In other words, AOL is indeed a perfect case study of the Internet itself and of online shopping's true potential.

AOL is now so big, maybe it is indeed the Internet!

eBay

Totally misjudging the eBay phenomenon, I did not include it as a likely online winner in the first edition of this book. Remember, eBay started out as a place where collectors of Pez Dispensers (kid's candy toys) could buy and sell. Like many, I felt eBay would be a faddish, low-dollar-volume, online-garage-sale type of venture that would never grow large, even if it survived. How wrong I was!

Profitable since day one, eBay has 30 million registered "eBaysians," has posted its 500 millionth auction listing, and earned $48 million on gross sales of $5.5 billion in 2000. The company aims to grow revenues by 50 percent a year for the next five years, reaching a whopping $30 billion by 2005.

Initially an online auctioneer, eBay completely transformed and improved the way the auction business had been conducted offline: it provided a more convenient, efficient, and enjoyable way of trading merchandise than garage sales and classified ads. Now it has become much more, adding "eBay Stores," an e-commerce hosting service where businesses can sell products with fixed prices as well as offer auction-based listings. This recognizes a trend that auctions are moving away from person-to-person and toward business-to-consumer. See, I told you auctions were a fad.

Actually, that's why eBay bought Half.com that lets sellers offer items at set prices. eBay also does fixed-price selling with its "Buy It Now" feature which accounts for about 25 percent of items listed on the site. So what was a "collectibles" site can now mediate the sale of any product. Indeed, the company is moving into many fixed-price segments, including automobiles, plus the liquidation of excess inventory for the likes of IBM or Bloomingdales. Indeed, eBay already moves $1 billion worth of cars and car parts through its site.

The beauty of the eBay model, of course, is that the company never has to handle or ship the merchandise; it just mediates the sale, as an auctioneer does, with no merchandise to store or ship. As a result, the company earns a whopping 82 percent gross margin on sales and will be hugely profitable.

Quixtar

Quixtar was destined to be big. A subsidiary of privately held Alticor (the former Amway), Quixtar racked up first year online sales of $518 million — compared with Amazon's first year of $147 million and eBay's $32 million — and was profitable from the get-go. This success is based on a selection of reasonably priced, non-perishable, replacement-item consumables such as SA8 laundry detergent, Artistry skin care and cosmetics, and Nutrilite vitamins and wellness products — all perfect items for Quixtar's online

retail world. Indeed, the site offers "DittoDelivery" automatic shipment of repeat items.

When launched in late 1999, Quixtar.com's 15,000-page Web
site already was as big as that of General Motors. During its first
24 hours of operation, the site was overwhelmed by more than 20
million hits. Within two weeks, Quixtar was the fifth-ranked global shopping site, logging 52 million page views by 800,000 unique
visitors and racking up its first $1-million sales day. After one
hundred days, Quixtar sales topped $100 million and the Web site
was selling $2 million worth of product daily. The site ranked 15th
overall in terms of traffic during the 1999 year-end holiday shopping season. By January 2000, the site had moved up to 13th place
and was very close to being in the top 10.

Quixtar not only survived the dot-com shakeout but became a
big winner, quickly turning into one of the Internet's top e-commerce businesses — all without spending any money on advertising. In September 2000, the National Retail Federation ranked
Quixtar the seventh top e-commerce site based on what company
officials say was a low estimate of company sales. A month later,
Internet World magazine's ranking of the top e-commerce companies excluded Quixtar because it is not a publicly traded company.
Yet, comparing Quixtar's $518 million in sales to those of the "top
ten" listed companies, Quixtar would have ranked fifth largest.
The company had its biggest sales day ever during the year-end
2000 holiday shopping season — $5.3 million — and is expected to
double its sales in 2001 to reach more than $1 billion.

The Web site is a personalized "My Quixtar" shopping portal
that is functional, fun, easy to use, and offers just about anything
shoppers might ever need. Its thousands of products include the
full Quixtar range of over 10,000 products, plus those of nearly
one hundred partner stores such as Panasonic, Hickory Farms,
Reebok, OfficeMax, Fuller Brush and Lens Express. The site
offers "Quixtar Exclusives" of innovative, high-quality items and
"Hot Buys" of limited-time deals on nationally branded products.
A virtual department store called "The Store For More" carries
apparel, electronics and home furnishings. A "Virtual Tabletop"
helps shoppers select dishes, glasses, flatware and other accessories to create their own dining room ensembles.

The site also has interactive features such as "Ask the Expert,"
linked to Johns Hopkins University, that helps users select the

right nutritional products for their needs. As well, customers can fill out "personal assessments" of their eating habits, stress factors and overall lifestyle which Quixtar then analyzes, responding with a personalized portfolio of suggested products. Product shipment is arranged automatically on a predetermined schedule chosen by the customer.

Quixtar reaches tomorrow's consumers — the tech-savvy generations X and Y who are starting their own families and will consume lots of products during the next three decades. The Web site is fun to use and appeals to younger consumers because it doesn't so much sell products as a brand new lifestyle — a Web Lifestyle.

Quixtar's high-tech Web site also uses customer relationship management software to maintain its trademark "high-touch" customer interaction provided by Quixtar's super-enthusiastic independent business owners (IBOs). Quixtar pays commissions to IBOs on goods ordered through them. The IBOs build businesses that allow them to earn income through what Quixtar calls "Tridigital Commerce" — a synergy of personalized shopping, member benefits, and business ownership. This model gives entrepreneurs the chance to own a Web-based business without the expense of a Web site of their own or any product development or distribution headaches.

The new Quixtar model bears little resemblance to that of the old Amway or competitors such as Avon. These old multilevel or network marketing firms were built on the back of a single product that was vulnerable to copying and competition. Quixtar's model is based on sound, futuristic business criteria. And it is attracting successful people from the traditional business world who desire to achieve their personal and financial ambitions as independent business operators.

Quixtar's future success will stem not only from a superior Web site but because its new breed of IBOs understand how to build high-tech/high-touch communities of customers. They know that online success requires one-to-one, people-oriented, long-term customer relationship building and cooperative teamwork and mentorship among IBOs. Quixtar's IBOs are a key differentiator that will lead it to success over its brick-and-mortar, pure online, and hybrid retail competitors. Indeed, the enthusiasm and aspirations of the IBOs to tap into the Web, leveraging their success to its phenomenal growth, is creating a new 21st-century American cyber dream.

The company has built a loyal customer following, with a high rate of repeat business due to its innovative "Ditto Delivery" service (to-the-doorstep delivery of standing orders of things that people buy week in, week out). Indeed, Quixtar will be far more successful once all its IBOs fully embrace "Ditto Delivery" which, after all, is the core essence of what e-tailing is supposed to be all about. In 2001, Quixtar also arranged with InPhonic to distribute WebPhones and other wireless devices that IBOs would get free but would offer to their customers. The phones will carry promotional offers from Quixtar as well as news, weather, and sports information.

Quixtar also needs to grasp the opportunity to add more in-demand products onto its "Ditto Delivery" system (especially supermarket non-perishables) as well as more digital services, such as comprehensive financial services. Then, as the IBOs fully embrace more high-tech tools (including "Ditto" and InPhonic WebPhones), the company could easily and quickly become the leading player in mobile commerce.

Webvan: Out of Gas — and Delisted

Webvan, as described in the "Grocery" section, has run out of gas and is no longer listed either in this "Top 5" or even the "Top 50" Web sites of 2010. Forced to retrench on its nationwide expansion ambitions, Webvan ended up back where it started out, in San Francisco, a city that has the highest percentage of Web users in North America. The company met or exceeded every internal performance milestone it laid down for itself: sales growth, gross margin, repeat users, and customer satisfaction. Indeed, Bay Area customers loved the service and are distressed that it failed.

Webvan was way more efficient than the supermarkets — requiring only half the number of employees. But the company simply tried to go nationwide too fast without proving out its business model in San Francisco. Webvan did prove that shoppers are willing to pay for shipping in exchange for convenience, which is what online shopping is about. It is only a matter of time before online grocery shopping takes off.

Forecast of Online Sales to 2010
The total mass merchandising market is estimated at about $400 billion a year. Wal-Mart alone sells $165 billion worth of products annually.

By 2010, a majority of people will live a Web Lifestyle. Hence, general merchandisers that automatically deliver replenishment products to customers' doorsteps can only grow in popularity. They will take market share away from second-string big box stores and from retailers in specialized product categories.

Our forecasts for online mass merchandising sales, as a percentage of total category sales to 2010:

Online Mass Merchandisers as % of Total Sales		
2000	*2005*	*2010*
2%	14%	29%

Which Web Sites Will Win
Among general merchandisers, the "big 5" discussed here will battle it out for Web domination. Portals or online shopping malls, lacking brick-and-mortar presence or distribution systems, will not succeed. Neither will second-string big box stores such as K-Mart, which went online with its silly, no-name BlueLight.com site. The future of this category belongs to the big online and offline brands.

By 2010, we forecast this category's "Top 5" Web sites, listed alphabetically, will be

- ◆ **Amazon.com**

- ◆ **AOL Time Warner**

- ◆ **eBay.com**

- ◆ **Quixtar.com**

- ◆ **Wal-Mart.com**

19 SUMMARY
Total Online Retail Sales in 2010 and the "Top 50" Web Sites

This is simply the first step in the ongoing migration of the $4 trillion global retail economy onto the Net.
— Jeff Bezos, chairman
Amazon.com

EVERY DOLLAR SPENT ONLINE is a dollar not spent in a store. Total North American retail sales in 2000 were about $2.9 trillion but online sales were only $48 billion, accounting for less than two percent of total sales.

Most forecasts call for online sales to account for six or seven percent of total retail sales by 2003–2004. For all the various reasons stated earlier, these forecasts ignore future social and technological developments and are far too conservative.

A much closer approximation of the future of online sales potential comes from Martha Rogers, co-author of *One to One Marketing,* who believes that consumer-direct marketing will account for 24 percent of retail sales by 2010. Some analysts even predict that non-store retailing will account for 55 percent of general merchandise sales by then.

Considering the evolution of Web Lifestyles and the suitability of tomorrow's Web for online retailing, the truth lies somewhere between these extremes. As well, there will be major shifts in category dominance as the travel, food, healthcare, entertainment, household, and automobile categories rapidly move online.

We predict that 12 percent of total retail sales (on a category-weighted basis) will occur online by 2005, reaching 29.5 percent by 2010. Indeed, excluding the huge automobile and education sectors, online sales will be 41 percent of total retail sales by 2010.

These totals are tabulated in the 12-product category summary in the top figure on the next page. The forecasts for 2005 are in the same ballpark as those made by the Organization of Economic Cooperation and Development (OECD), the group of most developed countries. While many of their categories are not comparable, the five in the lower table opposite are typically relevant.

You will note that many of the OECD numbers are rounded off to the nearest five percent and thus clearly are somewhat arbitrary guesses. As well, the OECD forecast that as great a percentage of automobiles will sell online as books is not realistic. Nevertheless, our forecasts for 2005 are otherwise generally in line and, we believe, much more probable.

To give our forecasts a further "reality check," let's recall our earlier projections for online shoppers and how much they will spend. By 2010, we forecast that 79 percent of 115 million North American households will shop online, and that 66 percent of all households will be actively buying online. If those 76 million households on average each spend a modest $280 a week online, that tallies to $1.1 trillion in e-tail sales. By 2010, total retail sales will be about $3.7 trillion. Hence, 29.5 percent of sales will occur online.

Top 50 Retail Web Sites in 2010

Even if only 10 to 15 percent of retail sales occur online by 2010, there will be a radical rationalization of retailing. There will be many alliances, mergers, acquisitions and bankruptcies among online, offline and brick-and-click hybrid companies in all product categories. As 29.5 percent of retail sales go online, the upheaval during this decade will be horrendous.

While it is extremely difficult to forecast which Web sites will win out in a "winner-take-all" world, companies blessed with a big first-mover advantage, a great brand, or much capital and human talent will dominate their product categories in 2010.

All considered, in terms of dollar volume, any short list of leading North American sites will tend to include mass merchandisers and/or the top one or two players in the major product categories.

We continue to give the benefit of the doubt to today's biggest brick-and-mortar retailers on the assumption that they will make a successful and significant online transition and/or will gobble up

Online Sales as % of Total Retail Sales to 2010

(Figures in parentheses are from the first edition of this book)

Category	2000	2005	2010
Apparel & Footwear	**2** *(4)*	**12** *(16)*	**28** *(34)*
Automobiles	**2** *(2)*	**9** *(8)*	**19** *(16)*
Books	**14** *(12)*	**30** *(28)*	**70** *(57)*
Education	**2** *(1)*	**8** *(6)*	**16** *(14)*
Entertainment & Sports	**12** *(10)*	**24** *(21)*	**55** *(42)*
Expressions	**13** *(11)*	**26** *(23)*	**55** *(47)*
Financial Services	**7** *(8)*	**21** *(22)*	**39** *(43)*
Groceries	**1** *(1)*	**12** *(16)*	**27** *(34)*
Health & Beauty	**2** *(2)*	**12** *(11)*	**30** *(27)*
Home & Home Improvement	**3** *(12)*	**10** *(23)*	**20** *(45)*
Newspapers	**2** *(1)*	**15** *(15)*	**35** *(39)*
Mass Merchandise	**2** *(2)*	**14** *(14)*	**29** *(32)*
TOTAL RETAIL	**2** *(3)*	**13** *(14)*	**30** *(31)*
Excluding Autos & Education	**4** *(6)*	**20** *(21)*	**41** *(46)*

Forecasts for 2005
Online % Shares by Category

	OECD Forecast	Our Forecast
Automobiles	20%	9%
Books	20	30
Education	5	8
Newspapers	10	15
Financial Services	30*	21

*simple mathematical average of stock trading (60%), bill payment (36%), banking (16%), and insurance (10%)

many pure e-tailer competitors. Should they do neither, they will not survive to 2010 and hence will no longer be on the list by then.

Due to our North American focus, our list does not include names such as Tesco in the U.K., which clearly would be on any global list. However, companies such as Sony of Japan and Bertelsmann of Germany make the list because of their strong presence in the North American market and their aggressive online strategy in that market.

Here, then, is our list of the "Top 50" Web site companies that will dominate North American e-tail sales in 2010. We list both the "Top 5" and the smaller 45 in alphabetical order.

The Big 5

- ◆ **Amazon.com**
- ◆ **AOL Time Warner**
- ◆ **eBay.com**
- ◆ **Quixtar.com**
- ◆ **Wal-Mart**

The Next 45 Biggest

- AutoByTel.com
- AutoNation.com
- Bertelsmann/ Barnes & Noble
- CarsDirect.com
- Citibank
- CVS
- Dell
- Disney/ESPN
- Dow Jones
- EdisonSchools.com
- E*Trade
- Expedia.com
- Fannie Mae
- Ford/Carpoint
- Gap
- GMBuyPower
- Home Depot

- Intuit/Quicken
- JonesInternational.edu
- Kaplan
- KnightRidder
- Kroger
- Microsoft
- Morgan Stanley
- NewsCorp
- New York Times
- Nordstrom
- Office Depot
- JCPenney
- Realtor.com
- Safeway

- CharlesSchwab
- Sears
- Softbank
- Sony
- Travelocity.com
- UNext.com
- UoPhx.edu
- USAToday
- Viacom
- Virgin
- Walgreen
- Washington Post
- WebMD
- Wells Fargo

PART IV

— • —

e-Marketing Strategy
From Mall to "Mallennium"

Every business will be an e-business . . . or it will not be in business.

— Andrew Grove, chairman
Intel Corporation

D UE TO THE RAMP-UP OF ONLINE SHOPPING and the limited space available on the average e-consumer's favorites list, each and every retail category is facing a massive shakeout. Indeed, according to the Pew study *Internet & American Life* (February 2001), the dot-com shakeout caused only eight percent of users to lose even one site from their favorites lists. Any site not yet on surfers' favorites lists doesn't stand much chance.

By 2005, as online purchases reach at least 10 percent of total retail sales in most categories, that will be more than enough to wipe out the net profit of most retailers. In food retailing, for example, the net profit margin is less than two percent. Most supermarkets will go bankrupt if you take away just a small percentage of their sales. The same applies in varying degrees to other product categories. So, as online retailing surges to 30 percent of sales by 2010 — 41 percent in categories other than autos and education! — most retailers will get killed.

As Andy Grove asserts, the overwhelming implication for real-world companies as we enter the Internet millennium is that they will either become an e-business . . . or they will not be in business. Retailers have no choice but to join the "mallennium" of online retailing. And their chief executives need to wake up to their inevitable e-commerce future.

CEO — Chief E-commerce Officer

Corporate success in the online world requires executive management to think geo-strategically. Those who do not see the "big picture" and the long-term evolution of the Web will fail to master the strategic nature of e-business.

To be of any effective value, the CEO must be the "Chief E-commerce Officer." E-commerce initiatives cannot be left indiscriminately to information technology or marketing managers. A company's Internet strategy must be the paramount element of its overall corporate strategy. Web strategy must drive the business strategy.

Yet, in a 1999 survey of Internet "leaders and laggards" by Ernst & Young, only the leaders — who numerically are in the minority — agreed with this approach. The majority laggard CEOs do not even understand that simply using the Web as an internal and external communication tool is now more essential than picking up the telephone.

Let me tell you, CEOs who do not personally surf the Web have zero appreciation for the threats and opportunities that e-commerce represents to their business. You can't delegate Web surfing to an executive assistant. Such executives are simply blind to the future. Indeed, they do not qualify to be an "executive."

The most successful e-commerce companies recognize the overwhelmingly strategic importance of the Web to their future. Their executives see how the Internet is transforming their industry and their business. They see the company's future from the viewpoint of e-consumers who, drawn into a Web Lifestyle, will place radically different marketplace demands on their product and service providers.

To gain a keener appreciation for the Web's strategic marketing implications, this final section explores the following topics:

◆ Bricks vs. Clicks: Webify or Die

◆ Digital Rules: Strategic Web-Site Marketing

◆ The Future of Advertising: Pay-to-View Web Sites

◆ Branding the Web: Selling the "Web Lifestyle"

◆ Customer Service Management: Winning the Digital Race

20 BRICKS VS. CLICKS
Webify or Die

On the Web, all the physical constraints go away; shelf space is infinite.

— Jeff Bezos, chairman
Amazon.com

ONCE CLICK-HAPPY CUSTOMERS get used to hassle-free online shopping, there is little chance that they will still go to brick-and-mortar stores unless they need something right away. Let us consider how retailing will shift online, and the strategic implications of that, both for brick-and-mortar retailers and e-tailers.

Mass Customization

Today's most successful retailers — both online and offline — carry a minimum of inventory as manufacturing shifts away from mass production to mass customization. As more customers configure more and more products for themselves online, point-and-click prefabrication of everyday items zapped to people-less robotized factories could be commonplace by 2010. In turn, factories, warehouses, and distribution centers will converge into a single integrated facility that operates at the beck and call of online shoppers. Of course, any product that can be totally digitized will be simply downloaded from a central database, again in customized format.

By 2010, therefore, there likely will be only a handful of so-called manufacturers competing aggressively for the business of online shoppers. Indeed, with all the bargaining power in the hands of the consumer, it is possible that each product will be manufactured by a single entity — which will not be considered a monopoly because of its lack of power. Furthermore, that entity could be a single electronic mega-cooperative that is one hundred percent owned by its customers.

The evidence for this trend lies in the history of retailing itself, starting with the pre-industrial village market. Most villages were self-sufficient economic entities where the local population produced and consumed its own product and service needs. The massive "reversal" effect of the Webolution is highly likely to create a cyberspace version of that pre-industrial networked village economy.

The upsurge of the Internet is a major inflection point that represents a clean break from the past. It is somewhat like the introduction of the automobile and its impact on previous modes of transportation. The speed of the cars kept everyone on their toes and scared the hackney carriage horses and their drivers to death. Indeed, compared to the speedy upstart e-tailers, today's old-line merchants are very hackneyed. They plod along, blinkered to the major threats to their existence. Technology shifts economic power. And if you look at a list of industry leaders before a particular innovation came along, few if any of the names on that list are there 10 or 15 years later.

The Internet will have an impact on brick-and-mortar retailing similar to that of Wal-Mart. Wal-Mart's simple strategy was to move into a small town that had a reasonable number and mix of appliance, clothing, shoe, music, hardware and "five-and-dime" stores. Wal-Mart then effectively integrated those disparate stores into a single "big box" store that offered greater product breadth, lower prices, and convenience. It simply converged the shoppers into its store.

Today, the Internet is causing a similar form of integration that is leaving traditional brick-and-mortar retailers scratching their heads — perhaps even Wal-Mart included. As we have seen, Wal-Mart has been very slow to understand what, in effect, is the "Wal-Marting" of the Web.

Some analysts call this the "malling" of the Web. But that view is too linear, drawing too much of a parallel with today's shopping mall model. For example, since its IPO in 1993, America Online has yielded a return of more than 10,000 percent to its shareholders and cannot be compared with any kind of physical retail model. Its Web site is, at one and the same time, a shopping mall, a postal service, and an entertainment conglomerate, all rolled into one. Yet, unlike any of those, it has more than 30 million paying members — growing by one million a month — who provide an annuity revenue stream that none of its contemporaries can ever contemplate. AOL is not a shopping center developer nor a "big box" store but, thanks to webonomics, is outshining all of them.

Amazon.com, as we also just saw, is the next generation of retailing. It is Wal-Mart many times over, transformed into a new electronic model of retailing. As observed by Amazon founder and chairman, Jeff Bezos, "On the Web, all the physical constraints go away; shelf space is infinite." Indeed, Amazon.com has effectively put its bookshelves on display on every computer attached to the Web. And it has achieved this with one large computer database and a few highly sophisticated warehouses.

Thanks to Amazon.com, why do book buyers need thousands upon thousands of brick-and-mortar shops, each one with limited inventory? If a chain of 1,000 stores wants to double sales, it must open another 1,000 stores and incur the associated physical asset and labor costs. An online competitor, once established, can expand sales with very little extra expense.

The Internet thus disconnects info-based activity from physical location, just as the automobile disconnected shopping from residential neighborhoods and put it in shopping malls. The brick-and-mortar marketing maxim of "location, location, location" becomes one of locationless e-tailing: no warehouse, no store, no headquarters.

Irrational Fear of Cannibalizing Sales

The vast majority of brick-and-mortar retailers are reluctant to go online for fear of cannibalizing their offline sales. In the end, of course, they must face the question as to whether they want to eat their own business before a competitor does. Every time an online retailer sells something, an old-line retailer has lost a sale. Many retailers are simply in denial: they naively think that online shopping will merely be a niche market, just like mail order.

Although larger companies have capital, logistics, distribution, merchandising, cash flow, and an established brand, they have been afraid to cannibalize their established business, never mind consider shrinking it. All of these companies suffer from cannibalization inertia: they rationalize that online sales will cannibalize store sales, negating their Internet investment. Some of the weak-kneed excuses they give for not selling online are:

Conflicts with store investments	67%
Lack necessary info-technology	67%
Lack necessary distribution network	50%
Insufficient return on investment	33%
Product not suited for online sales	17%
Customers will not buy our product online	17%

Perhaps, as one wag put it, their inertia is better described as a bureaucracy-loving "PowerPoint inertia." This occurs where various levels of management repeatedly make the case through PowerPoint presentations about whether or not and, if so, how the company should go online. Meanwhile, their e-tailing upstart competitors have established first-mover advantage online. Consequently, online success may be inversely related to the number of PowerPoint presentations required to get a "go ahead" decision. Indeed, some e-tailers deliberately shun such presentations, and the successful online brick-and-mortar retailers say the difference is amazing once you break the PowerPoint ritual in the boardroom.

All trends start small. Big companies usually dismiss what at first appears to be a small market as being not worth their time and effort. For example, in late 1999, Dayton Hudson — which owns Dayton's, Hudson's, Marshall Field's, Mervyn's, and Target — scoffed at the notion that traditional retailers are slow to go online. The head of "new business" — who ought to know better — said, "We sold eight times as much as the entire online market in our categories." He also said he did not expect the Web to be a significant revenue channel for his company "any time soon." He is dead wrong! Just as fashion comes from the street up, the world of retail has no choice but to follow shoppers where they are going — online.

Let me repeat, the Web is a two-edged sword. It will make you or break you. Either side of the blade can cut any retailer's throat. For now, online sales as a percentage of in-store sales are tiny. However, a small loss in sales to another distribution channel will disproportionately reduce profitability because fixed costs remain unchanged. This will particularly be the case in some product categories. Moreover, the most profitable customers are often the first to switch channels and go online, leaving even lower revenues to cover costs.

So do you wait for somebody else to cannibalize your sales or do you do it to yourself first? Also, keep in mind that buying habits can change quickly, and a mere five percent shift of sales away from stores could slash your net profit in half. A 10 percent decline in sales could wipe out all your profits. If, as we are forecasting, online sales grab 30 to 41 percent of the total market by 2010, the vast majority of retailers — in every category type — will be swept onto the corporate trash heap.

Brick-n-Click Hybrids

Still, a few retailers, including Dayton Hudson, are venturing online to create a hybrid brick-and-click business model. One of the pioneers was stockbroker Charles Schwab, which first created a separate e-business called e-Schwab. It then decided this was the wrong path because it forced customers to choose between Schwab and e-Schwab. So it integrated the two models and unquestionably has become the best-positioned retail brokerage firm. The company not only blended the back-office efficiencies and product expertise of a traditional brokerage with a Web presence but created seamless options for its customers.

The Gap is another great hybrid example, this time of a traditional retailer that developed a solid e-commerce division in-house right from the start. Gap's strong brand made the online transition easier because customers quickly found it online. Gap.com uses Web interactions to track customers and knows when they visit the site, how long they stay, how often they buy, and how much they spend on which items. The company is an industry leader when it comes to displaying, selling and delivering online merchandise. Its popular jeans and tops transfer easily to e-tailing, taking much guesswork out of the process for shoppers who are familiar with Gap's apparel lines.

Another way to make the online transition is to acquire an existing complementary online business, just as the CVS drugstore chain purchased Soma.com. This was a great match-up because Soma.com was more oriented towards pharmaceutical products than CVS and had its own distribution system in place.

Alliances also offer a win-win opportunity for offline and online retailers to create a hybrid brick-and-click model. For example, PetCo allied with Petopia.com, each company contributing its core competency to the venture. Nike formed an arrangement with FogDog sports in a deal that allows the offline manufacturer and retailer to sell its products online. Global Sports allied with Sports Authority to run its online store. Microsoft is installing kiosks in RadioShack's 7,000 stores to demonstrate Microsoft software products and high-speed access to its MSN and WebTV online services. Microsoft has a similar deal with North America's leading shopping mall developer and owner, Simon Property Group, to install kiosks in its major malls.

One of the best examples of a multi-channel transition to the Web is RightStart.com in the baby product business. Its products include accessories, hard goods, childcare videos and books. The company has about 50 brick-and-mortar stores, mainly in California and Texas, plus a catalog that is mailed to about three million people. The company viewed its stores and catalog not as liabilities but as assets which could be leveraged online. After all, the company has millions of people who have seen its catalog and millions more who come into its stores. Willing to cannibalize its existing sales, both in-store and catalog customers were solicited to go through RightStart.com for a fully integrated experience of the brand. The physical stores act as customer service modules and as vehicles for customers who wish to return or exchange items they bought online. As a result, sales have not declined but have grown more rapidly.

In contrast to RightStart.com, many big-name retailers do not yet accept in-store returns purchased online. Examples are Wal-Mart, Barnes & Noble, Best Buy, and Victoria's Secret. This is one of the dumbest policies that retailers could possibly have. Encouraging in-store product returns is one way that brick-and-mortar retailers can promote their online presence and even generate additional in-store impulse purchases when the customer returns an item. Customers do not expect there to be any difference between a company's store and its Web site. Indeed, there should not be a difference. Customers expect all retail channels of one brand to work together seamlessly.

Given a choice between an online retailer that accepts returns in its stores and one that does not, online shoppers will simply choose the store that doesn't force them to re-package the product, trudge to the post office, and then tediously line up, just to mail back an unwanted item. By contrast, Nordstrom — as might be expected from that innovative retailer — has accepted returns of items bought online ever since it opened its Web site. The company views this as an important part of offering good customer service. Retailers who do not adopt such a policy are simply losing their customer base.

In the future, brick-and-mortar stores may be less like a place for selling merchandise and more like a showroom — with more offerings in smaller inventories — which also serves as a product pickup and return center. Circuit City, the electronics giant, gives its online customers the option of picking up locally any merchandise they order over the company's Web site. The Sharper Image, meanwhile, opened stores as showrooms for its catalog merchandise. These approaches help customers save money on shipping costs and let them experience the joys of instant gratification. These smart retailers also realize that customers who walk into their stores are prospects for additional purchases, impulse or otherwise. As Internet shopping grows, many retailers are likely to use such models for future stores.

Whatever model they choose, traditional retailers must realize that building an online presence means more than hanging up a "dot-com" shingle or printing a Web site name on their shopping bags. The traditional brands have a big advantage in their customer base which they can introduce to the online world before somebody else does. Yet, many retailing brands are too slow to do so. Consider Toys 'R' Us, which revolutionized toy retailing through the "big box" retail concept but ignored the next generation of retailing. It sat back while eToys essentially built its entire brand on the concept of, "We're not Toys 'R' Us." This is reminiscent of the marketing success of Seven Up which positioned itself as the "un-Cola."

Economics of Going Online

If the foregoing arguments are not persuasive enough, the economics of going online are compelling. For example, it costs about $2.25 to process a catalog order versus only 25 cents or less for an Internet order. But that is just a trifling micro-detail of the differences between online and offline retailing. Conventional marketing is four times as expensive as e-marketing, which generates 10 times more sales for 10 percent of the advertising budget. E-commerce offers huge competitive advantages: lower costs, product customization, faster time-to-market, zero inventory, market reach, targeted promotion, and immediate transaction completion.

As well, the amount of inventory that e-tailers need to carry is substantially reduced, if not eliminated entirely, in most instances. At a minimum, e-tailers can eliminate the duplicate inventory that must be carried by each brick-and-mortar store of a retail chain. At a maximum, e-tailers can eliminate inventories completely by relying on wholesalers. In addition, of course, an online store can offer a much wider choice of product than could ever be carried in any brick-and-mortar store. Thus, for example, even though it is building its own distribution warehouses, Amazon.com turns over its book inventory weekly versus Barnes & Noble's once every 26 weeks.

The relatively low overhead of e-tailing is a huge cost advantage over brick-and-mortar stores. Obviously, other than for any necessary warehouses, the need for stores in high-cost, high-traffic areas — whether owned or leased — as well as fixtures, checkout terminals, and employee salaries, is considerably reduced if not eliminated. The occupancy cost of a downtown or shopping mall store is perhaps 20 times higher than the $3 per square foot of a spartan warehouse in a rural area.

> Conventional
> marketing costs
> *four times*
> as much as
> e-marketing.

On the sales side, a JCPenney or Wal-Mart typically generates sales of $150 to $350 per square foot versus $2,500 to $3,000 per square foot at an Amazon warehouse distribution center. As a result, e-tailers can grow sales much faster than retailers. For example, it took Wal-Mart 12 years and 78 stores to reach $150 million in sales. Amazon did it in three years, with one Web site and one warehouse.

All things considered, a 1997 study by Booz-Allen & Hamilton found that the investment cost to reach a market area of 10 million potential customers would cost a traditional brick-and-mortar retailer about $1 billion. Conversely, the study said that an Internet retailer could reach that same market at a cost of only

$1 million — that is, for a mere 0.1 percent of the investment. This vast difference is again starkly illustrated in the book industry. Barnes & Noble and Borders combined have more than 2,100 stores and about 24 percent of the market while Amazon.com with a single Web site has already grabbed about 20 percent of the market. Brick-and-mortar retailers typically generate two to three dollars in sales for every dollar tied up in fixed assets while e-tailers are able to at least triple that.

Using the same argument, it seems inevitable that all retailers, regardless of what strategy they adopt, are going to be forced to rationalize their brick-and-mortar presence, closing perhaps as many as 80 percent of their outlets by 2010 to survive.

Customer Acquisition Costs

Moreover, Amazon.com has acquired more than 20 million customers and is able to spread its lower fixed costs over a larger customer base. The company can therefore grow faster. Indeed, Amazon.com's investment in new warehouses can potentially support $15 billion in sales compared with Barnes & Noble's current annual sales of about $1.5 billion. Of course, the argument is made that pure e-tailers are currently spending about twice as much as brick-and-mortar stores ($42–$48 versus $22) in customer acquisition costs.

However, it also costs a brick-and-mortar retailer another $11 to convert an existing customer to its Web site. Moreover, e-tailers such as eBay.com are recouping their customer acquisition costs in about 12 months. And, despite the ignorant carping by many stock market analysts, Amazon is now profitable in its book division and its customer acquisition costs are only 65 percent of those of Barnes & Noble, as follows:

Customer Acquisition Costs

	2000	**2001 (est.)**
Barnes & Noble	$42.00	$30.00
Amazon.com	$27.60	$20.00

Brick-and-mortar retailers with Web sites are in fact doing better than pure e-tailers at converting browsers into buyers, as the following table shows:

	Pure E-Tailer	Multi-Channel Retailers
Buyer Conversion rate	3%	6%
Repeat Buyers	17%	26%

When done right, multi-channel retailers blend reach, segmentation, and economic advantage with product breadth, personal service, and in-store ambience. When they add the immediacy and interactivity of the Internet, supported by known brands, their potential is outstanding.

Price Leverage

Nevertheless, as e-tailers try to rapidly build a customer base, they are presently spending about 75 percent of revenues on marketing and sales expenses, compared with about 15 percent for multi-channel retailers. Moreover, until their customer base reaches a certain critical mass, e-tailers are not able to exact the same price discounts from manufacturers and distributors that a multi-chain retailer can command. Yet, unless they make the leap and ramp up their customer base fast, they will finish up with a customer base that buys the least but costs the most to service.

Obviously, though, these factors will change as e-tailers gain in competitive strength. Online retailers can harness the Web's power to track data on what customers buy and can then use that data in two ways: to cross-sell and up-sell other products to customers; and to gain pricing power over manufacturers by sharing their customer data with them.

In terms of retail price competition, most customers naturally prefer to buy products at the lowest available price. However, in a brick-and-mortar world, time-pressured customers are not inclined to shop around, enabling many retailers to charge higher prices. On the Internet, price comparison is easy, thus forcing prices down and ultimately making them a less-important competitive differentiator.

The Future of Shopping Malls

As a result of all these changes, the regional shopping mall faces significant challenges. Almost anything for sale in a shopping mall can be bought online faster and often cheaper.

Even before the Internet, the average shopping mall was

becoming less popular. The average visitor spends about an hour at a conventional mall, but this is much less than a decade ago and people are going to malls less frequently. Less than 10 percent of Americans shop frequently at malls, down from 16 percent in 1987. As recently as 1994, shoppers averaged 2.6 trips per week to the mall but that plunged to 1.7 times a week by 1999.

As a result, sales volumes have basically stagnated and, in some categories, are beginning to decline. The poorest growth is occurring in the strongest online sales categories such as books, music, toys, and greeting cards. While stores in these businesses occupy only about five percent of the retail space in a mall, two other vulnerable categories — clothing and shoes — occupy about 50 percent of a mall. Shopping mall sales average about $315 per square foot, but this is declining and the malls need to modify their merchandise mix as online sales penetrate every product category. Incidentally, Web site effectiveness used to be measured by the number of "hits" on the site. A more realistic measure would be "sales per Web page" comparable with "sales per square foot" for old-line retailers.

To maximize sales, it is not enough to change the product mix. As online shopping becomes increasingly attractive, the physical shopping environment must be transformed from routine necessity into something that both informs and entertains. As Simon Property Group is demonstrating, shopping malls are not real estate but a medium; they must position themselves as a shopping experience and entertainment destination. Malls and their tenants must combine speed, convenience, immediacy, and outstanding customer service with the thrills of an amusement park. They must provide a family atmosphere with new things to do and new entertainment to experience.

Some mall operators simply don't get it. In the fall of 1999, the upscale Galleria shopping mall in suburban St. Louis outraged its tenants and gained widespread notoriety for a stupid attempt to defend itself against potential online sales.

The mall owner, Hycel Partners, issued a notice to prohibit its retailers from "displaying any in-store signs, insignias, decals or other advertising or display devices, which promote and encourage the purchase of merchandise via e-commerce." The company said it was trying to avoid losing income to online sales, rationalizing its decision with a linear logic that "a sale rung up on the Internet is not rung up in the store." Within days, the mall had come to its senses and gave up the battle declaring, "We accept the inevitable."

Other shopping malls are more enlightened. Indeed, the International Council of Shopping Centers asserts that "the Internet is here to stay and mall owners had better find ways to get on-board and tap into it if they hope to offset its impact." In line with that thinking, America's second-largest mall owner, General Growth Properties, has an online site called Mallibu where customers anywhere in the U.S. can purchase goods from any store in any of the company's 135 malls.

America's leading mall owner, the Simon Property Group, has more than 250 malls, including the Mall of America. Already mentioned above in an alliance with Microsoft, Simon has launched a series of programs that combine e-commerce with brick-and-mortar shopping by encouraging consumers to window-shop at the mall and buy later online. The programs, run by Simon's Clix'nmortar.com subsidiary, use bar-code scanners fitted into hand-held devices that shoppers use to roam the malls, scanning in codes of products they like.

The bar-code scanner — called YourSherpa for adults and FastFrog for teenagers — creates a list that the customer can review online before deciding what to finally purchase over the Web. Consumers can set a time for home delivery or arrange to have items gift-wrapped and shipped to multiple places. Simon has also joined forces with Time Warner's Turner Broadcasting to form Live Media to merge the retail and e-tail experiences through a network of kiosks, broadcasts, Web sites, print media, and live entertainment.

Simon's flagship Mall of America is a mega-themepark composed of dozens of mini-themeparks: Enchanted Tales stuffed animal store, Rainforest Cafe, Lego Imagination Center, Warner Bros., and so on. To further lure shoppers, the mall also has an entertainment complex, a walk-through Underwater World aquarium, and the huge Camp Snoopy amusement park. Not surprisingly, Mall of America attracts more than 40 million people a year, more visitors than Walt Disney World and Disneyland combined.

Mall of America is in the process of doubling in size, adding two more anchor stores, hundreds more boutiques, a 1,650-room hotel, an 11-story office tower, 300 condos, a spa and fitness center, and a 5,000-seat domed performing arts arena. The three- to five-year expansion will cost about $1 billion, making it larger than the West Edmonton Mall and by far the world's largest shopping complex.

This idea of "shoppertainment" has caught on in Europe. Trafford Centre in suburban Manchester, England, is a series of four malls that resemble a small town. Covering an area equal to 30 soccer fields, the mall's 280 shops are almost incidental to the abundant entertainment choices: a 20-screen cinema, a bowling alley, an interactive computer game arcade, a gigantic TV wall, and 6,000 restaurant seats. The "Orient Leisure Dome" of the mall is part food court, part theme park, with 25 restaurants and architecture from around the world. An adjoining fitness complex has indoor and outdoor tennis courts, a swimming pool, a gym, an aerobics studio, and a health and beauty spa.

One of the earliest U.S. theme-parked shopping malls was The Forum Shops in Las Vegas, fashioned after an ancient Roman marketplace. Visitors can watch Atlantis rise and fall on the hour and Roman gods prance around. Opened in 1992, it now racks up more than $1,200 per square foot in annual sales — more than double that achieved at Mall of America. The Disney-like experience of these and other shopping complexes, such as Ontario Mills Mall near Los Angeles and West Edmonton Mall in Alberta, represent whatever future is left for brick-and-mortar retailing. Certainly, the old formula of building a mall around "anchor" department stores is obsolete.

The Future of Stores

People are shopping less in stores and are switching channels to go online, as the following preferences show.

	Online	Catalog	Shop	Mall
Preferred Place to Shop				
Software	49%	22%	68%	42%
Books	49%	23%	63%	51%
Clothing	18%	22%	66%	68%

Web surfers and experienced online shoppers both indicate that they will shop much less at brick-and-mortar establishments, as shown in the table on the following page. Experienced online shoppers shop even less than they expected at many outlets, with only warehouse stores, mass merchandisers and off-price discounters retaining some favor. Clearly, many brick-and-mortar outlets are losing custom and many product categories will face widespread closures.

Even today, North America simply has too many stores and, even before the Internet's upcoming impact, their number has begun to decline. For example, between 1975 and 1995, the number of apparel stores increased by about 50 percent. Of course, this was the phase of market specialization where niche players took business away from lackluster department stores. Now, however, the number of apparel stores has begun to decline. During the same two decades, thanks to increased affluence and the Baby Boomer desire to stay young-looking, the number of beauty shops also increased steadily. But they too are now in oversupply and their number is falling.

Meanwhile, the Boomer pre-occupation with health and fitness caused a 150 percent increase in the number of sporting goods stores between 1970 and 1991, most of them chain stores. Since then, the number of outlets has declined 12 percent and continues to fall due to aging Baby Boomers simply exercising less aggressively. Bookstores, even in the face of superstores and Amazon.com, open more outlets each year and, by 1995, there were three times as many as in 1975. Clearly, that situation cannot endure.

A similar picture can be painted for most, if not all, brick-and-mortar retail categories, especially at the small retailer level. In turn, it is difficult not to agree with Amazon.com chairman Jeff Bezos that "strip malls are history!"

Smaller retailers clearly have felt the impact of the specialization efforts by retailers such as Gap and Barnes & Noble. The specialty store model has had a 20-year run and likely has another 20 years of life, probably in formats targeted at consumers by age and lifestyle. But the specialty retailer also must go online to survive.

Smaller retailers also have particularly been affected by "big box" retailers such as Wal-Mart, Home Depot, and Toys 'R' Us. However, these so-far successful big box outfits look blockheaded in their faltering steps to go online. After all, regardless of the

Web Users Shop Less At Brick-and-Mortar Locations			
	Web Surfers will likely shop less at	*e-Shoppers already do shop less at*	*Actual vs Likely*
Mail Order	56% less	62% less	+ 6
Warehouse Stores	42% less	27% less	-15
Strip Malls	37% less	43% less	+ 6
Local Shops	23% less	34% less	+11
Consumer Electronics	35% less	37% less	+ 2
Mass Merchandisers	30% less	19% less	-11
Off-Price Discounters	28% less	11% less	-17
Department Stores	24% less	27% less	+ 3
Shopping Malls	22% less	26% less	+ 4
Factory Outlets	22% less	34% less	+12

Internet challenge, these bare-bones outlets aren't exactly places where you take your family for the ambience. As a shopping "experience," their long checkout lanes make for a dismal adventure. Facing market saturation offline, they have reluctantly gone online but have done so without distinction. Toys 'R' Us, for example, lost out to the now extinct eToys start-up until it partnered with Amazon.

The most venerable may be the most vulnerable. The cold and cavernous big box model does not easily extend itself to the more experiential Web. After all, what is experiential about shoving a shopping cart around a 100,000-square-foot "airplane hangar" to restock cat litter, dog chow, detergent, and toilet paper? These stores are so big that they would be more valuable for their cubic foot storage space than their square foot retail space.

Still, these heavy hitters cannot be counted out as they ponderously step up to the online batting circle. They could well hit a grand slam home run and knock everybody else out of the game. According to Lou Gerstner, chairman of IBM, the existing flurry of dot-com upstarts is merely "fireflies stirred up before the real storm ahead." He believes — perhaps with vested interest — that the real revolution will be created by traditional retailers such as Wal-Mart as they gear up to take the Internet by storm.

A successful online retailing venture requires merchandising, technology, and customer service skills. But those skills are different than those that work in the brick-and-mortar world. Many retailers will not successfully make the transition online, as we have seen with faltering steps by Levi Strauss, P&G, Nike, and other stalwarts. The entire brick-and-mortar retail industry is at risk and the Webolution could be catastrophic for them.

Many traditional retailers are going to strike out because they no longer understand the rules of the game, which have changed dramatically. Any company that thinks the way it did business in 1990 will cut it with future consumers is going to be blown away. My own forecast is that a handful will be very successful online but that the rest will end up in the corporate graveyard.

The retailing shakeout — online and offline — will continue. Pure-play retailers have had the market primarily to themselves over the past three years. Now that the big brick-and-mortar retailers such as Wal-Mart are lumbering online, pure e-tailers will face more severe competition. Many will merge, be bought out, or disappear. When the dust finally settles, we'll find a few big winners who will join the ranks of the world's premier 21st-century retailers.

21 DIGITAL RULES
Strategic Web-Site Marketing

The winners will be the ones who develop a world-class digital nervous system.

— Bill Gates, chair, Microsoft
in *Business @ the Speed of Thought*

AS BILL GATES OBSERVES in his 1999 book *Business @ the Speed of Thought,* very few companies are using digital technology to radically improve their competitive position. He estimates that even those companies that have invested in information technology are realizing only 20 percent of its potential benefits. Perhaps the major shortcoming — and hence the greatest opportunity for improvement — is to use digital technology to help customers solve problems for themselves and, in turn, allow the company to respond immediately to complex customer needs.

In his book, Bill Gates outlines a dozen rules for success in the digital age, four of which are particularly pertinent to online marketing strategies. These four rules are abstracted and re-interpreted for digital marketing as follows:

Bill Gates' Four Rules for Online Marketing

1. Use Real-Time Sales Data: Study sales data online across the company so as to share insights easily. Sales data need to be collected in real time along with data surrounding every customer interaction. When data are digitized, employees can examine them at any level of detail and from any viewpoint, circulating their ideas for collaborative and instantaneous response decisions.

2. Give Immediate Customer Response: Use digital systems to handle customer complaints immediately and to capture various elements of a complaint that might lead to a product or service improvement. Indeed, Gates argues — and I agree — that companies should examine customer complaints more often than company financial statements. Tell that to the accounting department!

3. Disintermediate Middlemen: Use digital delivery to eliminate the middleman. In his earlier book, *The Road Ahead,* Gates coined the term "friction-free" capitalism to describe how the Internet was creating a marketplace where buyers and sellers could operate in the minimum of time — and possibly while spending much less money. For example, if products are sold online, middlemen of various kinds can likely be bypassed, thereby getting the product to market more efficiently and at a lower cost.

4. Provide for Customer Self-Service: Use digital tools to help customers solve problems for themselves. Gates cites the example of Dell, which allows customers to configure their own computer purchase online. Michael Dell, company founder and chairman, characterizes the business as "different combinations of face-to-face, ear-to-ear, and keyboard-to-keyboard," where each interface serves its own unique purpose in doing "meaningful things" with customers. This essentially high-tech/high-touch approach again optimizes value creation and digital competitiveness.

The Internet clearly is reinventing the basis of competition. The Web's ubiquity of information implies that all companies have access to the same market intelligence. The companies that survive and prosper will be those that do the best job of converging ubiquitous information to their unique advantage. Companies that do not keep up with breakneck advances in online technology are simply not digitally competitive.

The "4 Rs" of Digital Competition Strategy

The four major business forces in the Internet marketspace are buyer leverage, digital competition, convergence, and divergence. These are easy to understand in the following four-element array.

Buyer Leverage
- Online customization
- e-Community buying
- Comparison shopping

Convergence
- Product transformation
- Channel disintermediation
- Value web creation

Digital Competition
- Online start-ups
- Low entry barriers
- New e-channel

Divergence
- Global market reach
- Market specialization
- One-to-one markets

In response to these forces, companies need a four-pronged, Web-driven general strategy where they restructure, reframe, revitalize, and renew their customer value proposition, as follows:

"4 Rs" of Digital Competition

Restructure
(to Boost Productivity)
- Exploit e-channels
- Embrace open standards
- Network the organization

Revitalize
(to Generate New Revenue)
- Create e-products
- Enter new high growth markets
- Forge lifetime customer relations

Reframe
(to Change Paradigm)
- Become virtual organization
- Focus on information not product
- Operate in real-time

Renew
(to Change Competencies)
- Develop online capability
- Invent new processes
- Become an e-business

"Value Chain" to "Value Web"

In terms of the customer value proposition, successful e-commerce businesses will recognize that the Internet is deconstructing the "value chain" and reconfiguring it into a "value web." Distribution channels will radically change and Web-driven competitors will reframe the industry value equation. In sum, in a digital economy business simply must be digitally competitive and, to be digitally competitive, must go online.

The digitally competitive strength that the Web brings to a company rests on the correlation between its Web market reach and the value web proposition that it offers. In turn, this correlation depends on four variables, listed below and shown in the subsequent "Value Web" Matrix:

- **Customer Base:** built through Web site affiliations and links;

- **Cost and Efficiency:** online product ordering, distribution, and delivery;

- **Product Transformation:** commoditized information redefines product value;

- **Online Experience:** web site flow of context and content are compelling.

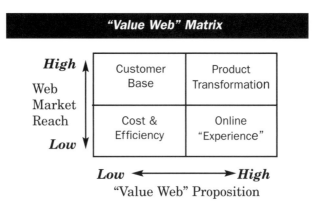

"Value Web" Proposition

This "Value Web" Matrix transforms buying, selling, and information flow, driving Web site traffic so as to maximize share of customer and corporate profits. In turn, the value web makes Web site design imperative.

Next-Generation Web Site Strategy

A very recent study by Deloitte & Touche found that only two-thirds of traditional retailers and consumer product manufacturers even have a Web site. Even worse, only one-fourth are selling online. Astonishingly, 31 percent of those with Web sites said their sites have "no strategic purpose" and another four percent couldn't even articulate their strategic purpose. How can they possibly hope to compete in tomorrow's retailing environment?

Good customer service stems from interpersonal experience. And the great online equalizer is the quality of the Web site experience. As Wal-Mart has shown, you can be a huge business but if your Web site sucks then people will be dissatisfied and will go elsewhere. Conversely, as Amazon has shown, the start-up that delivers a great site and follows up with startling customer service not only out-competes but beats established businesses.

Implicit in achieving an online leadership position is the need for a next-generation Web site. Several comprehensive books have been written on how to build a next-generation Web site, and this is not the place to regurgitate their excellent advice. However, we need to understand the past, present and future of marketing in order to anticipate future Web site design requirements. The following matrix looks at the Web site marketing medium through its three primary purposes: to inform, to facilitate exchange, and to entertain.

Evolution of Web Sites		
Past (Mass Market)	**Present** (Internet I)	**Future** (Internet II)
Inform Brochure or Catalog	Form & Content	Multi-Sensorial Simulation
Exchange Filing Cabinet Telephone Marketplace	Data Bank e-Commerce Search-n-Click	1:1 Data Base e-Marketing e-Tailing
Entertain Print Radio/TV Market "Haggle"	Monologue Infomercial Mall "Chore"	Interact Multimedia Content Web Site "Flow"

(Note: The overall trend is from top left to bottom right.)

The next phase of the Internet will be more about interactivity and relationships and less about attracting eyeballs and keeping them. The intersection or point of convergence between information, exchange, and entertainment is the Internet "flow experience."

The "Flow Experience"

The richest Web site experiences are Disneyesque: they integrate the active and the passive to absorb and immerse the customer in a memorable experience that makes them want to come back again and again. That experience combines information-rich content with entertainment to yield an experience that is so aesthetically pleasing that it provides an exhilarating escape from mundane offline shopping.

This experience can be described in terms of "flow." To understand the "flow experience," we again need to see technologies as extensions of human capabilities. For example, hammers are extensions of our hands, wrists and arms — which is why weapons are called "arms." The telephone is an extension of the mouth and ear. Microscopes and x-rays are extensions of the eyes. Roller skates, skate boards, bicycles, automobiles, and airplanes are extensions of our feet and legs.

Technologies extend human abilities and, implicitly, we extend our abilities and senses into the technologies we use. For example, we become engrossed in a good book, movie or TV program, often to the exclusion of everything else. (Note also that all technologies are media.) This level of engagement with technologies or media is described by University of Chicago psychologist Mihalyi Csikszentmihalyi as a "flow experience." He and other consciousness researchers define this as the "flow state" — a seamless, intrinsically enjoyable, self-reinforcing, captivating experience. Anyone who has spent a serious amount of time surfing the Web knows exactly what this feels like.

"Web Lifestyle" Hierarchy of Needs

Psychologist Abraham Maslow advanced the theory that people's needs are arranged like a ladder, with basic survival needs — air, food and water — at the bottom and self-actualization at the top. Maslow's hierarchy of needs is paralleled in our use of the Internet, with flow experience being the ultimate achievement for those who live a Web Lifestyle, as follows:

Maslow's Hierarchy	Web Lifestyle
• self-actualization	• flow experience
• esteem/ego	• surfing prowess
• belonging/social	• community of interest
• safety/security	• privacy/security
• basic survival	• no Web access

The concept of "flow" is an excellent way to describe the interaction experienced by an online shopper with an e-tailer's Web site. When you become engrossed in surfing, you extend your mind and consciousness across the Web. Content is not merely downloaded to you or uploaded by you. Rather, the Web is an e-mediated environment that you "experience" in the "flow" of your online immersion. You literally "screen out" irrelevant thoughts and distractions — whether they be off-screen noises or onscreen banner advertisements. Those who live a Web Lifestyle immerse themselves in virtual worlds. As this occurs, their neurons spark faster, creating a transformative experience that carries them to another plane.

There is nothing nerdy or New Age about this. The product or service under consideration of purchase simply gets transformed into the context of how it will enhance the surfer's Web Lifestyle. As with an absorbing book, Web sites that generate the most flow will, in turn, generate the most repeat visits. As explained by Elaine Rubin, the founder of 1-800-Flowers, "Duplicating the look of a flower shop is not as important as trying to recreate the moods and emotions that usually motivate the purchase of flowers. We designed an interface oriented around various emotional occasions; click on 'Birthday Party' and you're greeted with the sights and sounds of a party where you can see various flower arrangements appropriate to that occasion."

Thus, the greatest amount of flow is generated when the interaction at the site is intuitive and subconsciously navigable — like driving a car — and where the content is both intriguing and of high value. The best Web sites generate a flow experience that captures one hundred percent of a visitor's attention. Online shoppers who become engrossed in a flow experience will learn and retain the content with which they interact. Remember, a product is merely content.

But content itself is not sufficient consideration. Companies that successfully capture the Web's digital advantage will build 10 key strategic elements into their Web sites. These "10 Cs of Web-Site Marketing" are listed in the figure on the next page, along with example Web sites to make them self-explanatory.

"Flow Experience" = "Favorite" Web Site

Those Web sites that optimize these "10 Cs" will stand the best chance of creating the flow experience for the online shopper. In turn, surfers who experience flow will impulsively bookmark that site and add it to their favorites list for ready access in future. This again raises the most important point of this book: The sole object of any business is repeat sales. The object of a Web site is repeat visits. Hence, the primary goal of any e-tailer is — pure and simple — to get their Web site added to their customers' favorites lists.

The "10 Cs" of Web Site Marketing	
"10 Cs"	**Sample Web Site**
1. Content	Expedia.com
2. Context	HomeAdvisor.com
3. Choice	Amazon.com
4. Comparison	PriceLine.com
5. Convenience	1800Flowers.com
6. Customization	Dell.com
7. Cost Savings	eBay
8. Community	iVillage.com
9. Cool Experience	ESPN.com
10. Confidence	Schwab.com

Clearly, then, the battle for online market share is going to be won by a few e-tailers whose Web sites generate the most compelling flow experience. Thus, the strategic dilemma for any company is whether to be a first mover by going online early, or a fast learner by going online later and playing catch-up.

In that regard, while first-mover advantage will not overcome the disadvantage of a poorly designed Web site, it will be a major factor in online success. Since only a few online brands are going to make it onto surfers' favorites lists — thereby granting attentive mind share — it becomes critical for an e-tailer to drive hard to be Number One in its category. The sheer number of e-tailers and intense competition in many product categories means that there soon will be a major shakeout of the weak and the latecomers.

Friction-free markets tend to evolve into winner-take-all markets. That is, networked markets tend to enable a single competitor to gain an overwhelmingly dominant market position over time, pre-empting new entrants and thwarting competition. As we've seen, the Web is indeed something of a "winner-take-all" world. Being No. 1 in a product category will be awesome. Being No. 2 will be pretty good. Beyond that, the chances of success and meaningful profits appear meager.

Against this background, anything less than a well-designed, easy to navigate, uncluttered Web site will destine an e-tailer to oblivion.

22 ADVERTISING
Pay-to-View Web Sites

The Internet will do to advertising what the telephone did to letter writing.

— Keith Reinhard, chair and CEO,
DDB Worldwide

I T'S LONG BEEN SAID THAT 50 percent of advertising is wasted but we don't know which half. Well, now we know much more about what "clicks" with content users and what doesn't. Imagine being able to send ads of interest only to those individual users who are interested in them, and then have those users touch an ad on their WebPhone and have that ad suddenly come to life.

Well, now you can. However, just as the telephone took the post out of the post office, the Web takes the advertising out of the advertisements.

From Mass Advertising to
One-to-One Web Site Messages

The Webolution smashes the era of "mass" advertising to smithereens. Mass production, mass consumption, mass marketing, and mass advertising are fast becoming obsolete. Consumers are as individual as fingerprints, and PCs and WebPhones are empowering personalized consumption.

In the Agricultural Age, the producer was the consumer. There was no advertising. Marketing was local and based on individual consumer tastes and buying patterns. The Industrial Age brought mass production. The automobile shaped urban society, with its high street markets and suburban shopping malls. We entered the impersonal world of mass marketing, mass consumption and mass advertising. But the Webolution changes all that; it reverses previous processes. We now have a Global Village full of individual buyers who, thanks to computers, are again reachable by marketers on a customized basis.

As our consumer webographics data revealed, tech-savvy buyers expect to be fully informed about product benefits, and their search for value is best satisfied through information. Sales pitches and hype are counter-productive in an era when people want to buy knowledgeably. Bombarded with 60,000 ads a year, they tune out and search for tailored information about their buying needs.

After all, the consumer is paying for the ad. Consumers indirectly pay for the cost of ads through the cost of the products they buy. In future, this will be reversed. Advertisers are starting to pay consumers directly for their attention to ads; paying for their attention (which is scarce, and hence valuable) with rich content (which is abundant, and hence inexpensive). This trend completely reverses today's advertising model.

Mass advertising thus is largely a waste of time and money. According to Deloitte & Touche, less than 20 percent of advertising dollars spent by retailers actually affect sales performance. Mass media should only be used for "halo," or overall image, branding. In any event, TV is constantly losing its audience as people increasingly get their information from the Web. As this occurs, ad dollars will flow from TV to the Net. Ad dollars always go where the consumers are — and people are flocking to the Web.

Effective advertisements create added value for both the brand and the consumer; they create intellectual capital in consumers' heads in the form of brand recognition. Such ads work because they are genuinely useful, or personally relevant. That implies 1:1 marketing. The future of marketing will dictate the future of advertising, and the future of marketing is about serving smaller and smaller consumer audiences, down to individual customers at the individual point of purchase. On the Net, every ad that is clicked on is a one hundred percent direct response; mass ads are 99 percent non-response. Web ads reach those most interested in them; mass ads get zapped, muted, or flipped over.

The Web Site is the Advertisement

With the rapid growth of the Internet and online retailing, it is obvious that the old models of selling advertising no longer apply. Traditionally, the cost of advertising has been based on how many people might see the advertisement. This is usually expressed as a CPM or "cost per thousand" ratio. Television companies sell advertising based on the estimated viewing audience. Newspapers and magazines sell advertising space on the basis of how many thousand readers are reached by the publication's circulation.

Marketers do not go onto the Internet for exposure but for results. Rather than delivering eyeballs, a Web site should deliver a fully qualified customer lead. Traditional advertising is based on telling the customer that a product exists and selling its benefits. The Web goes further, linking qualified buyers to a virtual showroom and giving them enough personally relevant information to help them make an actual purchase decision. Therefore, it is not the quantity of people attracted to the site that counts but rather the quality of their experience while interacting at the site. A relatively small number of loyal consumers can be far more valuable to a Web site than millions of hits by people who never return. Hence, Web site design is far more important than advertising ever was.

Indeed, a Web site in and of itself best optimizes the various advertising objectives of all other media. As shown in the matrix below, the four purposes of advertising are to create awareness, to educate through information, to prompt a customer purchase, and

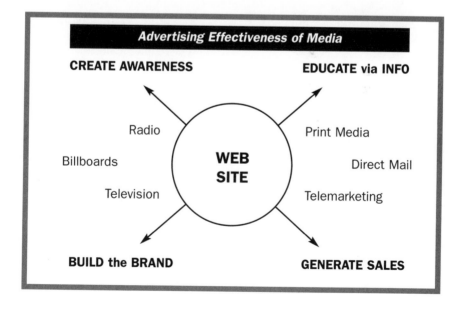

to create and build brand image. The best tools for building awareness are radio and billboards. The best educators are print publications. The most effective response media are direct mail and telemarketing. Television is best at creating and maintaining a strong product image.

A Web site does it all: builds awareness, creates image, educates, and generates not only a direct response but a sale. In fact, the Web is the only medium where the user can see an ad, inquire about the product quickly and in detail, compare prices, and then decide to buy — either then and there online, or later offline — and save time and money doing it.

Internet Achieves Best Reach and Frequency

Moreover, in terms of message reach and frequency, as more millions flock online, the Web integrates all the elements of traditional media and will outmatch radio, TV, print, and billboards combined. More important, a Web site has the power to reach an individual consumer, no matter where they are, either globally or locally, and in a personally relevant manner.

As shown in the matrix below, the media with lowest reach and frequency are billboards and radio, followed by print publications and television. However, the Internet far surpasses TV in both reach and frequency.

In comparison with traditional advertising, the Internet makes vast amounts of information readily available and easily accessible to customers on a permanent basis rather than through infre-

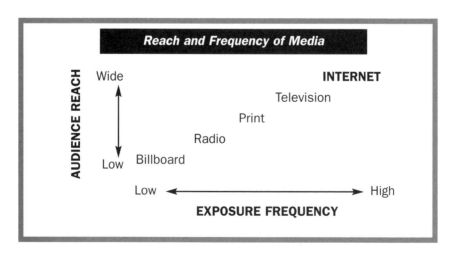

quent 60-second radio or TV ads or daily/weekly print ads. Internet content is always available 24 hours a day, 365 days a year, creating a permanent presence to a global audience. Indeed, it might be said that the Internet is a *less expensive* but a *more expansive* medium. In addition, because the user is interactively involved with the information being contemplated — as opposed to passively listening to a radio ad or reading a print ad — the Internet offers the opportunity for dynamic, customized, personally relevant messages.

Word of Modem

Just as word-of-mouth was the most effective mode of advertising in pre-industrial times, so will word-of-modem be the most effective mode of advertising in the Internet Age.

Vilely named "viral" marketing, word-of-modem spreads like a virus, replicating exponentially by doubling at each iteration, as follows:

```
             X
            XX
           XXXX
          XXXXXXX
       XXXXXXXXXXXXXXX
   XXXXXXXXXXXXXXXXXXXXXXXXXXXXXX
```

The oft-quoted classic example of viral marketing on the Web is Hotmail.com, now part of Microsoft. It is a free e-mail service where each e-mail automatically carries the message "Get your private, free e-mail at http://www.hotmail.com" — thus inviting the recipient to switch to the free service. The more people joined up, the more messages were sent out, and the service grew by feeding on itself. For example, once the first member subscribed in India, within three weeks another 100,000 had joined up, making Hotmail.com the largest e-mail provider in India without ever spending one rupee to market its service there. In its first 18 months, Hotmail.com gained 12 million subscribers in the U.S.A. and still signs up 150,000 a day.

The End of Mass Advertising

Hence, in its purest form, advertising on the Web is not required and has no value. More important are Web site design and what users say to each other online. Just as word-of-mouth is and will remain critically important, in the future word-of-modem will be vital. Yet advertising agencies, their heads deep in the sand, persist in desperately attempting to justify their own traditional existence in a media space where advertising probably has no future.

This bundling of media will blur the line between content and advertising and will radically redefine what advertising — if it survives at all — will become. Recall that there was no advertising to speak of until P&G began sponsoring TV soap operas, where ads interrupted the story to build a brand. But there are no soap operas on the Web. And interrupting people with messages they don't want, about products in which they have no interest, backfires on the brand. Customers are searching for informed relationships, not brands. So companies need to build emotional connections with consumers through ideas. On the lonely Web, interaction and connectivity will be of primary importance. After all, unengaged online shoppers can leave the store in a mouse click.

Indeed, in 1994, the then chairman of P&G, Ed Artzt, gave a watershed speech to the American Association of Advertising Agencies where he said, "From where we stand today, we can't be sure that ad-supported TV programming will have a future." Obviously, few people were sufficiently rattled by that comment to seek a new future for advertising.

The old model merely hypes products with millions of dallars of largely wasted advertising spending that not only inflates the price of the product but does not guarantee a single sale. Instead, e-marketers will give consumers an incentive to buy the advertising they actually wish to receive on an as-needed basis.

Pay-to-View Advertising

Nearly 40 years ago, media guru Marshall McLuhan predicted that the electronic age would eliminate advertising. At that time, he described newspaper reading as a form of paid employment; that ads mixed with content were "paid learning." Advertisers, he said, pay for space and time and thus effectively buy our attention as surely as if they had rented our homes for a public meeting. He also suggested that advertisers would gladly pay the reader, listener, or viewer directly for their time and attention if there was a way to do so.

The Internet provides just such a way. A few years ago, an

Internet start-up called CyberGold began paying users to click through ads on the Web. Advertisers paid CyberGold at least 50 cents for each ad that a consumer read through to the end. This approach recognizes that the Web is about developing mutual relationships with consumers at the time when they are most interested and ready to buy. By the end of 1999, there were more than a dozen such cash-for-clicks programs of various kinds.

Of these, AllAdvantage.com was most prominent, then ranking in MediaMetrix's top 30 most popular Web sites with more than three million members and boasting advertisers such as Microsoft and eBay. It has since closed down but its model was valid. Members downloaded a Viewbar ribbon that stayed at the bottom of their PC screen and showed banner-style ads when the PC was connected to the Web. Members were paid only when they were actively surfing and received 50 cents an hour for a maximum of 25 hours a month. A green light on the Viewbar indicated when money was being earned, turning red whenever the computer was idle. AllAdvantage.com also tried to capitalize on the benefits of multilevel marketing by paying members an additional 10 cents per hour if they got their friends to sign up. If, in turn, those friends signed up more members, the original member got a further five cents an hour for those referrals.

The benefit to advertisers of this model is that surfers can be tracked wherever they go, building profiles about their interests and targeting ads accordingly. In other words, the advertiser gets to truly "know" the customer. Ultimately, this "knowability" feature of the Web will wipe out marketing and advertising as we know it.

This "incentivized" approach also contrasts greatly with simplistic Web banner advertising, which merely mimics old-fashioned billboards. Indeed, as with drive-by billboards, the click-through rate on surf-by banners and the subsequent purchase rate are extremely small. Research shows that for every one million hits, only 0.50 percent of surfers will respond to a banner ad. Of those 5,000 "lookers," just two percent are likely to buy. In sum, there are only a hundred buyers for every million banner impressions, resulting in a trifling 0.01 percent conversion ratio.

Need one say more?

In the end, pay-to-view may be the model, but it applies not to advertising — which now will become a historical curiosity — but to the Web site.

23 BRANDING THE WEB
Selling the Web Lifestyle

Brands will either be distinct or extinct.

— Tom Peters,
management guru

ONLINE CONSUMERS demand instant satisfaction or they quickly move on to another Web site. In such a click-intensive environment, is it possible to build and maintain a distinct brand online?

To begin answering that question, let's just recall some characteristics of a brand. According to Michael Eisner, chairman of Disney, great brands exhibit these 10 traits:

- Monopolizes "share of mind"
- Is the perceived category leader
- Has human face (people know what to expect)
- Has a strong icon (e.g., Mickey Mouse)
- Typifies the entire company
- Promises and delivers meaningful emotional rewards
- Stays close to customer (each guest comes first)
- Does what the customer expects
- Has a clearly differentiated identity (describable in 10 words or less)
- Seeks the company of other brands

We will not address all of these traits, but will focus on "share of mind" and the high-touch, personalization elements of branding the Web.

We live in an age of accelerating product proliferation, enormous customer choice, and growing clutter and clamor in the marketplace. The Internet is compounding these characteristics, thereby making it necessary for marketers to build stand-out brands. Indeed, the Internet makes it possible for almost any product to create a unique "share of mind" by leveraging emotional responses. Great brands always tap into our emotions; they reach out to the consumer and make powerful connections at deep personal levels of experience.

A brand is a cult: it creates a deep emotional bond with consumers and becomes a cultural icon. These emotional connections transcend the product; they *are* the brand. Products are built in factories; brands are built in the consumer's mind.

The flow experience of the Internet thus offers marketers the opportunity to surprise the consumer by adding a new dimension to the brand, re-energizing it. When you shop online, the look and feel of the brand are just as important — if not more so — as when you walk down Main Street. Online brands need to deliver an enjoyable and straightforward shopping experience from the comfort of the customer's home.

However, as we have repeatedly noted, online customers quickly align themselves with just a few brand names. This creates a challenge for marketers. For example, while Amazon.com broadens its scope into many product categories, it already is fixed in most customers' minds that it is a bookstore. As company founder and chairman Jeff Bezos has observed, "Brands to a certain degree are like quick-drying cement; when they are young, they are stretchable and pliant, but over time they become more and more associated with a particular thing and are harder to stretch." Whether Amazon can successfully become a Wal-Mart type of brand which offers a complete array of products is still to be seen. But it surely will be on many surfer's favorites lists.

Similarly, Yahoo became an established Internet brand by making the Web useful for millions of people. People first started using Yahoo as a search engine to cut through Web clutter. Then they used Yahoo for local weather, news, stock quotes, sports scores, classified ads, and so on. Yahoo thus branded itself as a part of the Web Lifestyle and managed to extend its brand beyond that of merely a search engine. Therefore, while the Web — in contrast to television — makes it difficult to establish universal meaning, branding across a wide audience is clearly possible even in the one-to-one world of the Internet.

Indeed, the Internet is the most powerful medium for communicating the essence of a brand in a personalized way. While the Internet is used in uniquely individual ways by each of us, it is possible to create an online experience that grows richer with time so that the consumer's experience of a brand is expressed through a particular Web site. As repeat visits occur, a bond of trust is created that fosters consumer intimacy.

Such intimacy is achieved through the dynamic experience conveyed by the Web site's contextual content that is presented in a personal, one-to-one, up-to-date, live presentation. Again, then, the overall goal of Web site design is to make the customer want to come back again repeatedly — and to bookmark the site as one of their few favorites that they will visit frequently.

In the traditional world, as brands got bigger, they frequently became impersonal. Consumers increasingly found it difficult to relate to brands. This was mainly due to a paradoxical failure to communicate through mass media because consumers developed a built-in resistance to advertising. The intimacy of the Internet, however, allows brands to take on a personal face that is relevant to each individual customer through personalized information, experiences and products. This actually allows companies to capture consumer interest at lower cost and lets them focus not on mass market sales but on the repeat business and lifetime value of each customer. Therefore, it is in the interest of companies to build online intimacy with their customers by putting control of product and service information directly into the customer's own hands at the Web site.

My Agent is My Brand

An excellent way to do give customers that control online is to offer the shopper a "smart" agent. Smart agents — also called "bots" (short for robots) — greatly empower the consumer and take the legwork out of online shopping. Already, smart agents allow customers to search for products according to their own specifications, including pricing. It therefore becomes increasingly difficult to differentiate products on the basis of advertising, selection, service, or price. Indeed, some retailers have specifically barred agents from entering their Web sites, presumably because their prices or product selection were not competitive enough to stand scrutiny.

Even branding may not differentiate products in the future because smart agents ignore brand in favor of specific consumer requirements. For example, MySimon.com was a smart agent that gathered prices from about two thousand stores but proved difficult to use. Nextag.com goes a step further: after searching for product prices, you can negotiate with the various sellers and get an almost immediate reply from each merchant and then renegotiate.

Some agents can be programmed to track the availability of specific products based on pre-defined preferences. For example, if a new musical comes to town, the smart agent can automatically reserve tickets for shows in which it knows you will definitely be interested. The smart agent then sends an instant message to alert you that the musical has been reserved, along with a seating diagram that shows where you will be sitting, and requests authorization to actually buy the tickets.

Buy.com sends out intelligent agents daily to scan Web pages for prices on the same items that Buy.com offers. Upon their return, the agents automatically trim Buy.com's price below the lowest competitive price. Another agent, Netbot's Jango, finds the best price it can on any specified item from deep inside other sites. Jango brings back a detailed report on where to find the item and how much it costs.

Another site, Compare.net doesn't use agent technology but provides a searchable database of product specifications and a unique interface that allows easy comparison of the various features of competing products. Many shoppers use Compare.net to decide which item they want and then send Jango to find it. Another agent, RUSure, sits on your computer in the Windows system tray at the bottom of your screen and wakes up when you visit a supported Web site. It pops on screen and starts querying other sites for the same product, returning with the best price found and a hot link directly to the site where it was found.

Smart agents also threaten the brick-and-mortar retailer. Bar-Point.com turns barcodes into shopbots by letting consumers pull up product and price information from the Internet on a wireless PDA or WebPhone. The unit's scanner swipes the barcode price tag and thus lets users compare and save money right under the shopkeeper's nose.

Smart agents effectively put a dedicated virtual sales clerk at the beck and call of every online shopper. In the near future, an online shopper will be able to say, "Find me a red sweater, $30–$35 range." The smart agent will take that request, match it against the customer's historical preferences stored in a database, and come back with a list of all they might wish to consider. The list will contain a range of sweaters — wool, blended, cotton, polo neck, vest, and other types — in the entire red color range, all in the consumer's exact size. In addition, the smart agent will identify which of these options will best go with existing items in the customer's wardrobe database and will recommend which one to buy. Then, once you decide which to buy, the agent will go out and negotiate a suitable price — not everything is price sensitive online — and delivery time.

Such agents clearly will not react to advertising and will have no brand loyalty unless the customer specifies that they prefer certain brands. To have any effect, advertising and branding will need to operate differently than before. For example, the more frequently a shopper uses a smart agent, the less the shopper will visit an online merchant's Web site and, hence, will not be exposed to what is displayed there.

The End of Web Sites as We Know Them?

The more this occurs, e-shopping agents might even eliminate Web sites as we now know them. Online products can simply be stored in a massive database that, of course, does not require any user interface. This is already the case with 99.9 percent of the products carried by Amazon.com, where most products are not displayed on the site until you bring them forward by searching for them.

Since shopping agents will be able to query huge databases of products, there will be little if anything to differentiate one merchant from another. In other words, the Web will be dominated by a few major database e-tailers such as Amazon. The merchants who succeed will become effective personal agents for their customers by forming relationships both with the customer and her smart agent and by providing high-touch personal service through on-demand videoconferencing. In the future, therefore, marketing becomes more a matter of content interaction and transaction.

Imagine, then, what the Internet will be like when one billion e-shoppers' agents are constantly scouting for products that those shoppers say they want or which their agent thinks they want. A huge virtual economy will evolve where one billion e-consumer agents are constantly interacting with each other. For example, a smart agent representing Amazon.com could repeatedly submit millions of bids to consumers on a non-stop basis until the consumer agents accept the price. As that occurs, a true friction-free economy will emerge where each agent has perfect market knowledge; an economy where agents both maximize value for each consumer and provide reasonable profits for merchants.

The Customer Gets Branded

Indeed, thanks to e-shopping agents, each customer is "one in a billion." They are both an individual market and an individual brand unique unto themselves. On the Internet, therefore, everything again gets reversed: the consumer gets branded because she is more unique than the products she buys.

Brands used to represent a single message to a mass market of customers. Future brands must offer context to a global multitude of individual consumers. As already mentioned, getting attention in an info-laden Web world is not a question of more content; it is an issue of context. Future brands must offer a context within which to live a Web Lifestyle. As the e-tailing sector takes off, the "e" in an e-brand must stand for engagement, entertainment, enjoyment, empathy, and emotion — that is, *experience.* Experiences make brands; brands are experiences! E-tailers thus must become marketers of experiences and Web Lifestyle brands. Successful brands will sell the Web Lifestyle.

Focused vs. Diversified Branding

A critical element in online branding will be to decide whether to pursue a focused or a diversified branding strategy.

Focused brands generally succeed by owning and broadening a specific product category, just as Gillette broadened razor blades into shaving cream and after-shave. A good online example is E*Trade, which is broadening its brand into every type of financial service. Focused brands also succeed by capturing sales through a wide range of channels, just as Coca-Cola sells through supermarkets, convenience stores, fast food chains, and vending machines.

A key to becoming a category leader is the creation of trust with the online consumer. By specializing in one category, a new brand establishes category leadership and hence attracts a growing following of customers. Online examples are AutoByTel.com and E*Trade. Offline brands also can succeed online by being category focused. Comparable examples are GMBuyPower and Charles Schwab.

Diversified brands create a special value proposition of high credibility and reputation and then leverage that brand image across a variety of products. Good examples of this strategy are Sears and Wal-Mart, with the leading online example being the newly diversified Amazon.com. The most successful new online brands focus on a product category, dominating that category by becoming the expert in that market. Amazon.com began this way, dominating the online book-selling category. But now it is trying to become a diversified brand, rolling out its product strategy in stages. After 30 months as the market leader in online book sales, Amazon.com added music and then other products to its Web site offerings.

An offline store can be a valuable asset in creating an online brand by seamlessly weaving them together so that the customer can interact either online or offline. Branding thus must put the customer at the center of the process. The discount broker Charles Schwab has proven that physical stores can drive traffic to Web sites and the company continues to open retail outlets because customers are comfortable there when signing up for accounts. Then, once the relationship is established, the majority of customers move online where they are more easily and less expensively served.

Budgeting for Brand Building

Traditionally, creating brand loyalty and brand equity has been an expensive and lengthy process. It required heavy spending in print and broadcast media in order to make a product become a household name. The Web has changed the brand-creation process. It is simply faster and cheaper to reach a wider audience with user-relevant information on the Web. The Internet is an ideal tool for creating brand loyalty due to the ability to interact directly with the customer.

The future winners on the Internet will not necessarily be the

Web sites with the most traffic. The winning brands will be those that establish strong one-to-one relationships with their customers. On the Internet, brands are perceived less in terms of their image and more in terms of how companies respond to customer needs. Indeed, an online shopper who is intensely focused on a specific product requirement will pay little or no heed to brand images.

In a strategic sense, therefore, it is essential to spend significant money branding the Web site. It is advisable to allocate marketing budgets to online branding based on the brand's offline strength, where such already exists. Indirect marketers of products such as chewing gum or running shoes should continue to spend more on media advertising than on Web site development, perhaps in a 75:25 ratio, because consumers rarely need much information for this type of product and spend little time buying it. Direct marketers of products such as cars or airline tickets should spend 50:50 on advertising and Web site development and focus heavily on customer service, since the Web site is where transactions will primarily occur.

Traditional retailers, on the other hand, have much to lose from online competitors because brick-and-mortar stores can suddenly become much less convenient places to shop vis-à-vis a compelling Web site. Retailers should spend much less on advertising and much more heavily on Web site development, perhaps in a 25:75 ratio, focusing on customization and customer service and in trying to leverage the advantage of their real world presence and brand awareness.

Still, the Internet is a great leveler that can rapidly raise upstart brands alongside long-established brands. The key difference between old branding and new branding is the need to connect with consumers based on a one-to-one relationship rather than through a mass-market appeal that emphasizes product benefits.

This represents a big shift away from an "in-your-face" to an "in-your-Weblife" strategy. It is now critical to understand the online consumer's Web Lifestyle and how the brand enhances it.

24 CUSTOMER SERVICE MANAGEMENT
Winning the Digital Race

With data mining, you can present your products and services in a way that's most likely to increase your value to your customers . . . and their value to you.

— Bill Gates, chair, Microsoft
in *Business @ the Speed of Thought*

ON THE WEB, each customer is a market unto herself. And the Web is a perfect medium for both customizing and personalizing customer service offerings as well as fostering lifelong customer relationships.

Customization and Personalization

Research shows that, once a Web site offers customization and personalization features, it boosts its customer base by about 50 percent a year — and its revenues by about 55 percent. Moreover, people who use personalization features return to such Web sites five times more often than other sites and they view at least twice as many pages, spending more time on the site.

Customization and personalization are customer-driven features that can be used in at least four different ways:

- **Personal Profiling and Filtering Systems,** such as MyYahoo where users can display their favorite news, stocks, sports scores, etc.

- **Shopping Baskets and Ordering Processes,** such as Amazon.com's "one-click" ordering system and the inescapable shopping basket icons.

- **Configuration Systems,** where shoppers can design or

select a product that suits their particular needs, such as Dell's custom-configured computers.

- **Recommendation Systems** that automatically suggest products based on previous customer behavior at the Web site vis-à-vis that of customers with similar characteristics, such as Amazon.com's suggestions that allow it to cross-sell other products.

As a result of these Internet-enabled features, the market for specialized products will be much larger than in the past. Until the Internet came along, there really was no effective distribution channel for products that sell in small volumes. It was virtually impossible to reach a small number of buyers who were interested in niche products but who were scattered across the marketplace. The self-segmenting Internet almost automatically brings these scattered customers together in a "community of interest" around niche or specialized products. Therefore, e-commerce is returning us to niche products and brands. While a brick-and-mortar retailer cannot afford to stock slow-turning items, an e-tailer can. And that means multiple varieties of multiple products and multiple brands, each very specialized to individual tastes.

Conversely, products that were previously mass market can now be mass-customized for markets of one. For example, a manufacturer of cosmetics can only display about 10 products on store shelves. But on the Web, 50,000 different combinations of product can be offered. Perhaps the best example of this is Reflect.com, the Web site of Procter & Gamble, which allows women to customize their own cosmetics. As observed by Andrew Swinand, director of marketing at Reflect.com, "Reflect.com itself is not the brand; we allow women to create their own unique brand of customized beauty."

You can even purchase custom-size golf clubs on the Web. At ChipShot.com, you input four basic parameters — your height, wrist-to-floor distance, glove size, and how hard you hit the ball — to obtain just-for-you golf clubs in any one of 500,000 different permutations. Each club can be specified differently, so that you can have shorter shafts on irons or longer ones on putters, for example. In a similar way, MusicMaker.com lets you select 40 CD tracks to make your own custom CD from a huge assortment of available songs and artists. Clothing can also be bought in this way. At Levi

Strauss, an optical scanner automatically measures your body and, once you pick a style and fabric, your order is zapped to a factory where lasers cut the cloth precisely to your size.

In the near future, a huge variety of goods — from cars and computers to clothing and cosmetics — will be manufactured in these ways to match each customer's taste, specifications, and budget. As such, the Internet clearly reconfigures the entire retail value chain into a one-to-one global e-tail value web.

This really is what the one-to-one concept is all about. One-to-one is not a matter of having a relationship with your toothpaste manufacturer. Rather, it is about one-to-one customization and personalization of the online shopping experience. Many people wonder if — in a vast continent of 300 million people such as North America or Europe — it is possible for manufacturers or retailers to have a personal relationship with all their customers. Those in doubt should just consider, for example, that the U.S. Postal Service has a relationship with every American household. It will be the same for manufacturers and retailers on the Internet once everyone has a home page — which they will, well before 2010.

Customer Loyalty: To Bookmark or Not to Bookmark?

So far, pure e-tailers are spending about twice as much as brick-and-mortar retailers to acquire a new customer. However, they only spend about three percent of their marketing budget to retain customers versus sixteen percent spent by traditional retailers. Hence, customer loyalty becomes increasingly important online where the nearest competition is but a click away.

> Customer loyalty is more important online, where the nearest competitor is just a click away.

To try to increase customer loyalty, e-tailers are using programs such as the PointClick Network, which pays cash to online shoppers. E-tailers in the network pay for surfers who click on their site, thus increasing shopper traffic and online sales. Users only get paid for clicks they make on a network merchant's site. Similar programs are offered by companies such as Netcentives.

Clearly, the loyalty programs devised in the 1990s such as frequent flyer points are becoming less effective. Initially introduced to help differentiate one merchant from another, they were quickly copied by competitors. It also was thought that loyalty programs would increase barriers to entry and protect higher margin goods by countering price sensitivity, thus protecting profit margins. However, the Internet allows inexpensive and rapid entry into a market and makes it easy for customers to compare prices.

On the Internet, then, the main purpose of a loyalty program is to foster customer traffic and repeat business, thus building customer relationships. Again, however, such loyalty programs are easy to copy and their main benefit is to reinforce first-mover advantage by establishing a Web site literally as a "customary" place to go. Beyond that, loyalty programs will not build Web site loyalty and, in and of themselves, will become commoditized as to be worthless.

Customer Relationship Management

E-tailers are also finding that good customer service on the Web amounts to much more than posting a few answers to FAQs. Indeed, research shows that about two-thirds of online shoppers abandon their shopping carts at the checkout, many because they cannot get quick answers to their personal questions. One of the best responses to this problem is the "Lands' End Live" feature at LandsEnd.com which allows shoppers to interact immediately with a customer service agent over the Web by videoconference.

Thanks to the Internet, marketers also can read their customers' minds and predict their changing needs by using tools such as Customer Relationship Management (CRM). CRM helps marketers attract, anticipate, influence, and repeatedly satisfy high-value consumers.

Online marketers must do three things well:

- Predict the changing needs, wants, behavior, and expectations of individual e-consumers;

- Pursue an e-marketing strategy that is personally relevant to each e-consumer; and

- Identify high-value e-consumers and repeatedly satisfy them better than competitors.

Modern marketers need consumer insight and foresight, and that means they must converge on the "future-consumer.com" or e-consumer. Ultimately, all consumers will be e-consumers. And they want to better understand companies and their products, to better know themselves and their needs — through their interaction with their product and service suppliers.

As marketers converge on the e-consumer, they must of necessity embrace a "techno blueprint" that converges all customer "touch points" (wherever the customer comes into contact) on an enterprise-wide, real-time basis. The Web is a two-way interactive multimedium that redefines the very nature of products and services. Marketing, sales, and customer service must be a unified dialog not a monologue. The Net is a "product pull," individual-user multimedium, not a "product push," mass marketing medium. Companies need to become customer-driven, not product-driven.

The best way to boost shareholder value is to boost customer value. Information about each customer interaction, gathered at each customer touch point, creates a collective customer "memory base" (not a database). This customer memory base, when shared seamlessly across the enterprise will, over time, be far more valuable than the profit on any single end-transaction or sale. Indeed, each customer file must be seen as a profit center.

In this context, separate customer silos such as call centers are counter-productive. Today's $7-an-hour call center "drones" no longer cut it; they must be upgraded to profit-oriented CRM agents. Similarly, data mining actually is primitive, stone-age marketing; information refining and interpretation for company-wide access is what creates real value.

So how much should you invest in CRM? You can't budget it as "x% of sales" or "$x per customer." The CRM "techno blueprint" must relate to the lifetime value of each customer's business. For low-value customers, companies shouldn't invest much, if anything; in fact, they should get rid of most such customers. As a general rule, 20 percent of customers are high-value and generate 80 percent of profits; another 20 percent of customers are low-value and generate 80 percent of costs.

High-value, tech-savvy customers need and deserve tech-savvy CRM. Companies should give each customer their own special premium homepage on the corporate Intranet. The higher the value of the customer homepage content, the higher will be the lifetime sales and profits on that account — on that profit center.

Clearly, then, ROI now means "Return on Information" and

"Return on Internet." Indeed, ROI becomes e-ROI and the e-ROI of CRM is quite simply the difference between superior profits and corporate bankruptcy.

Winning the Digital Race

To generate superior e-ROI and e-profits, companies need to do the following five things:

1. Redefine the Business

E-consumerism restructures each industry and redefines the very nature of business. For example, the financial service sector is no longer the "money business" but the "business of information about money." The telephone industry is transformed into one of providing ubiquitous instant homepage access to rich multimedia content — something no telco yet understands! The old marketing maxim of "Location, location, location" becomes "Homepage access, anyplace, anytime." And no company can offer that without enterprise-wide CRM.

2. Become Web-Centric/Customer-Centric with CRM

In response to the convergent restructuring of business, companies must define their techno blueprint around the customer, using smartcards, touch screens, and interactive systems at the point-of-sale terminal — probably a WebPhone. Then companies can model future consumer behavior based on comprehensive, company-wide CRM. With CRM, they can satisfy customers with unparalleled convenience, control, and choice.

3. Drive Sales with CRM

CRM generates better-qualified sales leads and helps companies close sales faster, at lower cost and with greater customer satisfaction. CRM lets companies precisely target new product offerings, customize them, optimize channels, and maximize customer service payback. Since implementing a CRM system, for example, FedEx has 20,000 fewer people handling 68 percent more business. At FedEx, Web page views now outnumber calls to the company's free 1-800 telephone number. As a result, staff at FedEx call centers focus on customer service and problem solving. FedEx says that without the Web it would need twice as many call centers worldwide. Does CRM drive sales and profits? You do the math!

4. Bond Consumers with CRM

Competitors can copy products, they can match prices, and use similar channels such as Web sites. But they will never duplicate that very special personal bond a company has with its best customers. CRM doesn't just build relationships; it fortifies them. CRM helps companies deliver a consistent customer experience that builds brand equity, loyalty and trust. In turn, trust leads to more info sharing, more interactions, and more profitable transactions. And when companies truly bond with their customers, the privacy issue becomes a non-issue, and the company Web site gets bookmarked by customers as one of their favorites.

5. Compete Digitally with CRM

CRM is not new but it is sweeping across all industry sectors. It is a powerful weapon that lets companies compete for e-consumers in real time. Coupled with a winning Web site, CRM is a distinct market differentiator that separates winners from losers in the digital race. In the Web world, companies need to let consumers click, walk, and talk — and then lock them in with CRM. It is the only way to be digitally competitive in the new digital marketspace.

In sum, companies are engaged in a digital marketing race. They need to allocate major resources to CRM because it literally lets companies read their customers' minds. CRM provides a "digital dashboard" on each customer and lets companies predict and act on what customers need and want, and how they wish to do business online.

Those companies that embrace CRM will win the digital race — leaving competitors to eat digital dust — because they will do the best job of building "share of customer."

Share of Customer

Whether online or offline, to stay in constant touch with each customer e-marketers need to use CRM on a real-time basis. CRM becomes e-CRM. They must use e-CRM to constantly re-evaluate and anticipate customer needs and measure lifetime customer value. Traditional marketers focus on yesterday's one-time sale and the total monthly sales of whoever decided to buy something last month. E-marketers focus on future earnings streams. They focus on building tomorrow's "share of customer," not on yesterday's share of market.

As shown, to gain share of customer, e-tailers must first attract customers to their Web sites and then get bookmarked on surfers' favorites lists. In doing so, they will focus on acquiring high-value customers in high opportunity segments. Then, through the flow experience of their Web site, e-tailers will retain their customers through superior value and scintillating service, constantly adjusting to the customer's individual needs by maximizing the mutual value of the relationship with the customer.

Lifetime Value of Customers

Few companies ever consider how much a customer is actually worth. On the Web, you cannot afford not to do so; indeed, it becomes easy to do so. Clearly, the expected lifetime value of a customer — that is, the amount of net profit a company might expect to earn on the sale of products to that customer over their lifetime — will depend on the customer's available purchasing power, which will vary by product category.

Income generally rises with age, then levels off and declines. Factors other than age, such as education level, family size, and so on, are also important variables. Using e-CRM, however, an e-marketer can model the lifetime value of similar customers and then, based on an individual customer's buying behavior with the company, forecast that customer's lifetime value to the company.

Other things being equal, as shown in the chart below, the prospective lifetime value of a customer starts high and then declines as they mature. This is because the customer simply has

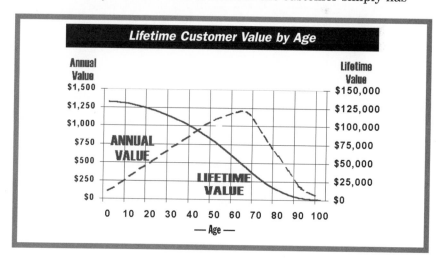

Lifetime Customer Value by Age

fewer years to live and hence less accumulated spending ahead of them. Conversely, as mentioned, annual income and spending tends to rise, then level off in middle age, and finally decline rapidly in later years.

Obviously, this profile will differ for each customer for each product category. Some products are bought less frequently than others (e.g., a new car every few years) and at different stages of life (e.g., post-retirement travel packages). Hence, a travel company will view lifetime value as increasing rather than declining in the post-retirement years.

But regardless of product category, the key is to attract customers early in life. And the Web is the obvious tool for doing that.

The "6 Ps" of e-Marketing: Value and Flow Experience

What's the benefit you couldn't get before? And what's the emotional connection?

— Meg Whitman, chair
eBay.com

AS A RESULT OF THE FOREGOING ISSUES, savvy e-tailers need to rethink the most basic relationship of their business — that with their customers — and reposition themselves online using the "6 Ps" of e-marketing.

My 1993 book *The Future Consumer* forecast how the traditional "4 Ps" of a marketing mix would be transformed (by what then was called "the information superhighway") into a "New 4 Ps" of marketing, as follows:

1. Product becomes Mass-Customized Product

2. Place becomes AnyTime + AnyPlace

3. Price becomes Total Value Price

4. Promotion becomes Precise (1:1) Positioning

That book preceded the Internet, the first Web browser (Mosaic) coming out in the same year. While the initial six years of the subsequent Webolution have shown the "4 P" model to be valid in forecasting the next 10 years of online shopping, it is clear that some slight modifications are called for. I also believe two new "Ps" should be added.

For example, the Internet severely intensifies price competition, dynamically driving prices down and making them much more negotiable than anyone anticipated. Hence, while the total value package of the final transaction is still a valid part of the mix, "price" should be seen as "Dynamic Value Price."

In addition, high-touch customer service will become increasingly paramount in managing customer relations, whether in the click-and-order online world or the traditional brick-and-mortar store. This means we need a new "P" of "Personalized Service." The concept of personalization thus closes the loop with product and service customization. Indeed, customization and personalization overlay all parts of the new e-marketing mix.

Finally, as stated, the over-arching goal of online marketing is to persuade the customer to bookmark your Web site as one of their favorites to which they will readily return. The emotive flow experience of Web site design thus is critical — much more critical than traditional product packaging, product display, or advertising.

Hence, we need to add a sixth "P" of "Profound Experience" to the e-marketing mix. The resultant "6 Ps" of e-marketing can be viewed in two systemic clusters, as follows:

Product "Value Web"	*Customer* "Flow Experience"
• Mass-Customized Product: Built on-demand to custom specifications, often by the customer themselves in real time, through personalized Web sites.	**• Precise 1:1 Positioning:** Real-time data collection and lifestyle profiling to leverage customer's lifetime value to build "share of customer" via permission marketing.
• AnyTime + AnyPlace: Ordered and delivered from/to the customer's choice of WebPhone, PC, doorstep or local store, thus achieving maximum market reach and penetration.	**• Personalized Service:** High-tech/high-touch service to anticipate and enhance each customer's "Web Lifestyle" needs and aspirations via personalized, customized lifestyle solutions.
• Dynamic Value Price: Dynamically priced in discussion with the customer, often through an online bidding or auction process.	**• Profound Experience:** Web site design that optimizes the "flow experience" to ensure a bookmark on customer's favorites list.

The three product-related "Ps" are largely self-explanatory. As shown by Dell or Amazon.com, these aspects of the e-marketing mix can be highly automated activities that the manufacturer and/or retailer is able to carry out routinely at low fixed and variable cost. The main point is to recognize that the linear supply chain is a defunct concept. Mass-customized products, e-channels, and dynamic pricing become interwoven into a "value web" that must function flawlessly and seamlessly in real time. It must be a truly friction-free interdependent network that the customer can take for granted as a reliable part of their daily routines.

The three customer-related "Ps" will require most attention from manufacturers and retailers. In turn, this will cause dramatic shifts in marketing and advertising budget allocations. The Web amplifies word-of-mouth through word-of-modem. Hence, marketers must allocate most resources to the building of profound customer experiences. To optimize the customer's flow experience, much time and money must be invested in database marketing, customer relationship management, and Web site design — design that doesn't just create a Web site but builds a meaningful, distinctive, and compelling online presence.

With such an e-marketing mix, the objective is to enable speedy, interactive, personalized, ongoing customer relationships that accumulate both online and offline traffic and sales. This e-marketing mix converges or blurs the lines between traditional advertising, marketing and selling which, as separate functions, now become obsolete. The objective is to focus holistically through the Web's e-multimedium on what each customer experiences with the e-brand.

In the e-tailing world, e-marketing must occur in real time. Monthly or quarterly marketing campaigns and related sales reports are useless. Each customer is a "market of one" and the "campaign" with each customer must be adjusted on the fly in response to each individual Web site interaction and transaction. Moreover, since the Web is a self-segmenting medium, similar customers will automatically re-cluster and be re-segmented at least daily as their purchase profile changes in the virtual marketspace.

The "6 Ps" of e-marketing also apply to brick-and-mortar retailers. Offline and hybrid retailers must develop in-store formats that relate to their customers' Web Lifestyles. They should focus on "experience" products, dramatically exploding their offerings into every facet of the shopping experience, creating in-store "happenings" that converge relevant and valuable content or entertainment with the purchase process. They should severely de-stock "non-experience" products, instead offering them through in-store online kiosks. In this way, they can combine local and virtual presence in a hybrid format that leverages high-touch products in a high-tech way — thereby creating a flow experience in their stores.

In sum, a sales channel — whether a Web site or a brick-and-mortar store — is a multimedium. It should be used as such.

— • —

This book has explored how the Webolution will dramatically reshape the retailing industry over the next decade. I urge you to consider its findings as they apply to your own situation.

To get you started, on the next few pages are "50 Random Questions for Monday Morning" that are intended to provoke your thinking. Work your way through these questions and I virtually guarantee that you will find your own answers to your future online success.

Good luck!

"TO DO" LIST
50 Random Questions for Monday Morning

1. What are we waiting for?
2. What are the implications for us if 50 percent of families are living a Web Lifestyle?
3. When the Web goes wireless and m-commerce predominates, where and how will our customers want to buy from us?
4. If individuals are going to have their own home pages or Web sites, and if every household has its own Web address, what does that imply for our business?
5. When the Web becomes an always-on "Evernet," how will that change human behavior?
6. If everything gets reversed by the Webolution, what does that imply for us?
7. If the car is an information appliance or WebMobile, how will our customers use it and how will that affect our business?
8. When a large portion of the workforce no longer "goes" to work, what does that portend for how work gets done and how people use their time?
9. If most people always have a WebPhone at hand, what does that imply for communications and commerce?
10. How do Web economics change our business model?
11. How might we take advantage of "winner-take-all" economics?
12. Which intermediaries can we eliminate? What new mediation roles might we play?
13. How might the housing and commercial property markets be changed by the Webolution?
14. If most families legally incorporate, what are the implications of that?
15. What are the webographic factors of our own customer base, and how are they changing?
16. Which e-communities do our customers participate in and how might we best reach them?
17. How does the "Millennium Effect" influence our business?
18. How might we help our customers optimize their "TIMES" factors of technology usage?
19. Are we going to be a first mover or a fast follower?
20. Are we going to be a pure clicks e-tailer or a brick-and-click hybrid? What role, if any, will bricks play in our e-business?
21. Which of our products are most vulnerable to online cannibalization and what should we do about that?

22. Which of our products are most suitable for online sale, why, and how might we make them more suitable?

23. Are any of our products destined to become museum curiosities?

24. What brand new, previously impossible product offerings does the Internet allow for us?

25. Can our products be mass customized online and, if so, how?

26. What products or processes are we able to digitize, either partially or completely?

27. What does individualized, lifelong online learning imply for us?

28. What does the digitization of money imply for us?

29. What role will smartcards play in our future?

30. How might we best webify our organization?

31. How might we come to own the customer's doorstep?

32. What is our "value web" and how can we enhance its value to our customers and ourselves?

33. As old media fade away, how will that impact our business?

34. If all products are merely content, what are the implications for our products in a context-centric world?

35. How might we mediate e-commerce and m-commerce — our own and that of others?

36. How do we become an e-business?

37. What is the role of the CEO as "Chief E-commerce Officer" in our organization in the future?

38. Who will be the winners in our product category?

39. How do the digital rules of strategic Web site marketing apply to us?

40. How might we become more digitally competitive?

41. How might we optimize our customers' "flow experience"?

42. What role, if any, will advertising play in our future?

43. Other than through advertising, how might we maximize the reach and frequency of our business?

44. How might we exploit viral marketing?

45. In what ways might we best sell the Web Lifestyle?

46. How might we best e-brand ourselves?

47. How might we optimize customer service in the Internet Age?

48. What is our e-ROI strategy?

49. What are our "6-Ps" of e-Marketing?

And last, but most important of all . . .

50. How do we ensure that our Web site gets "bookmarked" onto surfers' "favorites lists"?

APPENDIX A
Web-Based Research Methodology

Five empirical "content analysis" and "trend monitoring" techniques have been used to compile the evidence for the coming explosion in online shopping.

1. Internet Content Analysis Program (ICAP):

In 1997, the author commissioned a proprietary software package called "Internet Content Analysis Program" (ICAP). He uses this package to conduct "computerized content analysis" of the Internet, via the Internet. Content analysis is a longstanding technique used by the CIA and other intelligence organs; it was effectively used in simplified form by John Naisbitt in scanning traditional media for his "Megatrends" best-sellers. However, the author believes that his ICAP package is second only to that used by the CIA itself in that it was developed by someone who once worked on their software — someone who approached the author after a speech and offered his services. He thus believes this to be the most sophisticated futures research methodology now in use.

2. Netrends Smart Agents:

In conjunction with ICAP, the author's software developer also created several "Netrends Smart Agents" that constantly roam the Internet and e-mail their results into a database which automatically sorts and ranks the trend findings. These results are analyzed by the ICAP software, thus relieving the author of an otherwise burdensome and probably impossible task. He can simply overview and probe the info to readily draw inferences and make trend projections and impact assessments.

3. Delphi Study:

An extensive five-round Delphi study was conducted via the Internet itself to develop a scenario on the future of the Internet and that of various e-commerce sectors, particularly online shopping. Participants in this study are over a hundred key thought leaders, executives, and industry analysts from today's leading e-commerce markets. The Delphi study was used as a basis for the book's lead-off "Web Lifestyles 2010" scenario and the socio-economic and sectoral e-commerce effects of online shopping.

4. Webographics:

Future online consumer spending power is evaluated on the basis of novel consumer "webographic" variables and the inevitable "time–money" trade-off which consumers will make in an "attention-based" economy (see also Appendix B).

5. 2,000 Web Sites Evaluated:

Based on a composite of criteria used by web design experts, over 2,000 worldwide web sites have been evaluated on a multi-element matrix, from a "Web Lifestyle" perspective and the likely value-added expectations of online shoppers.

APPENDIX B
Forecasting Online Sales

The volume of future e-tail sales can be predicted by forecasting five variables. These variables, which compound on each other, are:

1. How many people will use the Internet?
2. What percentage of them will buy online?
3. How much will they spend and how frequently?
4. On what items will they spend it?
5. At which Web sites will they spend it?

To answer these five questions, each variable has been forecast by complex computer models and there is no point in spelling out long calculations. In simple terms, however, the forecasting process is as follows:

1. How Many Online:
The trend in the number of Internet users is widely tracked by a variety of published methods and our own proprietary ones. Statistical forecasting techniques have been applied to these trend data to estimate the number of users in every year through to 2020. Yes, this book forecasts online retail sales only to 2010, which, by the way, is six years farther out than any e-tail forecasts published elsewhere. However, since the Internet is still in its infancy, the most profound impact of the unfolding Webolution will not be fully evident until 2020. Hence, long-term forecasts about the Internet's future actually can be made with more definitive certainty than short-term ones. Our internal forecasts to 2020 thus help validate the near-term projections in this book.

2. How Many Buyers:
To predict how many surfers will become shoppers by 2010, user demographic, psychographic and webographic trends, tracked since 1994, are also forecast to 2020. Generally speaking, the more tech-savvy the user, the less accumulated online experience they need

before making their first purchase. It is therefore possible to predict, with some precision, when online users will become shoppers.

3. How Much Spent:

The greater a consumer's accumulated online experience, the more frequently she buys and, in turn, the more she spends. The data surrounding these e-shopping habits are projected for each year to 2020. The result is applied to the likely number of e-shoppers in 2010 to forecast category sales volumes for that year. In addition, we conduct e-shopper surveys, over the Internet itself, to determine shoppers' changing perceptions and expected future e-buying habits. These accumulated survey profiles of some 3,500 accumulated Internet users, most of them compiled in 1999–2000, serve as a subjective reality check on all statistical projections.

4. On What Items:

Total online retail sales are then forecast, assuming certain retail sector trends and overall economic conditions. For example, if there are 500 million Internet users worldwide by 2010, half of whom shop online once a week and spend $200 weekly, then online sales in 2010 will total $2.6 trillion. (500,000,000 users x 50% = 250,000,000 shoppers x $200 weekly x 52 weeks = $2.6 trillion online sales). Sales for each product category — both online and offline — are forecast, thus determining what percentage of each category's total sales will gravitate to the Internet.

5. At Which Web Sites:

Projections are then made as to which Web sites will most likely capture what percentage of those online sales dollars. These forecasts are based on a variety of factors. These include: changing customer preferences, prevailing and expected retailing trends, likely new e-tailing entrants, the design of Web sites, and the marketing strategy now being and likely to be adopted by the key players. The magnitude of future online shopping is much easier to grasp by looking at the percentage of sales rather than their dollar volume. To publish dollar volume forecasts would generate irrelevant argumentative comparisons with other published forecasts, which is not fruitful. Hence, we adopt the simple convention of forecasting the percentage of online sales by category to 2010.

FURTHER READING

Since this book was researched and written almost entirely on the Web, a fully detailed bibliography or set of footnotes is impossible to provide. References from journals, magazines, newspapers, online databases, and Web sites are far too numerous to document. However, the following texts in particular enlightened my thinking and I recommend them as further reading.

Brockman, John, *Digerati: Encounters with the Cyber Elite,* San Francisco: HardWired, 1996.

Cairncross, Frances, *The Death of Distance: How the Communications Revolution Will Change Our Lives,* Boston: Harvard Business School Press, 1997.

Casson, Herbert N., *The History of the Telephone,* Chicago: A. C. McClurg & Co., 1910.

Castells, Manuel, *The Rise of the Network Society*, Malden, Mass: Blackwell, 1996.

Christensen, Clayton M., *The Innovator's Dilemma: When New Technologies Cause Great Firms to Fail,* Boston: Harvard Business School Press, 1997.

Davis, Dorothy, *A History of Shopping,* London: Routledge & Kegan Paul, 1966.

Davis, Stan, and Meyer, Christopher, *Blur: The Speed of Change in the Connected World,* Reading: Addison-Wesley, 1998.

———, *Future Wealth,* Boston: Harvard Business School Press, 2000.

Decker, Charles L., Winning with the P&G 99: 99 Principles and Practices of Procter & Gamble's Success, New York: Pocket Books, 1998.

de Kerckhove, Derrick, *Connected Intelligence: The Arrival of Web Society,* Toronto: Somerville House Publishing, 1997.

Dertouzos, Michael, *What Will Be: How the New World of Information Will Change Our Lives,* San Francisco: HarperEdge, 1997.

Dholakia, Ruby Roy, et al, eds., *New Infotainment Technologies in the Home: Demand-Side Perspectives,* Mahwah, NJ., Lawrence Erlbaum Associates, 1996.

Downes, Larry, et al, *Unleashing the Killer App: Digital Strategies for Market Dominance,* Boston: Harvard Business School Press, 1998.

Dyson, Esther, *Release 2.0: A Design for Living in the Digital Age,* New York: Broadway Books, 1997.

Evans, Philip, and Wurster, Thomas S., *Blown to Bits: How the New Economics of Information Transforms Strategy,* Boston: Harvard Business School Press, 1999.

Gates, Bill, *Business @ the Speed of Thought: Using a Digital Nervous System,* New York: Warner Books, 1999.

Gilder, George, *Life After Television,* New York: W. W. Norton, 1994.

Greenfield, Jeff, *Television: The First Fifty Years,* New York: Harry N. Abrams, Inc., 1977.

Grove, Andrew S., *Only the Paranoid Survive: How to Exploit the Crisis Points That Challenge Every Company and Career,* New York: Currency/Doubleday, 1996.

Hagel, John III, and Armstrong, Arthur G., *Net.Gain: Expanding Markets Through Virtual Communities,* Boston: Harvard Business School Press, 1997.

Hayward, Philip, and Wollen, Tana, eds., *Future Visions: New Technologies of the Screen,* London: BFI Publishing, 1993.

Innis, Harold, *The Bias of Communication,* Toronto: University of Toronto Press, 1951.

Jager, Rama Dev, and Ortiz, Rafael, *In the Company of Giants: Candid Conversations with the Visionaries of the Digital World,* New York: McGraw-Hill, 1997.

Johnson, Steven, *Interface Culture: How New Technology Transforms the Way We Create and Communicate,* San Francisco: HarperEdge, 1997.

Jones, Glenn R., *Cyberschools: An Education Renaissance,* Englewood, CO., Jones Digital Century, 1996.

Kelly, Kevin, *New Rules for the New Economy: 10 Radical Strategies for a Connected World,* New York: Viking Press, 1998.

Leebaert, Derek, ed., *The Future of the Electronic Marketplace,* Cambridge: MIT Press, 1998.

Lévy, Pierre, *Becoming Virtual: Reality in the Digital Age,* New York: Plenum Trade, 1998.

Lopiano-Misdom, Janine, and de Luca, Joanne, *Street Trends: How Today's Alternative Youth Cultures Are Creating Tomorrow's Mainstream Markets,* New York: Harper Business, 1997.

Lowery, Joseph, *Netrepreneur: The Dimensions of Transfering Your Business Model to the Internet,* Indianapolis: Que Corporation, 1998.

McLuhan, Marshall, *The Gutenberg Galaxy,* Toronto: University of Toronto Press, 1962.

———, *Understanding Media: The Extensions of Man,* New York: Mentor, 1964.

Martin, Chuck, *The Digital Estate: Strategies for Competing, Surviving, and Thriving in an Internetworked World,* New York: McGraw-Hill, 1997.

———, *Net Future: The 7 Cybertrends That Will Drive Your Business, Create New Wealth, and Define Your Future,* New York: McGraw-Hill, 1999.

Martin, James, *Cybercorp: The New Business Revolution,* New York: Amacom, 1996.

Mougayar, Walid, *Opening Digital Markets: Battle Plans and Business Strategies for Internet Commerce,* New York: McGraw-Hill, 1997.

Negroponte, Nicholas, *Being Digital,* New York: Random House, 1995.

Papert, Seymour, *The Connected Family: Bridging the Digital Generation Gap,* Atlanta: Longstreet Press, 1996.

Perkins, Anthony B., *The Internet Bubble: Inside the Overvalued World of High-Tech Stocks — And What You Need to Know to Avoid the Coming Shakeout,* New York: Harper Business, 1999.

Porter, David, ed., *Internet Culture,* New York: Routledge, 1997.

Porter, Michael, "Strategy and the Internet," *Harvard Business Review,* March 2001.

Rheingold, Howard, *Virtual Communities,* New York: Addison Wesley, 1993.

Saunders, Rebecca, *Business the Amazon.Com Way: Secrets of the World's Most Astonishing Web Business,* Dover, NH.: Capstone, 1999.

Schwartz, Evan I., *Webonomics,* New York: Broadway Books, 1997.

———, *Digital Darwinism: 7 Breakthrough Business Strategies for Surviving in the Cutthroat Web Economy,* New York: Broadway Books, 1999.

Seybold, Patricia B., *Customers.Com: How to Create a Profitable Business Strategy for the Internet and Beyond,* New York: Times Business, 1998.

Shapiro, Carl, and Varian, Hal R., Information Rules: A Strategic Guide to the Network Economy, Boston: Harvard Business School Press, 1999.

Siegel, David, *Creating Killer Web Sites: The Art of Third-Generation Site Design* (First and Second Editions), Indianapolis: Hayden Books, 1996-7.

———, *Futurize Your Enterprise: Business Strategy in the Age of the E-customer,* New York: John Wiley, 1999.

Sterne, Jim, *Customer Service on the Internet: Building Relationships, Increasing Loyalty, and Staying Competitive,* New York: Wiley Computer Publishing, 1996.

Tapscott, Don, *The Digital Economy: Promise and Peril in the Age of Networked Intelligence,* New York: McGraw-Hill, 1996.

———, *Growing Up Digital: The Rise of the Net Generation,* New York: McGraw-Hill, 1998.

Toffler, Alvin, *The Third Wave,* New York: William Morrow, 1980.

Underhill, Paco, *Why We Buy: The Science of Shopping,* New York: Simon & Schuster, 1999.

Whitehead, Alfred North, *Adventures of Ideas,* New York: Macmillan, 1933.

Yoffie, David B., *Competing in the Age of Digital Convergence,* Boston: Harvard Business School Press, 1997.

ACKNOWLEDGMENTS

EACH AUTHOR owes an incalculable debt to all previous writers and thinkers. Many concepts in this book were prompted by several thought leaders, particularly by the farsighted media guru Marshall McLuhan and the pioneer futurist Alvin Toffler.

I make it a yearly habit to re-read the deeply penetrating and perceptive writings of these mental giants, particularly their *Understanding Media* and *The Third Wave* respectively. These two great guides to the 21st century were written decades ago, yet they provide all the essential keys to understanding the evolving global village and its third wave transformation by today's Internet Revolution, or Webolution as I prefer to call it.

As well, the reactions of various audiences to a multitude of conference speeches, corporate seminars, and international presentations have helped inestimably to shape my own thoughts as I developed the book over the past five years. In the latter regard, I especially want to thank my exclusive lecture agency, the Leigh Bureau, for facilitating such a fascinating and stimulating roster of engagements since 1989. Each one was a valuable learning experience.

In addition, I want to thank Jim Williamson and Nick Pitt at Warwick Publishing for eagerly continuing to publish my books. They are a joy to work with and I look forward to an ongoing partnership as we develop more ideas together.

Finally, I deeply appreciate the unfailing support, patience, and understanding of my wife Tammie and our daughters Melissa and Ashley, particularly during the culminating phase of the project when my time for them was little, but precious.

Thank you all!

INDEX

ABOUT THE AUTHOR

FRANK FEATHER is a global business futurist and public speaker who, in 1979, coined the now well-known phrase, "Thinking Globally, Acting Locally."

Formerly a strategic planning executive with three of the world's biggest banks, in 1981 Frank founded Toronto-based Glocal Marketing Consultants. In 1980 he was the organizing Chairman and Secretary General of the 1st Global Conference on the Future, and he is ranked by *Macmillan's Enclyclopedia of the Future* (1996) among the Top 100 Futurists of All Time.

Mr. Feather's 1989 book, *G-Forces: The 35 Global Forces Restructuring Our Future,* met wide acclaim in the USA, Canada, and Japan. Frank's 1993 book, *The Future Consumer,* extended his "Thinking Globally, Acting Locally" concept into one of glocal (global + local) marketing.

Mr. Feather has an uncannily accurate forecasting track record that often upturns the conventional wisdom. He is in demand worldwide across all industries by global corporations and has advised the Chinese government on market reforms since 1984. Even the world's big consulting firms regularly pick his brain.

Frank is married to Tammie Tan, a native of Shanghai, and they have a two-year-old daughter, Melissa, adopted from China in 1999.

Mr. Feather may be reached via the website

http://www.future–consumer.com